NO SALVATION OUTSIDE THE CHURCH?
A CRITICAL INQUIRY

NO SALVATION OUTSIDE THE CHURCH? A CRITICAL INQUIRY

NABPR Dissertation Series, Number 9

by
Molly Truman Marshall

Published for
The National Association of Baptist Professors of Religion
by
The Edwin Mellen Press
Lewiston/Queenston/Lampeter

Library of Congress Cataloging-in-Publication Data

This volume has been registered with The Library of Congress.

ISBN 0-7734-2854-2

A CIP catalog record for this book is available from the British Library.

National Association of Baptist Professors of Religion - Editors:

Rollin S. Armour, Sr., Mercer University
Journal - *Perspectives in Religious Studies*

Edgar McKnight, Furman University
Special Studies Series

James McClendon, Fuller Theological Seminary
Dissertation Series

David Scholer, North Park Theological Seminary
Bibliographic Series

The Edwin Mellen Press
Box 450
Lewiston, New York
USA 14092

The Edwin Mellen Press
Box 67
Queenston, Ontario
CANADA L0S 1L0

Edwin Mellen Press, Ltd.
Lampeter, Dyfed, Wales
UNITED KINGDOM SA48 7DY

Printed in the United States of America

FOR DOUGLAS
Wellspring of Joy
and Nurture

TABLE OF CONTENTS

PREFACE

This study was originally presented as a doctoral dissertation to the faculty of The Southern Baptist Theological Seminary in 1983. In the ensuing years, I have become even more convinced of the centrality of the theological question it explores.

Religious pluralism characterizes our world as it is poised on the brink of a new millennium Anno Domini. Recent decades have witnessed a resurgence of traditional religions as well as major "world religions"—Islam, in particular. Further, we can observe the flowering of new expressions of religious faith, for example, the nascent "goddess movement" and varieties of the amorphous New Age movement. All of these phenomena present a critical challenge to Christian doctrine.

Scholarly literature which addresses the tenability of Christianity's unique claims regarding Jesus Christ, a new theological context embracing a pluralist paradigm, the significance of religion for humans in a critical and post-critical world, current strategies for Christian mission and interreligious dialogue (to mention only a few concerns), has burgeoned. Perceptive essays and books have grown out of scholarly consultations such as the one held at Claremont Graduate School, Claremont, California, March 7-8, 1986; the mature fruit of that discussion has been published in *Christian Uniqueness: Toward a Pluralistic Theology of Religions*, edited by John Hick and Paul F. Knitter. An earlier conference, "Toward a Universal Theology of Religion," hosted by Temple University, Philadelphia, October 17-19, 1984, resulted in a substantive collection edited by Leonard Swidler, *Toward a Universal Theology of Religion*. These gatherings suggest that for many participants the word "ecumenical" now encompasses the larger spectrum of religious insights and hopes. Clearly, this topic engages Christian theologians with new urgency and clarity.

I must express gratitude to those who made this study possible. Financial assistance from my family and The Southern Baptist Theological Seminary allowed me to pursue intensive research at Cambridge University. I owe a particular debt to John A. T. Robinson for making my studies with him during the Michaelmas Term at Trinity College, 1980, both memorable and constructive. His keen interest in a theology of religious pluralism that yet retained a robust, incarnational christology enlarged my understanding and tempered my conclusions. My teachers and friends, Southern Seminary professors Wayne Ward, Dale Moody, Marvin Tate, and Hugo Culpepper, have shaped my theological vision and encouraged *fides quaerens intellectum* through percipient insights and graceful example. My own work as a teacher will always bear the marks of their investment.

Finally, I am grateful to the NABPR dissertation series, currently edited by James McClendon, for its courage and commitment to scholarship among Baptists. Indeed, the National Association of Baptist Professors of Religion not only nurtures collegiality, but offers the liberating leaven of honest inquiry to a Christian tradition often more marked by obscurantism than by openness in theological matters.

I have delayed releasing my study for publication for fear that it might create more of a firestorm than has already occurred. Yet my vocation as a theologian requires that I attempt to voice my own perspective on the difficult question of *extra ecclesiam nulla salus* amidst the welter of contemporary options. I am grateful to Jim McClendon for his encouragement to be faithful to my calling; I trust that those who read this will also be prompted to new dimensions of fidelity in the service of Christ.

Molly Marshall

Pentecost 1991

CHAPTER 1

INTRODUCTION

During the last one hundred years, a phenomenal growth in awareness of religious pluralism has occurred, for never before have the living faiths been in such close contact. Not too many years ago seemingly the whole of the West was professedly Christian, and non-Christian religions were distant or unknown. Now, the wide-ranging mobility of the earth's peoples—forced by technology—has made nonsense of religious isolation and rendered less plausible many of Christianity's affirmations.

The heightened awareness of religious pluralism is a greater threat and reason for greater unrest for Christianity than for any other religion because, in Karl Rahner's words, "No other religion . . . maintains so absolutely that it is *the* religion, the one and only valid revelation of the one living God, as does the Christian religion."[1] Soteriological problems are particularly acute because it has been a foundational axiom of Christian theology that salvation comes only through Christ and his church. Ecclesiastical exclusiveness has been among the persistent historical characteristics of the Christian church as, in its various forms and by varying degrees, it has insisted on a monopoly in the mediation of salvation. The Cyprianic theme of *extra ecclesiam nulla salus* ("no salvation outside the church") has not lacked occasion for re-utterance throughout the centuries, whether by the

---

[1]Karl Rahner, "Christianity and the Non-Christian Religions," *Christianity and Other Religions*, John Hick and Brian Hebblethwaite, eds. (Glasgow: Collins, 1980) 53-54. See the introduction to Russell F. Aldwinckle's *Jesus—A Savior or the Savior?* (Macon GA: Mercer University Press, 1982) 1-8.

pen of Augustine, Thomas, Luther, or Calvin, though the meaning has been modified by differing theological and ecclesiastical circumstances.

Yet, this *one* way of salvation excludes more than it includes[2] and it precipitates critical, theodicy-demanding questions: Why has this salvation been confined to a slender strand within human history? If God is Creator and Providential Sovereign of all, how can there be the provision of true religion only for a chosen minority? What about those who have never been given appropriate opportunities to respond to God's message of salvation in Christ? Does Christ's death have salvific efficacy for those responding to and "walking in the light" that they have been given? Is salvation to be denied to those who by cultural or geographical accident follow a life of faith other than Christianity's? A difficult theological agenda impatiently presses for critical reflection.

THE SIGNIFICANCE OF THIS STUDY

Some have suggested that Christianity is, in the main, theologically unequipped for living and ministering effectively amidst the religious plurality of the twentieth century.[3] Rather than reverting to the safe territory of old denouncements, theologians must now wrestle with the shape of the Christian self-consciousness vis-à-vis committed adherents of other ways of faith. Canon Max Warren put it graphically when he remarked that the impact of agnostic science will turn out to have been as child's play when compared to the challenge to Christian theology offered by other faiths.[4]

---

[2]Viewing the traditional exclusive approach in light of the contemporary religious situation, Heinrich Ott, "Existentiale Interpretation und Anonyme Christlichkeit," *Zeit und Geschichte: Festschrift für R. Bultmann,* E. Dinkler, ed. (Tübingen: 1964) 375, remarks: "Only a sectarian sensibility could manage to consider all men who do not explicitly confess Christ as automatically lost and excluded from the realm of God's saving actions. . . ."

[3]David Tracy, "Defending the Public Character of Theology," *Theologians in Transition,* James M. Wall, ed. (New York: Crossroad, 1981) 231.

[4]In an address at Scarborough, Ontario, 18 October 1958, cited by W.C. Smith, "The Christian in a Religiously Plural World," *Christianity and Other Religions,* 91. Gavin

Christians have dealt with the presence of pious non-Christians in a variety of ways—a few charitable, most less than charitable—in the protracted struggle to resolve the embarrassing dilemma that other faiths present. The struggle has been prompted by the apparent threat to the church's understanding of the gospel and the desire to promulgate the all-encompassing claims of that gospel. The contemporary situation seems to demand an end to the triumphal monologue of the Constantian era; however, switching to a praxis-orientation for mission strategy in order to sidestep the theological issues is a dubious substitute. Indeed, a growing number of Christian theologians of various traditions agree with W. C. Smith's assessment: "From now on any serious intellectual statement of the Christian faith must include, if it is to serve its purpose among men, some sort of doctrine of other religions."[5]

Many Christian theologians, confronted by these difficult issues, have found it necessary to reformulate their concepts of salvation and the church in order to lessen the starkness of the church's historic position as articulated by Cyprian. While still viewing the church as the primary sphere of the encounter between Christ and humankind, many now suggest that this primary way does not exclude other ways.[6] Due to the expanding concepts of salvation, ecclesiology has become one of the doctrines most studied recently. Likewise, additional theological assumptions must give way to fresh and creative thinking because "the

---

D'Costa, *Theology and Religious Pluralism: The Challenge of Other Religions* (Oxford: Basil Blackwell, 1986) 1-6, notes the new historical situation in which Christian theologians work.

[5]Ibid., 100. See John Hick, "Pluralism and the Reality of the Transcendent," *Theologians in Transition*, 65.

[6]Cf. Hans Küng, *The Church* (London: Burns and Oates, 1967) 403ff.; Karl Rahner, *Foundations of the Christian Faith* (New York: The Seabury Press, 1978) 176; W.C. Smith, *The Faith of Other Men* (New York: Harper and Row, 1962) 131f.; John Hick, "Jesus and the World Religions," *The Myth of God Incarnate*, John Hick, ed. (London: SCM Press, 1977) 181ff.; and John Hick, *God and the Universe of Faiths* (London: Macmillan, 1973); Paul F. Knitter, *No Other Name?* (Maryknoll: Orbis Books, 1985); and Rosemary Radford Ruether, *Faith and Fratricide* (New York: Seabury, 1974).

religious history of mankind is taking as monumental a turn in our century as is the political or economic."[7]

Thus the problem posed by the doctrine "no salvation outside the church" merits extensive consideration in light of the contemporary religious situation. Although the development of the axiom itself is worthy of attention,[8] this study proposes to use the formula as an interpretative key to deal with the soteriological implications of religious pluralism.[9] Traditionally, Christianity's negative view of other faiths has been enshrined in the dogma *extra ecclesiam nulla salus*. All traditions within western Christianity, not just the Roman Catholic that nurtured the classic formula, are experiencing ferment in questioning whether other religions provide ways of salvation.

THE PURPOSE AND METHODOLOGY

The purpose of this dissertation is to make a critical inquiry into the question of whether Christianity, realized in the church through Christ, provides the only way of salvation. In order to accomplish this, three subsidiary tasks are necessary. First, against the background of the historical and theological development of the doctrine and the reasons for its questionable status today

---

[7]W.C. Smith, *Christianity and Other Religions*, 89.

[8]See for example John J. King's, *The Necessity of the Church for Salvation in Selected Theological Writings of the Past Century* (Washington: The Catholic University of America Press, 1960); Jerome P. Theisen, O.S.B., *The Ultimate Church and The Promise of Salvation* (Collegeville MN: St. John's University Press, 1976), offers a helpful history of the axiom. He argues that it has remained a traditional doctrine from the earliest centuries to the present time; however, in the Roman Catholic Church today, careful revision in interpretation is underway.

[9]As will be demonstrated in chapter two, the formula has been broadly used by both Roman Catholic and Protestant traditions. Hick proposes the "Protestant missionary equivalent" (developed during the Reformation) to be "no salvation outside Christianity," but the early Reformers continued the historic usage, appropriating the same language as the Roman Catholics when evaluating the non-Christian religions. The formula is sufficiently inclusive for the present study.

(chapter two), the writer will present a critical analysis of three contemporary methods of engaging the question of *salus extra ecclesiam.* To that end, the writer has delimited three main theological positions. The first position is Christian Exclusivism which holds that there is no other way of salvation than through Christ and his church. Emil Brunner will represent this position.[10] The second position, designated as Christian Inclusivism, holds that there are other ways of salvation but that these are subsumed into the Church's universal vocation, for example, all ways of salvation are implicitly, though perhaps secretly, Christian. Karl Rahner is the architect of this position. The third position, Christian Relativism, represented by John Hick, views salvation through Christ and his church as one way among other ways.[11]

Second, the writer will evaluate the adequacy of each of these positions theologically in terms of soteriology and ecclesiology. The goal of the evaluation will be to determine whether and how well each position does justice both to the church's historic affirmation of the means of salvation and to the contemporary religious situation.

Chapters three, four, and five will present a critique of the chosen theological paradigms. After a descriptive analysis of each model, each will be evaluated internally by a series of questions constructed to elucidate the theologian's distinctive understanding of the relationship of the church and

---

[10]Brunner was selected for this position over against Karl Barth because his dialectical attitude toward other religions is more contemporary than Barth's absolutist and totally negative attitude toward other faiths. Barth's interpretation of "religion" is more a theological abstraction than a sensitive analysis of the complex reality of the religions of humankind. Brunner's "missionary theology" offers a better way forward. See Karl Barth's "The Revelation of God as the Abolition of Religion," in *Christianity and Other Religions,* John Hick and Brian Hebblethwaite, eds., 32-51. This article consists of extracts from *Church Dogmatics,* Vol. I, Pt. 2 (English translation, 1956).

[11]Since the original submission of this dissertation, Gave D'Costa has published *Theology and Religious Pluralism: The Challenge of Other Religions* (Oxford: Basil Blackwell, 1986), which follows a similar typological approach. He refers to the third position as Christian pluralism rather than relativism, believing it more adequately reflects Hick's position. This issue will be addressed in chapters five and six.

salvation. The following questions serve as guidelines and background for this author's evaluative task:

1. What is the nature of salvation?
2. Is salvation primarily of an individual or corporate nature?
3. What is the nature of the church?
4. What is the mission of the church?
5. What is the church's role in salvation?
6. What is Christ's relationship to the church?
7. In what way does the church continue the work of Christ?
8. Can the continuing work of Christ in the world be conceptualized only through the instrument of the church?
9. Is there any other sphere to encounter his redemptive benefits?
10. What implications for the possibility of salvation outside Christ and the church can be drawn from this position?

After summarizing each theologian's response to the questions, his position as a whole will be evaluated in terms of biblical consistency, coherence, comprehensiveness, and applicability to the contemporary religious situation, characterized by pluralism.

Finally, this writer will present a comparative evaluation of these positions in order to develop the norms and criteria for a tentative solution to the question regarding the possibility of salvation outside Christ and the church. Chapter six will summarize the strengths and weaknesses of the three positions, assessing each theologian's respective contribution to the construction of an adequate and comprehensive treatment of the question. In dialogue with these positions, the writer will then venture her response to *extra ecclesiam nulla salus*.

The criteria for the selection of the three theologians, Emil Brunner, Karl Rahner, and John Hick, were these: (1) a broad and continuing sphere of theological influence, and (2) the availability of books, articles and monographs dealing expressly with the concern of this dissertation. Each of these theologians has produced significant major works related to the possibility of salvation through means other than Christ and his church,[12] and each represents a clearly identifiable position that contrasts with the other two. A variety of primary sources are available for each; moreover, Hick and Rahner have offered many recent contributions to the ongoing discussion. Secondary resources abound as these seminal thinkers have been the subject of numerous studies and have sparked the attempts of other writers to deal with related issues.

A Swiss Protestant dialectical theologian, Emil Brunner (1889-1965), is one of the leading figures in the Neo-orthodox movement of the twentieth century. A hallmark of his long academic career, first as Professor of Dogmatics at the University of Zürich and then in the chair of Christian Philosophy in the International Christian University in Japan, was his concern to enter into dialogue with both the secular world and the non-Christian religions. Brunner advocated the apologetic role of Christian theology, believing it to be the paramount task in a post-Christian world. Theology, therefore, must always be "the understanding of the message of Jesus Christ in view of man's problems today. . . ."[13] More than his contemporaries in the Neo-orthodox stream, Brunner desired to carry his theological insights further than the orbit of Christianity.

At the forefront of Roman Catholic theology today, Karl Rahner (1904-1984), a German Jesuit, has contributed creatively to most of the concerns of modern theology. Among his chief interests has been the problem of reconciling

---

[12]See especially Emil Brunner, *Die Christusbotschaft im Kampf mit den Religionen* (Stuttgart und Basel: Evang. Missions Verlag, 1931); *Die Unentbehrlichkeit des Alten Testamentes für die missionierende Kirche* (Basel: Evang. Missions Verlag, 1934); and *Revelation and Reason. The Christian Doctrine of Faith and Knowledge* (Philadelphia: The Westminster Press, 1946). See Karl Rahner's *Foundations of the Christian Faith*, William V. Dych, trans. (New York: The Seabury Press, 1976); *Theological Investigations*, Vol. 4 (Baltimore: Helicon Press, 1966), and *Theological Investigations*, Vol. 5, Karl Kruger, trans. (Baltimore: Helicon Press, 1966). Two of Hick's books are especially important: *God and the Universe of Faiths* (New York: Macmillan Press, 1973), and *God Has Many Names* (London: Macmillan Press, 1980).

[13]Emil Brunner, "Toward A Missionary Theology," *Christian Century* 66 (1949): 816-18.

the church's historic pronouncements of the means of salvation and the plurality of twentieth-century religious traditions. Instrumental in designing Vatican II's "Declaration on Non-Christian Religions," Rahner has devoted many of his theological writings to *salus extra ecclesiam* and has fashioned the category of the "anonymous Christian" as a means of resolving the theological dilemma.

Standing within the English Presbyterian tradition, John Hick has, in recent years, focused his theological concerns primarily on the theme of religious pluralism. He credits his journey toward theological relativism to living in Birmingham, England, a multiracial, multicultural, and multifaith city.[14] His knowledge of the other great world faiths has led him to believe that *extra ecclesiam nulla salus* is "unacceptable to all except a minority of dogmatic diehards."[15]

Although much attention has been devoted to the theologies of Brunner, Rahner, and Hick, there has been no intensive theological critique in the broadened context of religious pluralism. There is a need for a thorough critical analysis of the options these theologians present for the problems engendered by "no salvation outside the church" and the current challenging factors. A comparative study is especially needed; analyzed alongside one another, the contours of each position should emerge more sharply and thus make a more comprehensive theological critique possible.

Most recent studies of religious pluralism either survey the breadth of Christian "attitudes toward other religions"[16] or focus more specifically on

---

[14]See his *God Has Many Names*, 4f.

[15]John Hick, "Pluralism and the Reality of the Transcendent," *Theologians in Transition*, 65.

[16]Cf. Owen C. Thomas, ed., *Attitudes Toward Other Religions* (New York: Harper and Row, 1969); Hick and Hebblethwaite, eds., *Christianity and Other Religions*; and Gerald Anderson, ed., *The Theology of the Christian Mission* (Nashville: Abingdon Press, 1961).

methods for dialogue,[17] or on the history of religions in general,[18] without any sustained theological engagement. Several collections of position papers have also been published recently,[19] which sketch a general approach without wrestling with some of the more difficult theological issues.

Since soteriological concerns are at the heart of the church's ministry, an intensive theological treatment of the problems raised by the non-Christian religions is needed. Usually, systematic or biblical considerations of the relationship of salvation and the church have relegated the problems presented by religious pluralism to an almost addendum status.[20] Within the evangelical wing of Christianity, with its continuing mission endeavors, there is a particular need for rethinking *inter alia* the church's soteriological position.

The problem of the limits and means of salvation has been of concern for the writer for nearly all of her Christian pilgrimage. Like so many others, the questions about "those who have never heard" and the possibility of salvation

---

[17]Cf. Stephen Neill, *Christian Faith and Other Faiths: The Christian Dialogue with Other Religions* (London: Oxford University Press, 1961); Raimundo Pannikar, *The Intra-Religious Dialogue* (New York: Paulist Press, 1978); and Kenneth Cragg, *The Christ and the Faiths* (Philadelphia: Westminster Press, 1986).

[18]Joseph M. Kitagawa, ed., *The History of Religions: Essays on the Problem of Understanding* (Chicago: University of Chicago Press, 1967).

[19]John R.W. Stott and Robert Coote, eds., *Down to Earth: Studies in Christianity and Culture: The Papers of the Lausanne Consultation on the Gospel and Culture* (Grand Rapids: Eerdmans, 1980); Gerald Anderson and Thomas F. Stransky, C.S.P., eds., *Christ's Lordship and Religious Pluralism* (Maryknoll: Orbis Books, 1981); Donald G. Dawe and John B. Carman, eds. *Christian Faith in a Religiously Plural World* (Maryknoll: Orbis Books, 1981); and Leonard Swidler, ed., *Toward a Universal Theology of Religion* (Maryknoll: Orbis Books, 1987).

[20]Two recent systematic theologies are excellent exceptions to this generalization. Dale Moody's *The Word of Truth* (Grand Rapids: Eerdmans, 1981), gives sustained attention to the issues of religious pluralism and its implications for soteriology throughout his study. See also Geoffrey Wainwright, *Doxology: A Systematic Theology* (London: Epworth Press, 1980). Another useful contribution is Aldwinckle's *Jesus—A Savior or the Savior?* which offers a helpful analysis of the biblical understanding of salvation and its applicability to grace and salvation in a non-Christian perspective (see especially chapter seven).

being constituted by "responding to the light one has been given" have never been answered satisfactorily for her. Interest in this area of study has been heightened through dialogue with committed Jews and Muslims while a student worker in Jerusalem and in extensive conversations with Buddhists, Muslims, and Hindus while studying at Cambridge University. The confidence they expressed in their faiths, evidenced in the quality of life pursued, furthered the writer's critical reflection. Moreover, participating in a comparative religions seminar at Cambridge where John Hick was both a guest speaker and frequent focus of discussion served as the catalyst for an academic concern to formulate a more responsible answer. Finally, this writer's commitment to personal evangelism in the name of Christ has ignited a burning desire to clarify what that task entails vis-à-vis committed adherents of other religious traditions. Does He alone offer the bread of life for which all hunger?

The formulation of a comprehensive, intelligible, and biblical answer to the question of salvation outside Christ and the church is of vital significance to contemporary Christian theology and the ongoing life of the community formed by biblical faith. Without some more satisfactory answers than have been given for this problem, the fundamental tenets and identity of Christianity may be seriously eroded. And particularly, the mission enterprise of the church needs firmer ground than is presently at hand.[21]

---

[21]Max L. Stackhouse pursues some of these key issues in his recent *Apologia: Contextualization, Globalization, and Mission in Theological Education* (Grand Rapids: Eerdmans, 1988).

CHAPTER 2

THE HISTORICAL AND THEOLOGICAL DEVELOPMENT OF *EXTRA ECCLESIAM NULLA SALUS*[1]

The formula "no salvation outside the church" has a checkered history in the development of Christian doctrine. Historically it has been a readily recognizable means of delimiting both the nature and instrument of salvation, that is, through Christ and his church, although it has been modified and qualified in various dimensions as theological climates have differed.[2] Moreover, the axiom does not lack for contemporary attention.[3] Rooted in the patristic era, the formula was a constant until the seamless robe of Medieval Christianity began to shred under the bombastic influence of Luther and other Reformers. In the crucible of

---

[1]The famous maxim is from Cyprian, Epistola lxxiii, and is usually misquoted as *nulla salum extra Ecclesiam*.

[2]For a history of the question, see Louis Capéran, *Le Problème du Salut des infidèles: Essai historique*, 2 vols. (Toulouse: Grand Seminaire, 1934); and H. Pinard de la Boullaye, S.J., *L'Étude Comparèe des Religions: Essai critique*, 2 vols. (Paris, 1929-1931); or, more briefly, Yves Congar, O.P., *The Wide World My Parish* (London: Darton Longman, and Todd, 1961), especially chapter 10 "No Salvation Outside the Church," 93-154.

[3]As Joseph E. Fenton, *The Catholic Church and Salvation* (Westminster: The Newman Press, 1958) ix, observes, "Few dogmas . . . have been commented upon and interpreted in twentieth-century theological and religious literature as frequently and extensively as that which teaches us that there is no salvation outside the true Church of Jesus Christ." Cf. Jerome P. Theisen, O.S.B., *The Ultimate Church and The Promise of Salvation* (Collegeville MN: St. John's University Press, 1976).

the Reformation was born the Protestant missionary equivalent: "no salvation outside of Christianity," which was a theological adaptation of no little consequence. Luther and Calvin both spoke of the church as the locus of salvation, using the familiar image from patristic theology of the church as a "Mother." Fundamental ecclesiological and soteriological issues separated the Reformers from their Roman Catholic heritage, yet they shared their insistence that salvation was offered only through Christ and refused to imply that any Protestant tradition would separate professing in Christ from implicit membership in Christ's church.[4] It is fair then to say that the maxim "no salvation outside the church" is as much a part of classic Protestant theological thought as it is of Roman Catholic.

In the Modern Period that flowered after the constructive influences of the Renaissance and Reformation, the synthesis of opinion about the means and extent of salvation began to crumble. Trade and travel spawned interest in other faiths and challenged long-held presuppositions. The development of critical methods, giving greater precision to historiography and comparative approaches, furthered the critique of what for many centuries had stood as the keystone in the theological structure of the church.

The purpose of this chapter is to give a historical overview of the theological development of the doctrine "no salvation outside the church," and it will devote particular attention to the interrelated theological problem of the Christian evaluation of the non-Christian religions.[5] The chapter will examine key figures from four periods: Patristic, Medieval, Reformation, and Modern. This background will enlighten the further task of analyzing current theological responses to the intent of the formula.

---

[4]Indeed, the maxim was held quite as firmly by Protestants as by Roman Catholics and was stated in nearly the same language.

[5]The term "non-Christian" will apply both to those of another religious tradition and to those belonging to none. It is not meant to hold pejorative connotations. "Pagan" and "heathen" are used at times, reflecting the usage of a particular era; they are never meant to imply a "godless one," but simply one who is not an adherent of any of the world's chief religions.

PATRISTIC PERIOD

The beginning of the church's theology is usually dated from the time of the Greek Apologists (ca. 120-220).[6] In seeking to commend and defend the claims of Christianity to a variegated public, the apologetic works of Justin Martyr, Aristides, Tatian, Theophilus of Antioch, and others, revealed both the consonance with current philosophical schemes and Christianity's distinctiveness when placed alongside religions of the heathen world.

The relationship between Christianity, Judaism, and Heathenism was of paramount concern to the early Apologists.[7] Innovative theology was not their task; rather, they reflected, for the most part, the New Testament materials[8] and did not "add anything to the general faith of the church."[9]

Justin stands out among them as a creative thinker in his use of the biblical materials and the philosophies with which secular thinkers were acquainted. Justin affirmed that all knowledge that persons have is the product of the Logos. Thus combining the philosophical and biblical traditions regarding the Logos, he concluded:

> Those who live reasonably are Christians, even though they have been
> thought atheists; as, among the Greeks, Socrates, and Heraclitus, and men

---

[6]Biographical information and dates which appear in this chapter are, unless otherwise noted, drawn from the *Oxford Dictionary of the Christian Church*, F.L. Cross, ed. (Oxford: Oxford University Press, 1974). Hereafter referred to as *Oxford Dictionary*, with appropriate page numbers.

[7]See especially Justin Martyr's *The Dialogue with Trypho*. The best edition of this dialogue is by E.J. Goodspeed, *Die ältesten Apologete* (1914) 90-265. See also A.L. Williams, *Justin Martyr: The Dialogue With Trypho* (London: S.P.C.K., 1930). Also excerpts and notes are found in A.L. Williams's *Adversus Judaeos: A Bird's-Eye View of Christian Apologiae Until the Renaissance* (Cambridge: Cambridge University Press, 1935) 167.

[8]Geoffrey Lampe, *"Christian Theology in the Patristic Period," A History of Christian Doctrine*, Hubert Cunliffe-Jones, ed. (Philadelphia: Fortress Press, 1978) 30.

[9]Reinhold Seeberg, *The History of Doctrines in the Ancient Church*, vol. 1, *The History of Doctrines*, Charles E. Hay, trans. (Grand Rapids: Baker Book House, 1977) 111.

> like them; and among the barbarians, Abraham and Ananias, and Azarias,
> and Misael, and Elias, and many others whose actions and names we now
> decline to recount, because we know it would be tedious.[10]

According to Justin, Christ, the first-born of God, is the Word in whom all persons are partakers; those who live in accordance with reason (*meta logou*) are Christians.

Greek Fathers

Hans Küng traces the roots of the axiom "no salvation outside the church" to Ignatius of Antioch, Irenaeus, Clement of Alexandria, and Origen, all prominent Greek Fathers.[11] Their formulations moved beyond those of the Apologists as the church gained more structure, becoming what is usually called the "Old Catholic Church."

The influential Bishop of Lyons, Irenaeus (ca. 130-200), adumbrated the greater clarity of Cyprian by maintaining that the Spirit and faith are imparted only through the preaching of the church.

> For this gift of God has been entrusted to the church, just as that of
> breathing at the creation, to the end that all members receiving it should
> be vivified; and in it is included the communication of Christ, i.e., the
> Holy Spirit, the pledge of incorruptibility and confirmation of our faith
> and the ladder of ascension to God.[12]

Irenaeus was expressing a common conviction when he said: "Where the Church is, there is the Spirit of God; and where the Spirit of God is, there is the Church

---

[10]*I Apol.* 46. 3-4. *The Ante-Nicene Fathers,* vol. 1, Alexander Roberts and James Donaldson, eds. (New York: Charles Scribner's Sons, 1913) 178. Hereafter cited as *ANF* with appropriate volume and page numbers.

[11]Hans Küng, *The Church* (Garden City: Image Books, 1976) 404. See also Küng's "The World Religions in God's Plan of Salvation," *Christian Revelation and World Religions,* Joseph Neuner, S.J., ed. (London: Burns and Oates, 1967) 25-66.

[12]Irenaeus, *Adv. Haer.,* III, 24.1, *ANF* 1:458.

and every kind of Grace."[13] As the head of the church, Christ has given it the continuing work of recapitulation, through baptism and the eucharist.

In contrast to Irenaeus's essentially positive formulation is that of Origen (ca. 185-254), Alexandrian biblical critic and theologian of expansive interests. He is in the best tradition of the Apologists in his comprehensive definition of Christianity as a universal religion, as opposed to the more provincial religions of Judaism, and those of the gentile world. As the superior religion, it will overcome these lesser ones.[14] Origen warned against the danger of seeking salvation in ways other than the Christian; he also cautioned believers of the judgment they would incur if they departed from the provision of redemption through the church.

"Let no one persuade or deceive himself," he writes, "outside this house, that is, outside the Church, no one will be saved; for if someone leaves, he is himself guilty of death."[15] Origen proclaims the role of the church and of the sacraments in the plan of salvation, yet this is difficult to balance with his doctrine of *apocatastasis*, the view that ultimately all free moral creatures will share in the grace of salvation.[16] Others will be forced to deal with this contradictory logic.

Another Alexandrian Father, Clement (ca. 150-215), stressed that one secures his or her salvation only in connection with the church. Indeed, in one statement he seems to equate human salvation with the church; "His desire is the salvation of men; and this has been called the church."[17] Clement did show appreciation for the values of Hellenistic culture and went further than Justin when he suggested that philosophy was given to the Greeks with the same purpose with

---

[13]Ibid.

[14]See *Contra Celsum, ANF* 4:497-669.

[15]*Homili i Jes Nave* 3.5. J.P. Migne, ed., *Patrologia Cursus Completus, Series Graecae*, vol. 12, col. 841. Hereafter cited as *PG* with appropriate volume and column numbers.

[16]*De Principiis* I. 6.2, *ANF* 4:260-61.

[17]*Paed.* iii. 12 fin.; i.6 123, 114, as cited in Seeberg, *History of Doctrines*, 1:145.

which the law was given to the Jews: "to serve as a handmaiden to lead them to Christ."[18] Like Origen, he took an optimistic view of the ultimate destiny of even the most wicked and wanted to extend God's gracious care to those who had not received the Judeo-Christian legacy.

A provocative theologian in the Greek tradition, Gregory of Nyssa (ca. 330-395), put his distinctive stamp on the Eastern Church in his writings on the Trinity and his interaction with Origen's thought. He, too, shows evidence of the interweaving of biblical motifs and philosophical presuppositions.

Gregory's soteriology reflected the central thought of Greek theology: since God has entered the human race in Christ, humanity has been deified and made immortal. Because Christ assumed human nature, all persons are drawn into the divine nature. Thus Gregory proposed:

> Just as when any one of all the race is alive, the resurrection of the part, being communicated from the part to the whole, penetrates the whole in consequence of the continuity and unity of the nature.[19]

Gregory, like his mentor Origen, was at times influenced more by Platonic philosophy than Scripture, particularly in his notion of the immortality of the soul.[20] He based universal salvation on the fact that all persons were created in the divine image; therefore, it was unthinkable that all should not eventually be brought to perfection. The salvific process was a gradual development of the human soul, the attaining of the "vision of God." The church occupied a less than fundamental role in this design; in the eucharist, Christ continued the work of purification that his incarnation had begun, but a person's relationship to the visible church would not ultimately determine his or her destiny. Its sacraments

---

[18]*Stromata* 1.20, *ANF* 2:323.

[19]*Catechetical Oration*. 13, 16, *PG* 45, col. 46.

[20]See Jaroslav Pelikan, *The Emergence of the Catholic Tradition (100-600)*, vol. 1, *The Christian Tradition* (Chicago: University of Chicago Press, 1971) 128-29, 151-52.

anticipate the general purification that those outside the church will ultimately experience, that is, through death and fire.

A distinctive economy of salvation is found in the tradition of Greek thought that began in Justin Martyr, developed in Origen, and achieved orthodox expression in Gregory of Nyssa. It stressed the "general availability of the means of terrestrial and heavenly salvation. . . ."[21] These theologians recognized a universal operation of Christ and found the fullness of his effective presence in the church, without limiting it to that sphere.

Latin Fathers

During the third century, practical problems forced North African Christian theologies to hammer out a more refined ecclesiology. The chief architect for Western theology was Cyprian, to whom history credits a major development in the Catholic conception of the church.[22] Perhaps because they were dealing with a different set of problems or simply were related to a less structured ecclesiastical form, the Greek Fathers during this period tended to be more optimistic about the divine purposes in the varieties of religious options confronting them than were the Latin Fathers. The role of the church in effecting salvation always bulked larger in the Western tradition.

At the headwaters of the Latin tradition stands that great Carthaginian lawyer and theological polemicist, Tertullian (ca. 160-225). The permeation of his foundational views in the thinking of subsequent theologians has earned for him the title "Father of Latin Theology." Tertullian's writings not only afford "an

---

[21]J. Patout Burns, S.J., "The Economy of Salvation: Two Patristic Traditions," *Theological Studies* 37 (1976): 598-619.

[22]R.P.C. Hanson, "St. Cyprian," *A Dictionary of Christian Theology*, Alan Richardson, ed. (Philadelphia: Westminster, 1969) 86.

incomparable source of material on the church life of his time,"[23] but, they can also inform and give direction to contemporary ecclesiastical needs.[24]

The consuming passion in his many treatises was the holiness of the church—it was not to be spotted by contact with secular learning and worldly enterprises. Tertullian's early writings were in the tradition of early Christian thought which bound together church and Spirit, bishop and Spirit, and tradition and Spirit. The one true church, visible since the time of the apostles and maintained through episcopal succession, is the only authoritative bearer of the revelation of Christ.[25] Tertullian was, however, always more concerned about the continuity of the faith than about loyalty to an institutional form.

Tertullian's rigorous church discipline and hardline stance on post-baptismal penitence led him to Montanism, with its exclusive sectarian concept of the church. In his later writings, he set up an opposition between the church as defined by the succession of bishops and the church as the gathering of "spiritual persons." Indeed, he pushed his new understanding to the point of saying: "The Church itself, properly speaking and principally, is the Spirit itself."[26] Tertullian anticipated Cyprian's question about the "authenticity of the vehicles by which the Spirit is made present among men."[27] For Cyprian the church is the guarantor of the Spirit; for Tertullian, the Spirit is the guarantor of the church. The continuity between Tertullian and Cyprian is quite striking, however.

Many of the concerns of his great mentor are reflected in Cyprian's practical treatises. While Bishop of Carthage, the Decian persecution and Novatian

---

[23]Hans von Campenhausen, *Men Who Shaped the Western Church*, Manfred Hoffman, trans. (New York: Harper and Row, 1960) 10.

[24]See Dennis E. Groh, "Tertullian's Polemic Against Social Co-optation," *Church History* 40 (1971): 7-14.

[25]*Oxford Dictionary*, 1352.

[26]*On Modesty* 21, *ANF* 4:99.

[27]Robert L. Wilken, "The Making of a Phrase," *Dialogue* 12 (1973): 174-81.

schism (249-250) profoundly challenged his theological understanding of the church. Due to these crises, Cyprian's quest for the proper ecclesiastical structure became an all-encompassing issue and the "whole heart of the great bishop was bound up with this idea."[28] Cyprian is traditionally known as the classic exponent of the doctrine of the visible church as the one and necessary ark of divine salvation.

Cyprian did not attempt to develop a doctrine of the church in a systematic manner; but, through controversies and his corresponding treatises, he laid significant foundations for the history of the church. As a result of the Decian persecution, many Christians lapsed from their faith, presenting a problem for the church leadership. Under what conditions should these be restored in the church? Cyprian was strongly opposed to reconciling the lapsed without proper penitential discipline and felt that the bishops should be in agreement about the method of restoring those apostatizing under persecution. By allowing the possibility of restoration, pending a council, he was in direct conflict with Novatian who retained "the ancient praxis in relation to the lapsed."[29] Novatian believed that the church should be comprised only of the pure (*catharoi*) and, thus, had no room for post-baptismal sin. Novatian deemed it theologically necessary to re-baptize those who came to him from the church at large, since that church would grant reconciliation sooner or later to "all sinners who have given adequate tokens and pledges of repentance,"[30] Rejecting this rigorism and that of the later Tertullian, Cyprian and the main body of the church in Africa held that the church was always a mixed society, wheat and tares together. Cyprian insisted that the clergy must be holy and catholic, and he refused to recognize baptism that was received from heretical or schismatic hands.

---

[28]Seeberg, *History of Doctrines*, 1:180. Cf. M.F. Wiles, "The Theological Legacy of St. Cyprian," *Journal of Ecclesiastical History* 14 (1963): 139-49.

[29]Seeberg, *History of Doctrines*, 1:179.

[30]Lampe, "Christian Theology," 171. He explains: "Cyprian's policy established distinctions among those who had lapsed in the Decian persecution and laid conditions for reconciliation varying with the gravity of the offence" (61).

Theologically, the Novatian schism was of great significance because "it confronted theologians with the need to mark out the limits of the true church since these were not now necessarily coterminous with the boundary between recognized orthodoxies and heresies."[31] Cyprian championed the strict view that there is no salvation outside the visible church. The church is the indispensable ark of salvation,[32] the one undivided garment of Christ.[33] Forgiveness of sins, direction of the Holy Spirit, true eucharist or true baptism, do not occur outside the church. Spiritual vitality is not to be found elsewhere; one must remain in the church to enjoy its spiritual benefits. "Whatever departs from the womb will not be able to live and breathe separately; it loses the substance of salvation."[34]

Cyprian maintained that the limits of the true church are to be found primarily in its episcopate. Through it, the church was directly linked with the apostolic faith and the apostolic institutions by its use of the apostolic scriptures. Moreover, Cyprian saw in the episcopal succession the primary guarantee of true doctrine. He elevated succession to the status of the "foundation on which the Church itself rests, and the continuing life and ministry of the Church is made to depend on it."[35] The bishops are necessary to the very being of the church; without them the church lacks the saving grace it exists to share.

Cyprian did much to outline and buttress the parameters of the church in a time when conflict threatened to obliterate its distinctiveness. His key contention in the face of schismatics was that there was only one visible communion, the church, which the Lord had established. Apart from Christ's church, one "will not

---

[31]Ibid.

[32]*De. unit. eccl.* 6, *ANF* 5:423.

[33]Cyprian echoes the thought of Ignatius who maintained that the church is *one*; Ignatius of Antioch is usually noted as the first to speak of the "catholic church," *Smyrna* 8.2.

[34]*De. unit. eccl.* 23, *ANF* 5:428-29.

[35]Lampe, "Christian Theology," 173.

come to Christ's rewards" but will be "an alien, an outcast, an enemy."[36]
Cyprian predicted the same fate for those who would break the unity of the
church, which was meant to express the "peace and concord of Christ."[37]

Differing with the Greek universalism of Origen and Gregory, Tertullian
and Cyprian assumed that the salvation accomplished in Jesus Christ could be
attained only through his church. One must believe the teachings of Christ, be
baptized, and belong to the communion of the proper church in order to
experience salvation. Cyprian's formulations prevailed; and, until the time of
Augustine and Gregory the Great, he was acknowledged as the theological
authority of the Western church.[38]

The key transitional figure between Cyprian and Augustine was Ambrose.
One of the four traditional "Doctors" of the Latin Church, Ambrose (ca. 339-397),
Bishop of Milan, is said to have largely presaged Augustine in his teaching,[39]
specifically in his understanding of the Fall and Original Sin. Ambrose was less
an innovator than a rigid guardian of orthodox Christianity.[40] The nature and
authority of the church were not problematic for him; he was content to build
upon the foundations of Cyprian as he pondered the relationship of church and
state in his own era. Ambrose, like Cyprian, saw the ultimate power and
responsibility for the church invested in the bishops of Christ, superseding even

---

[36]*De. unit. eccl.* 6, *ANF* 5:423.

[37]Ibid.

[38]See Berthold Altaner, *Patrology*, Hilda C. Graef, trans. (New York: Herder and
Herder, 1960) 201.

[39]Seeberg characterizes Ambrose as "an Augustine before Augustine," and he believes
that Ambrose was the "controlling authority in Augustine's thought," *History of Doctrines*,
1:308.

[40]See S.L. Greenslade, *Early Latin Theology, The Library of Christian Classics*
(Philadelphia: The Westminster Press, 1956) 176-77.

that of the emperor.[41] He also followed Cyprian's exclusivist position on the possibility of salvation outside the church.

In an extended allegorical passage, in *Letter* 41: *Synagogue at Callinicum*, Ambrose echoes the limiting refrain. Taking an almost pugilistic stance against the Jews, he compares the spiritual vitality of the church over against that of the synagogue. He declares that only the church has "oil"—that which heals and forgives and imparts the yoke of Christ; the synagogue has no "oil." The Spirit is absent from the synagogue; the pouring of special grace is upon the church alone.[42] There was no recourse for those outside the church, not even for the Jews.

Jerome furthers this exclusivistic tendency in Latin theology. Vacillating ascetic, vitriolic controversialist, prolific writer, and consummate scholar, Jerome (ca. 342-420) is better known for his biblical translations and commentaries than for his creativity as a theologian.[43] He skirted the doctrine of the church in his writings, preferring to devote his attention to the sanctity of the clergy,[44] which, in his mind, never measured up the exalted way of the monastic.

Jerome reiterated the familiar patristic theme of the church as Noah's ark.[45] In his "Appeal to Damasus for Light in His Doctrinal Darkness," he writes of the church: "This is the house where alone the paschal lamb can be rightly

---

[41]*Letter* 17: *The Altar of Victory, Letters* 10-14, and *Letters* 40-41: *The Synagogue at Callinicum*, Greenslade, *Early Latin Theology*, 195-97, 229-50.

[42]*Letter* 40: *The Synagogue at Callincum*, ibid., 15.

[43]Greenslade, *Early Latin Theology*, 288. Cf. von Campenhausen, *Western Church*, 181.

[44]*Letter* 14: *To Heliodorus*, Greenslade, *Early Latin Theology*, 292.

[45]This comparison of the church to the ark goes back at least to Callistus, Bishop of Rome (217-222), who justified the forgiveness of adulterers and fornicators by pointing out that the ark contained unclean as well as clean beasts. See R.H. Bainton, "The Parable of the Tares as the Proof Text for Religious Liberty to the End of the Sixteenth Century," *Church History* 1 (1932): 67-89.

eaten. This is the ark of Noah, and he who is not found in it shall perish when the flood prevails."[46] In the tradition of Latin theology, Jerome anchors any hope for salvation to one's relationship to the church.

The "Gracious Doctor" of the church, Augustine (ca. 354-430), stands as the unrivalled shaper of Latin Christendom. His deep piety and massive intellect enabled him to interpret and refine the thinking of the ancient fathers, which, in turn, was to give form and direction to Medieval theology.

The church's unity was central to Augustine's theology, as it was to Cyprian's, and, accordingly, he appropriates the axiom *extra ecclesiam nulla salus*. Augustine forged his ecclesiology in the heat of the Donatist controversy, a division that threatened the unity of the African church for nearly a century. The controversy was a combination of many influences arising out of the Diocletian persecution, which led to the formation of two warring churches, the Catholic and the Donatist.

Soon after he became bishop, Augustine began seeking to draw together the fragmented African church. The fundamental question the controversy engendered for Augustine was, "Where is the church, whether among us or among them?"[47] He rejected the rigorist Donatist doctrine of the church because it disallowed a mixed community. Rather, following the thrust of many of Christ's parables, he affirmed that good and evil would abide in the church until the time of final separation. Yet, this church is the *one* Catholic church, and he insisted that

---

[46]*Epistle* xv. 1-4, cited in *Creeds, Councils, and Controversies: Documents Illustrative of the History of the Church A.D. 337-461*, J. Stevenson, ed. (New York: The Seabury Press, 1966) 165.

[47]*De. unit. eccl.* 2.2 as cited by Seeberg, *History of Doctrines*, 1:318. Two very helpful volumes on Augustine's biography and theology are: Peter Brown, *Augustine of Hippo* (Los Angeles: University of California Press, 1967), and Eugene TeSelle, *Augustine the Theologian* (New York: Herder and Herder, 1970), respectively.

the Donatists lacked catholicity.[48] Furthermore, outside of this one Catholic church, the body of Christ, there is no truth or salvation.[49]

A distinctive theme of Augustine emerges as he analyzed the precipitating factors for schism. Since love is the essential characteristic of the church, schism is caused by lack of love and pride.[50] This perception is derived from Augustine's contention that it is only in the Catholic church that the Spirit and love are bestowed.[51]

Due to his different concept of the efficacy of the sacraments, Augustine rejected Cyprian's insistence that the baptism of Christ cannot exist among heretics or schismatics. The validity of the sacraments for him was not contingent upon the holiness or catholicity of the administrator; as gifts of God, the sacraments are actualized through the presence of the Holy Spirit, *ex opere operato*.[52] Augustine granted validity to each baptism administered by a Donatistic priest, with one demurrer: the baptism was not effectual until the baptized was united with the one Catholic church.[53] By broadening Cyprian's view, Augustine loses the organic wholeness of church and sacraments. He has been accused of depersonalizing the sacraments by giving them "an autonomous validity apart from the Church's actual life."[54]

One cannot fully comprehend Augustine's doctrine of the church or his understanding of the destiny of non-Christians without viewing them in the larger

---

[48]Lampe, "Christian Theology," 175.

[49]See Seeberg, *History of Doctrines*, 1:318.

[50]Lampe, "Christian Theology," 175.

[51]See *Ad. Simpl.* 1; *De. Bapt.* 1.8, 10; *Epistles* 185, as cited in Seeberg, *History of Doctrines*, 1:316-28.

[52]*c. Parm.* ii. II. 24, as cited by Seeberg, ibid., 1:316-18.

[53]See Seeberg, ibid., 1:320.

[54]Lampe, "Christian Theology," 175.

context of predestination. Conceding that the church presently is a mixed society, he distinguished the true, holy church as that known only to God, comprised of those predestined to eternal life. Although he professed the Cyprianic formula, the "logic of predestinarianism" made it impossible for him to deny that there may be salvation for some who are now outside the church.[55] Augustine did not believe that good works of faithful Jews were sufficient for salvation. Those who lived under the Mosaic law were justified by faith in the incarnation which was to come. Living in accordance with reason did not make one a Christian, as Justin believed; faith in Christ did.[56] Augustine's distinction between the visible and the invisible church allowed a greater openness toward the non-Christians while remaining true to Cyprian's formula. If the formula implied only the visible church, obviously there would be no hope for Jews, pagans, heretics—any person not a member of the one Catholic church. But only God ultimately knows those who are predestined to the City of God. Thus, Augustine stoutly opposed the system of Origen which speculated that all would be saved regardless of their relationship to the church.

Augustine assigned a greater role to the church in the economy of salvation than did any theologians in the Greek tradition. The church has both a mediatorial role in making forgiveness and charity available and is itself the community in which the Spirit dwells. One must remain a member of the Catholic communion to have the continuing grace of the Holy Spirit. The historical setting of Augustine's formulations precluded recognizing "subjective salvific acts without their public and explicitly Christian forms. . . ."[57] For Augustine the explicitly Christian forms could only mediate grace within sustained orthodoxy—the Catholic church. His view would prevail until the Reformation.

---

[55]Ibid., 176. See Eugene TeSelle, *Augustine*, 319-29.

[56]*De Civitate Dei*, X, xxv. *Nicene and Post Nicene Fathers of the Christian Church*, vol. 2, Philip Schaff, ed. (New York: Scribner's Sons, 1904) 8-9. Hereafter cited as *NPNF* with appropriate volume and page numbers.

[57]Burns, "The Ecology of Salvation," 615.

Gregory the Great (ca. 540-604) was the fourth of the traditional Latin Doctors of the church. Some historians consider him the last great figure of the patristic era, while others see him as the first representative of Medieval Catholicism. Gregory was particularly indebted to the writings of Augustine and can be regarded as the systematizer and interpreter of Augustinian thought, albeit a rather "emaciated Augustinianism."[58] A basic unity of thought exists between him and his forbears in Latin theology; he, too, postulated that all outside the church's bounds will by no means be saved.[59] The church became, in Gregory's thought, a bulwark of security in an age of superstition and fear. He elevated the power of the leadership of the church, almost making bishops and priests the dispensers of grace themselves.[60] Gregory's achievements lay in his practical leadership of the church, not in original theological thought.

Assessment of the Patristic Period

George Huntston Williams notes eight fairly distinct theories held in the patristic era about the meaning of non-Christian religions in the divine economy. The interest of these writers was primarily the religions prior to Christianity: Judaism and the Graeco-Roman religions. The Church Fathers postulated:

> 1) the doctrine of the individual elect persons amid the mass of fallen humanity and its numerous forms of *false religions*; 2) that Christianity was the republication of the aboriginal religion of Paradise and the Golden Age which had, here and there, survived from the beginning in the company of "the Friends of God" (the latter phrase combining both scriptural and pagan motifs); 3) that the eternal Word (Logos) has been guiding various groupings of humanity by means of religious philosophy

---

[58]Reinhold Seeberg, *History of Doctrines in the Ancient Church*, vol. 2, *The History of Doctrines*, Charles E. Hay, trans. (Grand Rapids: Baker Book House, 1977) 22. A bold new interpretation of Gregory has recently been published by Carole Straw. See her percipient study, *Gregory the Great: Perfection in Imperfection* (Berkeley: University of California Press, 1988).

[59]*mor.* xiv. v. 5; *ep.* xi. 46, as cited in Seeberg, *History of Doctrines*, 1:17-27.

[60]See Robert F. Evans, *One and Holy: The Church in Latin Patristic Thought* (London: SCPK, 1972) 146f.

and the moral law toward the plenitude of the revelation of the Word as incarnate in Jesus Christ; 4) that what was good in other religions and religious philosophies had been cravenly stolen or resourcefully borrowed from the Hebrews and then the Christians; 5) that other religions were Satan's tempting counterfeits of the true faith and cultus; 6) that national angels were, under God, guiding all peoples and their religious cults in various stages of obedience and disobedience on the part of both angels and men; 7) that the false religions were spiritual chastisements of various peoples for their having turned from an aboriginal universal monotheism and perfect cultus; and 8) that God intended the salvation of all men and would eventually bring about the *restitutio omnium* (Acts 2:21), including the fallen angels (universalism).[61]

The relationship of Christianity to Judaism was a pressing concern in the first five centuries, and virtually every major Christian writer either composed a treatise in opposition to Judaism, or included this theme in other collections.[62] The end result of these protracted disputes with Judaism and classical thought was a temporary resolution that provided a "schematization of the relation between Christianity and other religions that assured the finality of God's revelation in Christ while acknowledging the partial validity of earlier revelations."[63] The existence of the church and its role in salvation was evidence that in Christ the fullness of truth had come, and thus the vital question in these early centuries was "inside or outside the church."[64] *Extra ecclesiam nulla salus* had its genesis in

---

[61]George Huntston Williams, "Erasmus and the Reformers on Non-Christian Religions and *Salus Extra Ecclesiam*," *Action and Conviction in Early Modern Europe: Essays in Memory of E.H. Harbison*, Theodore K. Rabb and Jerrold E. Siegel, eds. (Princeton: Princeton University Press, 1969) 323.

[62]Pelikan, *The Christian Tradition*, 1:15. See especially Tertullian's *Adversus Judaeos*, *ANF*, 3:151-73; Cyprian's *Ad Quirinum*, A.L. Williams, 56-63; and Augustine, *Tractatus Adversus Judaeos*, *J.P. Migne, ed. Patrologiae Cursus Completus*, Series Latina, vol. 8, cols. 51-64. Hereafter cited as *PL* with appropriate volume and column numbers.

[63]Pelikan, *The Christian Tradition*, 1:55.

[64]S.L. Greenslade, *Schism in the Early Church* (New York: Harper and Row, 1950) 21.

the thought of the Latin Fathers as they sought to protect the church from heterodox influences. While it was early applied to those who had separated themselves from the unity of the Catholic church, by the time of Augustine, the formula was used as a delimiting means to exclude salvation through other means than Christ and his church.

MEDIEVAL PERIOD

The Middle Ages have been described as the "age of faith"; the church colored every sphere of life—architecture, music, philosophy, and education. The supernatural, although grossly caricatured at times, was an assumed component. The history of the church in the Middle Ages is the history of the "most elaborate and thoroughly integrated system of religious thought and practice the world has ever known."[65]

During the fifth and sixth centuries both the Greek and Latin traditions sought to articulate an orthodox consensus, derived from the patristic writers and conciliar actions. Although still parts of the one Catholic church, by the end of the sixth century it was apparent East and West were going their separate ways liturgically, administratively, culturally, and, not least, doctrinally.[66]

The Eastern tradition conceptualized salvation as divinization, which focused attention on christological issues, while the West dealt with ecclesiological and anthropological concerns, to which Augustine had largely devoted his attention. The doctrine of the church was never the subject of controversy in Greek Christianity and, consequently, was more loosely defined. The basic problem of Eastern Christianity from the ninth century on was survival. Always

---

[65]R.W. Southern, *Western Society and the Church in the Middle Ages*, vol. 2, *The Pelican History of the Church* (Middlesex: Penguin Books, 1970) 15.

[66]Pelikan, *The Christian Tradition*, 1:340. The differentiation between East and West first became pronounced in the Constantinian revolution, as Constantinople became the new Christian center (A.D. 330).

on the edge of Islam, the Greek tradition was not open to flux and change as was the West. The conservative Byzantine approach to theology is best expressed with the word *paradosis*, "that which is handed down."

It is possible to view Western Medieval theology as a "series of footnotes to Augustine,"[67] as Pelikan wryly observes. The Augustinian legacy was the theological agenda and each sought to adapt or interpret it, expand or correct it. The task of both Greek and Latin theologians was, in their thinking, not to discover truth—the councils had already decided that—but to systematize, harmonize, and defend the traditional dogma. They were preoccupied with restating the elusive *consensus patrum*,[68] which was a thoroughly backward-looking theological exercise. Most early medieval theologians made their doctrinal contributions by means of special treatises on individual questions or by way of doctrinal summaries more closely tied to the scriptural narrative or to patristic models. This *ad fontes* approach notwithstanding, there were dogmatic developments during this period, many of which were fostered by the impingement of non-Christian religions.

To the eight theories of the patristic age concerning the meaning of non-Christian religions in the divine economy, Byzantine and Latin (and Arabic) theologians added three new views:

> 9) [that] Islam specifically was a chastisement of Christians by God for their schisms and moral defections; 10) that Mohammed (or any other heresiarch) was, contrariwise, the instrument of Satan, or more precisely, of the Antichrist, since he misappropriated the revelation in Jesus Christ; and 11) that "Allah" was merely another name for the true God, and

---

[67]Jaraslov Pelikan, *The Growth of Medieval Theology (600-1300)*, vol. 3, *The Christian Tradition* (Chicago: The University of Chicago Press, 1978) 3.

[68]Jaraslov Pelikan, *The Spirit of Eastern Christendom (600-1700)*, vol. 2, *The Christian Tradition* (Chicago: The University of Chicago Press, 1974) 21f.

hence, God might well deign to accord to Muslims, by virtue of their obedience to the Qur'an, eternal salvation in the "bosom of Abraham."[69]

The earlier Middle Ages were little, if at all, troubled by the thought that those outside the fold (the church) had only the flames of hell awaiting them. "The harsh separation of the sheep from the goats was the axiom of its religious life, and discountenanced all attempts to enlarge the area of salvation."[70] The apologetic task vis-à-vis Graeco-Roman religions and Judaism, extensively engaged by the Fathers, fell into the background until the twelfth and thirteenth centuries.[71] Many practical problems begged for solution, however, as the interaction with pagan tribes became more frequent. Incorporating these tribes into the Catholic church made it necessary to define salvation in terms of a "bond between orthodoxy and morality,"[72] and the church denounced the heathen practices of these converts. The challenge of these tribes paled beside the emergence of Islam, by all measures the most far-reaching problem in Medieval Christendom.[73]

It will not be possible to trace even cursorily all the significant theological movements of this epoch[74] in a historical overview. The focus of this investigation is the theological development of the concept "no salvation outside the church" and the concomitant problem of the evaluation of non-Christian

---

[69]G.H. Williams, "Erasmus and the Reformers," 323-24.

[70]R.W. Southern, *Western Views of Islam in the Middle Ages* (Cambridge MA: Harvard University Press, 1962) 62.

[71]H.R. Schlette, *Towards a Theology of Religions*, W.J. O'Hara, trans. (London: Burns and Oates, 1963) 23.

[72]Pelikan, *The Christian Tradition*, 3:21f.

[73]Southern, *Western Views*, 3.

[74]The dating of the Middle Ages here being used is from 604 to 1350, i.e., from the death of Gregory I to the early advocates of reform.

religions. Hence, this section will include the approach of influential theologians in both Greek and Latin churches.

Greek Tradition

Meyendorff has observed that the predominant part of the theological literature of the Byzantine Church is either exegetical or polemical,[75] not an attempt at a "systematic theology." This was due, in part, to Greek Christianity's suspicion of the inadequacy of religious language, but in the main, because the church found itself in constant confrontation ideologically with Islam. Its claim to be the bearer of further revelation, establishing it as the true universal religion, provoked refutations of a more occasional nature from Byzantine theologians. Serious grappling with the primary source of Islamic theology, the Qur'an, did not occur until the ninth century, when a Byzantine scholar, Nicetas, attempted an extensive critique and refutation of the Qur'an, chapter by chapter.[76]

The leading Greek theologian of the eighth century and a continuing influence on the Byzantine Church, John of Damascus (ca. 675-749), is credited both with providing the classic exposition of Eastern theology, *De Fide Orthodoxa*, and with contributing significantly to Western theology. John's anti-Muslim polemics and disputations with Judaism figured prominently during this early period of the Middle Ages.[77] Indeed, the name of John of Damascus usually heads every list of Christian anti-Muslim polemicists.

Living in Arab-dominated Palestine, he held an essentially hostile attitude toward these "pagans." He spoke of Muhammad as the "forerunner of the Anti-

---

[75]John Meyendorff, *Byzantine Theology: Historical Trends and Doctrinal Themes* (New York: Fordham University Press, 1974) 4.

[76]Pelikan, *The Christian Tradition*, 2:229. For an explication of Nicetas's method, see Norman Daniel, *Islam and the West: The Making of An Image* (Edinburgh: The University Press, 1960) 5.

[77]See his "Against the Jews Concerning the Sabbath," A.L. Williams, *Adversus Judaeos*, 167.

Christ" (*prodromos tou Antichristou*).[78] Such acerbic language prevented real dialogue and caricatured the new religion "as nothing more than gross superstition and immorality."[79] Moreover, John listed Islam in his catalogue of Christian heresies,[80] believing that it was a conglomerate of the errors of the Arians, Nestorians, and Donatists.

Two strands emerged in Eastern Christianity's thinking about Islam: an extreme, closed approach that adopted an absolutely negative attitude, considering Islam a form of paganism, and a more moderate attitude that sought to affirm a common conceptuality and allegiance to monotheism.[81] Lapsing in consistency, John at times espoused the latter approach,[82] which always raised trinitarian issues, a key subject in all Islam-Christian disputes. Writing in the early years of the Islamic conquest, he began the long tradition of "arguing about the Persons of the Godhead in the context of Qur'anic Christology."[83] John maintained that Christian truth lies implicit in the Qur'an, and Christians must draw it out. It was a *corroboratio* of the Gospel, for it gave much involuntary witness to Christ.[84]

---

[78]*De. Haer. PG*, 94, col. 764. See Daniel J. Sahas, *John of Damascus on Islam* (Leiden: Brill, 1972) 68-69.

[79]Meyendorff, *Byzantine Theology*, 51. See Norman Daniel, *Islam and the West* (Edinburgh: The University Press, 1960) 4.

[80]Pelikan, *The Christian Tradition*, 2:230. For a full discussion of the ramifications involved in assessing Islam to be a Christian heresy, see Daniel, *Islam and the West*, 184-88. The tradition of deeming Islam a Christian heresy is undoubtedly due to John's expansive comments in *De Haeribus*. See Sahas, *John of Damascus*, 58-60.

[81]Pelikan, *The Christian Tradition*, 229. See Daniel's description of the two strands in the Oriental polemic tradition, *Islam and the West*, 2. The best example of John's more moderate approach is his *Dialogue between a Christian and a Saracen*, Anne Fremantle, ed., *A Treasury of Early Christianity* (New York: Viking Press, 1953).

[82]See James Kritzeck, "Moslem-Christian Understanding in the Medieval Times," *Comparative Studies in Society and History* 4 (1962): 338-401.

[83]Daniel, *Islam and the West*, 3.

[84]Ibid., 272.

Like other Greeks, John viewed Islam as a temporary aberration whose impetus would soon dissipate. Hence, he did not feel it necessary to examine its enduring ramifications in the economy of salvation. Another probable reason for his lack of theologizing about the ultimate destiny of the Muslims was his adherence to the Byzantine concept of *oikonomia*, which implied a certain flexibility in particular theological concerns. What is at stake in this stance is, in Meyendorff's observation, "an obligation to decide individual issues in the general context of God's plan for the salvation of the world."[85]

The Greek East rejected the West's juridical nomenclature when speaking about the nature of the church, personal redemption, or the communion of the saints.[86] Tradition and the sacraments were central for the Byzantines; however, they did not stress the character of the institution as did the Latins. They believed that the reality of God's church did not yield to simple definition or to exhaustive canon law. The Byzantine view of the church was:

> a sacramental communion with God in Christ and the Spirit, whose membership—the entire Body of Christ—is not limited to the earthly *oikumene* ("inhabited earth") where law governs society, but includes the host of angels and saints, as well as the divine head.[87]

Using the principle of *oikonomia*, the Greeks sought to ameliorate the austerity of Cyprianic strictures in order to remove obstacles to salvation for some.[88] They clearly manifested a greater tractability than the Latins when regarding the relationship of membership in the church to salvation.

---

[85]Meyendorff, *Byzantine Theology*, 88-89.

[86]Kallistos Ware, "Christian Theology in the East 600-1453," *A History of Christian Doctrine*, Hubert Cunliffe-Jones, ed. (Philadelphia: Fortress Press, 1978) 213.

[87]Meyendorff, *Byzantine Theology*, 79.

[88]Ibid., 88-89.

John of Damascus followed the central thrust of Eastern theology in his elaboration of what had been accomplished when the Logos assumed humanity,[89] but he departed from *apocatastasis*, condemned in 553 as Origenistic. Nevertheless, he shared Origen's view of the soul as immortal.[90] The fact that the Logos had assumed human nature as such implied the universal validity of redemption, but not universalism, which presupposed "an ultimate limitation of human freedom. . . ."[91] This element of freedom was essential to John's doctrine of salvation, as it was to his predecessor in Byzantine theology, Maximus the Confessor. John discarded the recapitulation motif which Maximus employed, for it did not sufficiently allow personal and free commitment. He also faulted Islam precisely at this point: the all-determining will of Allah did violence to the Christian understanding of free will and responsibility. He, like other Christian theologians of his era, believed that "Islam represented an out-and-out determinism."[92] The fact that he could affirm the universal salvific will of God did not mean that all were predetermined to choose salvation. In John's words:

> God gave us the power to do what is good; but he also made us free
> (*autexousious*), in order that the good might come both from him and
> from us; for whoever chooses the good, receives God's collaboration to
> do the good, so that, having preserved what is natural to us, we might
> receive what is supernatural—incorruptibility and deification—by union
> with God, by becoming members of his household by the power of our
> will. . . .[93]

---

[89]See John Meyendorff, *Christ in Eastern Christian Thought* (Washington: Corpus Books, 1969) 116-31.

[90]*Exposition of the Orthodox Faith*, Book 4, ch. 27, *NPNF*, 9:99.

[91]Meyendorff, *Byzantine Theology*, 163.

[92]Pelikan, *The Christian Tradition*, 2:234. See W.M. Watt, *Free Will and Predestination in Early Islam* (London: Luzac, 1948).

[93]*De duabus*, as cited in Meyendorff, *Christ in Eastern Christian Thought*, 210.

A ninth-century Arabic-speaking bishop, Theodore Abu Qûrra deserves attention in the history of early Byzantine polemics against Islam. He, along with John of Damascus, formulated the standard apologetic arguments for the Christian case against the Muslims. Better acquainted with the religious interloper than was John, he nevertheless maintained a "strictly negative attitude"[94] toward the religion of Muhammad. Abu Qûrra composed numerous "dialogues" that endeavored to engage the opposing parties at a very practical level.[95] More than any theologian before, he sought to explicate the differences in doctrine and thus to move toward rapprochement. His arguments were also conducted on a more philosophical and theological level, especially when discussing predestination and free will. As a well-schooled Byzantine theologian, Theodore used his sophistication in christological issues to refute the charge that "the Trinity represented a compromise of the monotheistic faith. . . ."[96] In his approach to these issues as well as others, a positive step is taken. Abu Qûrra genuinely worked for a greater degree of mutual understanding, and he cared more for constructive theological discussion than for careless invective.

From the eleventh to the fifteenth century, the knowledge of Islam gradually increased in Byzantium, and subsequent Islamic challenges were faced more realistically. Christian theologians took the persistence of Islam more seriously and shifted from praying for its destruction to praying for the conversion of the Muslims; Gregory Palamas was a significant artificer of this perspective.

Among the greatest "Doctors" of the Orthodox Church, Gregory Palamas (1296-1359), Archbishop of Thessalonica in the middle of the fourteenth century, is best known for his contribution to the Hesychasm movement in Eastern

---

[94]The Greek treatises of Abu Qûrra are published in *PG*, vol. 97, cols. 1461-1509. See also G. Graf, *Die arabischen Schriften des Theodor Abu Qûrra* (Paderborn, 1910).

[95]John Meyendorff, "Byzantine Views of Islam," *Dumbarton Oaks Papers* 18 (1964): 115-32.

[96]Pelikan, *The Christian Tradition*, 2:231. See Meyendorff, "Byzantine Views of Islam," 121.

spirituality. What is of importance for the present discussion is his attitude to Islam over against his understanding of the church.

Gregory manifests the shift that has occurred in Byzantium's stance toward non-Christian religions, notably Islam. In Meyendorff's eloquent study of Gregory's life and theology, he cites a conversation of 1354 in which Gregory describes his journey to Turkish-occupied Asia Minor in optimistic terms, "hoping for a subsequent conversion of Moslems and implying the acceptance, for the time-being, of a friendly co-existence."[97]

Another study of Gregory records the keen interest the Archbishop took in Islam. While on a voyage between Thessalonica and Byzantium, his ship was captured by Turks, and he was forced to stay in Asia Minor for nearly a year. He spent much time disputing irenically with his captors, working for a better understanding of their faith. In this he evidenced concern for the mission of the church, not the political interests of the empire.[98]

The doctrine of the church receives considerable attention in Gregory's writings—somewhat a precedent among Byzantine theologians. He attached great importance to baptism as Christian initiation; for him "neither Christian experience nor spirituality could exist outside the sacramental grace which, in the church, communicated the divine life to the faithful."[99] Gregory conceives the church as a real and visible community; those not incorporated in the church with Christ through baptism cannot experience redemption.

---

[97]Meyendorff, "Byzantine Views of Islam," 123. See J. Meyendorff, *Introduction à l'étude de Grégoire Palamas* (Paris, 1959) 157-62.

[98]John Meyendorff, *St. Gregory Palamas and Orthodox Spirituality*, Adele Fiske, trans. (Crestwood NY: St. Vladimir's Seminary Press, 1974) 106.

[99]John Meyendorff, *A Study of St. Gregory Palamas*, George Lawrence, trans. (London: The Faith Press, 1964) 160.

George Scholarius furthered Palamas's ecclesiological concerns. Appointed Patriarch of Constantinople[100] by its Turkish conquerors in 1453, Scholarius (ca. 1405-1472) was a gifted theologian and Aristotelian philosopher of enormous literary production.[101] Early in his career as a teacher and a monk, he had been involved in the Council of Florence's deliberation about the union of Latin and Greek churches;[102] however, his later theological activity revolved around his role as a Christian apologete to the Sultan Mahomet. At the request of the Sultan, he wrote a treatise summarizing Christian beliefs, *Concerning the Only Way for the Salvation of Men*, which was subsequently translated into Turkish.

The thrust of his apology was conciliatory, yet it delimited the method of salvation to be through the "one and only God in a Trinity of Persons."[103] He refuted the worship of Allah as inauthentic monotheism because it denied that the Son of God was the revealer of the one true God. Apart from the Christian doctrine of salvation, "it is impossible for man to reach his goal,"[104] he declared.

The goal of Scholarius's treatise was unabashedly the conversion of the Sultan and his followers. The way for them to be included in the economy of salvation was devotion to the Son of God—the only authentic monotheism.[105]

---

[100]At this time Scholarius adopted the name Gennadius II, under which superscription several of his writings were published. See *PG*, vol. 160.

[101]For further insight into this significant period see the revised edition of John Marenbon's *Early Medieval Philosophy (480-1150): An Introduction* (London: Routledge, 1988).

[102]See Joseph Gill, S.J. *Personalities of the Council of Florence* (New York: Barnes and Noble, Inc., 1964) 79-94.

[103]Geo. Schol. *Sal.* 21; Petit, *Oeuvres*, 3:452.

[104]Geo. Schol. *Sal.* 1; Petit, *Oeuvres*, 3:435.

[105]Pelikan, *The Christian Tradition*, 2:242. In Pelikan's judicious estimation there was "no such apologia over against Islam that succeeded more fully. . . ."

The patriarch's apologetic concern also extended to the Jews. To facilitate dialogue, he composed a summary of the doctrines of the Christian faith to be found in the New Testament and compiled a list of the chief passages in the Old Testament which foretold the coming of Christ and thus "proved" the truth of the Christian religion. In 1455 he issued a comprehensive treatise, "A Refutation of the Jews from Scripture and from History, in the Form of a Dialogue,"[106] which could both strengthen Christians and serve as an instrument for evangelism.

In the writings of these Byzantine theologians, the greater desire is for the conversion of the Muslims than for a peaceful co-existence. Living in religious isolation, it is understandable that they often reflected more of a siege mentality than a constructive Christian apologetic.

Latin Tradition

R. W. Southern divides western views of Islam in the Middle Ages into three stages: (1) the age of ignorance,[107] which dates from A.D. 700 to 1140; (2) the century of reason and hope, ca. 1150-1290; and (3) the moment of vision, 1290-1460.[108] This study will basically follow his divisions in the investigation of the Latin church's theological development vis-à-vis non-Christian religions, particularly Islam, and the further concretization of the maxim "no salvation outside the church."

Before 1100, Western writers knew practically nothing about Islam;[109] it was only one of many enemies threatening Christendom and clearly not as

---

[106]Excerpts from this treatise are found in Williams, *Adversus Judaeos*, 188-201.

[107]Southern, *Western Views*, delineates two kinds of ignorance manifested by the Christians with regard to Islam: "The ignorance of a confined space and the ignorance of a triumphant imagination" (14).

[108]Ibid.

[109]Ibid., 13, comments on this historical anomaly: "Nothing is more striking . . . than the extreme slow penetration of Islam as an intellectually identifiable fact in Western minds. . . ." See Kritzeck, "Moslem-Christian Understanding in the Medieval Times," 388-95.

menacing as the pagan tribes on their doorstep or the great cosmic struggle between good and evil. The most important sources of information reached Latin Europe by way of Spain; and, by the beginning of the twelfth century, Islam began to be treated seriously in works written in the West. Before that time, ignorance produced a body of scurrilous legends gleaned more from prejudice than scholarship or experience. Among the legends were these:

> Muslims were idolaters worshipping a false trinity; Muhammed was a magician; he was even a Cardinal of the Roman Church, who, thwarted in his ambition to become Pope, revolted, fled to Arabia and founded a church for his own.[110]

Before the twelfth century it had been primarily the Byzantine theologians who had outlined the apologetic case against the Muslims in the early centuries after the rise of Muhammad. The advent of the Crusades forced the Latins to take Islam more seriously as a theological issue, not just a military foe to be vanquished.[111]

The first line of argument to be developed among the Latins was, of course, the biblical, as the Bible was "the one effective intellectual tool of the early Middle Ages."[112] For the genesis of this overture, one must look to Bede, the great biblical master of England.

The Venerable Bede (673-735), English historian and theologian, is revered for his ecclesiastical history as well as his biblical commentaries.[113] The Bible, as the revealed Word of God, was the "ultimate foundation upon which the whole

---

[110]Albert Hourani, *Europe and the Middle East* (London: Macmillan Press, 1980) 9. Norman Daniel, *Islam and the West*, is the indispensable work on this subject. See also D.C. Munro, "The Western Attitude Toward Islam during the Period of the Crusades," *Speculum* 6 (1931): 329-45.

[111]Pelikan, *The Christian Tradition*, 3:243.

[112]Southern, *Western Views*, 15.

[113]See R.W. Southern, *Medieval Humanism and Other Studies* (Oxford: Blackwell, 1970) 1-8.

of Bede's world was built."[114] His entire lifework had been the prayerful study of Scripture; Bede confessed at the end of his long career: *omnem meditandis scripturis operam dedi.*[115]

When interpreting Scripture, Bede was especially insistent upon deriving the historical sense; the "spiritual" meaning could have no relevance if not based on history.[116] Bede's greatest historical problem was not England's church history; it was *sacra historia*, the biblical past.[117] Bede introduced into the medieval tradition of biblical exegesis the view that the Saracens were the descendants of Ishmael, the son of Hagar.[118] By using the Bible this way, a bridge was thrown over the deep ravine between Christianity and the Muslims; a niche was given to them within Christian history.[119] Thus, Bede influenced subsequent Carolingian scholars to place the Saracens in the Old Testament context.

Bede's understanding of the church was in concert with classical Latin theology. His reverence for and faithfulness to patristic tradition is without question, his zeal for orthodoxy renowned. For him, it was "only in that unity which is called 'catholic' that the gate of life is open to all."[120] That he placed

---

[114]Peter Hunter Blair, *The World of Bede* (New York: St. Martin's Press, 1970) 212.

[115]*Historia Ecclesiastica*, B. Colgrace and R.A.B. Mynors, eds. (Oxford: Oxford University Press, 1969) 566.

[116]Pelikan, *The Christian Tradition*, 3:39. For an opposite understanding of Bede's hermeneutical method, see Christopher Plummer's edition of *Historiam Ecclesiasticum Gentis Anglorum* (London: Oxford University Press, 1896) lvi-lxxi.

[117]See Roger D. Ray, "Bede, the Exegete, as Historian," *Famulus Christi: Essays in Commemoration of the Thirteenth Centenary of the Birth of the Venerable Bede*, Gerald Bonner, ed. (London: SPCK, 1976) 125. Ray notes the commonality that Bede felt with Augustine in viewing the Bible as the unparalleled book of history.

[118]See Bede, *Commentary on Genesis*, PL, 91, 189-90.

[119]Southern, *Western Views*, 17. See also Hourani, *Europe and the Middle East*, 24f., and Daniel, *Islam and the West*, 272.

[120]Bed. *Gen.* 1, as cited in Pelikan, *The Christian Tradition*, 3:15.

Muslims in a pre-Christian context indicated his posture toward the means of their salvation. They, too, must acknowledge the fullness of revelation that had come in Christ, fulfilling the vision of the Old Testament prophetic vision. This answer was sufficient for Bede, for his cloistered life in Wearmouth and Jarrow did not experience the shaking of Christendom's foundations,[121] yet his answer was not enough for those whose faith was presently being pummeled by the encroachment of Islam's powerful forces.[122] Those directly confronted in Spain made further strides in their biblical-theological reflection.

In addition to anchoring the Saracens in the biblical history as a means of identifying them, a strain of thinking emerged in Spain in the middle of the ninth century that looked to biblical prophecy as the means of interpreting Islam. Spanish apocalyptic thought handled the present oppression by looking to the future judgment of the Anti-Christ and the vindication of the church. Indeed, in this view, the appearance of Islam signalled the time of preparation for his destructive role.[123]

Between 850 and 860[124] a reaction to the rule of the Moors developed in Spain, known as the Martyr's Movement. Two similarly minded figures, Eulogious and Alvarus, were responsible for nearly all of the movement's literary production.[125] Because very few of their treatises remain,[126] it is possible only to ascertain the vague contours of their thinking.

---

[121]The Saracens had conquered Spain in the years 710-713. The Victory of Tours in 732, won by Charles Martel, saved Gaul from the fate of Spain.

[122]Hourani, *Europe and the Middle East*, 20; Southern, *Western Views*, 19-27.

[123]Southern, *Western Views*, 22.

[124]Ibid.

[125]Daniel, *Islam and the West*, 5-6, characterizes the brief literature of this movement as non-impressive and only important as a reflection of these Christians' ideas in this era. He also believes that these writings had no close literary ties with later Western writers.

[126]See *PL*, 115, 708-870; *PL*, 121, 397-566.

Alvarus interpreted Dan 7:23-25 and portions of Job and the Apocalypse[127] in a historicist manner, giving the symbols and images of these texts a literal referent within his historical era. With the help of the priest Eulogius, he proclaimed the imminence of the end, warning other believers against lax toleration of the religion of Islam.

These apocalyptic formulations had little to commend them;[128] nonetheless, they constituted the "first rigidly coherent and comprehensive view of Islam, related to contemporary circumstances, to be developed in the West."[129] It was not, however, factual. Their understanding of Islam was not based on reliable sources, but on the tormented projections of an oppressed, disenfranchised people.[130]

At the time of the First Crusade,[131] very little was known in the Latin West about the Muslims. Penetrating into Palestine did not afford the Crusaders knowledge of Islam; surprisingly, it only served to foster an attitude of triumph and contempt.[132] One effort to break out of the dual ignorance of a confined space and a triumphant imagination is noteworthy: the immense apologetic task of Peter the Venerable.

Standing on the threshold of the "century of reason and hope," Peter (ca. 1092-1156) gave inspiration and personal direction to a project as yet unattempted. On a trip to Spain in 1142, he conceived his plan to study intensively the original

---

[127]*PL*, 121, 535-36.

[128]Southern, *Western Views*, 24-25; Daniel, *Islam and the West*, 5-6.

[129]Southern, *Western Views*, 25.

[130]Not only was Alvarus concerned with the defection of Christians to Islam, but also the defection of Christians to Judaism. See A.L. Williams's *Adversus Judaeos*, 224-27.

[131]D.C. Munro, "The Western Attitude Toward Islam during the Period of the Crusades," *Speculum* 6 (1931): 330, cites Pope Gregory VII's announcement in 1075 of the plan for an "armed expedition against the enemies of God," which was "designed to go to the Lord's Sepulchre."

[132]Ibid., 337.

sources of the religion of Islam and a non-pejorative portrayal of the character of the Prophet. Undoubtedly, the contacts with beleaguered Spanish Christians on the boundary of Islamic and Christian-European cultures prompted him to initiate the study of Islam in Europe.

Peter believed that a weapon was needed to combat this heresy;[133] it could only be answered conclusively if the Qur'an were translated into Latin.[134] He saw it in the long-term interests of Latin Christianity to undertake this project.[135] At a time when the flush of crusading fever was epidemic, it seemed a curious, non-pragmatic concern, and drew very little support. Nevertheless, he hired three outstanding scholars and set to work on the translation that was to hold the field until the seventeenth century.

Peter pioneered in his insistence that the Muslims of his day "were as specifically intended as any of the Gentiles to participate in Christian salvation. . . ."[136] He believed that he could convert them by exposing the weaknesses of the Qur'an; he well knew they would not turn to Christianity under threat of the sword.

Peter denounced the Crusaders for forfeiting a grand opportunity for evangelizing the followers of Muhammad; instead, spiritual concerns had been trampled under Crusaders' horses in hot pursuit of political and military conquest. Suffice it to say, Peter was a lone voice insisting that he could justify the Crusades only if they were prompted for the conversion of the Muslims.[137]

---

[133]In *Liber Contra Sectam Sive Saracenorum*, translated in James Kritzeck, *Peter the Venerable and Islam* (Princeton: Princeton University Press, 1964), 226, Peter spoke of the heresy of Muhammad as the heresy that "exceeded all the heresies that have been aroused by the diabolical spirit in the 1,100 years since the time of Christ."

[134]The most significant study on this subject is by M.T. d'Alverny, "*Deux traductions latines du Coran au Moyen Age*," *Archives d'histoire et litteraire du Moyen Age* 16 (Paris: Mouton, 1948) 69-131.

[135]Southern, *Western Views*, 38.

[136]Kritzeck, *Peter the Venerable*, 24.

[137]Ibid., 20-23. See Giles Constable, ed., *The Letters of Peter the Venerable*, 2 vols. (Cambridge MA: Harvard University Press, 1967).

In addition to supervising the translation of the Qur'an, Peter wrote a summary of the beliefs of Islam[138] which, he hoped, would spur more enlightened study of the sources and theology of this "Christian heresy." As a Christian cleric writing for Christian clerics, Peter stood as a lighthouse pointing the way for others who would pursue the apologetic task. He was ceaseless in his proclamation of the significance of this mission for the church,

> believing that the church's credibility was at stake. If it refused to engage the threat of Islam, the church protrayed herself not only as scandalously ignorant, but negligent as well.[139]

Peter also directed an apologia toward the Jews. In his scholarly and zealous approach he was ahead of his time. He had sufficiently studied the Hebrew texts and talmudic sources and scholars as to be able to converse knowledgeably about differing biblical and theological points. His longest treatise, *Liber adversus Judaeorum inveteratam duritiem*, is the fruit of the "over-riding responsibility he felt toward non-Christians. . . ."[140] He attempted to convert Jews as he did Muslims: by showing them that their faith was *perfidiae*.[141]

Contemporary with the Cluniac Abbot, Peter the Venerable, was one of the more colorful characters of Medieval Latin Theology and an influential figure in the early Scholastic movement, Peter Abelard (1097-1142). Unrestricted by allegiance to a particular school,[142] he approached problems with freshness and insight, probing "some of the most firmly established religious convictions of his time,"[143] among them, *extra ecclesiam nulla salus*.

---

[138]*Summa totus haeresis Saracenorum*, Kritzeck, *Peter the Venerable*, 204-11.

[139]Cited by Kritzeck, ibid., 114.

[140]Ibid., 25. See *PL*, 189, 507-650, and the summary in Williams, *Adversus Judaeos*, 384-94.

[141]Daniel, *Islam and the West*, 189.

[142]*Oxford Dictionary*, 4.

[143]D.E. Luscombe, ed., *Peter Abelard's Ethics* (Oxford: Clarendon Press, 1971) xiv.

A significant concern for Abelard was the ultimate destiny of a person who did not accept God's salvific provision in Christ because of ignorance, not rebellious contempt. He states the problem in his *Ethics*:

> For if someone does not believe in the Gospel or in Christ for the reason
> that no preaching has reached him—as the Apostle says: "How shall they
> hear without a preacher?"—what fault can be ascribed to them on account
> of his unbelief?[144]

This person, he believed, should not be excluded from the pale of the righteous. If one sincerely sought to please God on the basis of the natural law[145] or reason, that one would be shown by God "what is to be believed about Christ,"[146] who is the saving truth. The strength of Abelard's proposal was its consonance with the historic faith of the church in allowing salvation only through Christ and his church without "having to consign the invincibly ignorant to a state that was beyond the grace and mercy of God."[147] After Abelard it became generally accepted in the Middle Ages that in case of invincible ignorance, the unbaptized can be saved.

That Abelard's theology had a distinctive "missionary" component has been observed.[148] All persons could gain a right sense of the rational meaning of Christianity, Abelard affirms, if they are allowed to interpret its reality by the

---

[144]Ibid., 65.

[145]In Abelard's *A Dialogue of a Philosopher with a Jew and a Christian*, Pierre J. Payer, trans. (Toronto: Pontifical Institute of Medieval Studies, 1979) 36, the philosopher, speaking for Abelard, claims that natural law consists in the love of God and neighbor.

[146]*Probl. Hel.* 13, as cited in Pelikan, *The Christian Tradition*, 3:255.

[147]Ibid. The extended argument of what constitutes "sinning ignorantly" is found in Abelard's *Ethics*, 63-67. See also D.E. Luscombe, *The School of Peter Abelard* (Cambridge: Cambridge University Press, 1969) 130-32.

[148]J. Ramsay McCallum, *Abelard's Christian Theology* (Merrick NY: Richwood Pub. Co., 1976) 24.

"logic of their own experience."[149] Abelard would instruct the missionary to follow the contours or structure of the individual person's religion when presenting the Gospel. Abelard was concerned with the proper definition of Christianity, and he desired the patterns which he employed to be commendable to all. Because he believed that Christianity, and thus a doctrine of the Trinity, is implicit in human understanding,[150] he held that through the operation of their reason, persons before the incarnation were numbered among the blessed. Here Abelard diverged from the majority of medieval theologians who had followed Augustine.

Ramon Lull, the Fool of Love, as he called himself, was a thirteenth-century visionary (ca. 1233-1315) who saw his chief mission in life to be the conversion of Islam and the Jews.[151] Like Peter the Venerable and Abelard, he believed in the possibility of the rational demonstration of the Christian faith to unbelievers; and, through intensive studies in Arabic[152] and Christian thought, and through holding disputations with Jews and Saracens, Lull attempted to redress the mutual ignorance between Jews, Christians, and Muslims. A prolific writer, he published more than two hundred works, many of them religious allegories which strove to effect his goal of first converting Islam, after which he believed the other religions would easily follow.[153]

Ramon's early writings and missionary activity illustrate the "moment of vision": that brief optimism about world unity, followed by the recognition that

---

[149]Ibid.

[150]Ibid., 25.

[151]The standard biography is that of E. Allison Peers, *Ramon Lull: A Biography* (London: SPCK, 1929).

[152]Daniel, *Islam and the West*, 7, observes that it was not until the thirteenth century that Arabic sources became directly available.

[153]*The Book of Contemplation*, chap. 36, quoted in Peers, *Ramon Lull*, 75.

his hopes were illusory.[154] In his first monograph of importance, *The Book of Contemplation*, he fervently pleaded for the evangelization of all non-Christians.[155] Instead of taking up arms against the infidels, Christians should preach the holy faith to them, Lull insisted. He was no isolated theorist, unwilling to apply his apologetic arguments, as his African incursions reveal. He believed that Islam was ripe for conversion and passionately committed his life to that task. Should one remain a Muslim, he or she would be damned;[156] such was the theological position that spurred Lull to a level of almost frenetic activity.

Lull's later writings reflected his gradual dis-illusionment with the effectiveness of a rational exposition of the faith; after 1290 he virtually despaired of his vision of converting the Muslims. They now appeared to him as an overwhelming enemy, threatening the whole of Christendom.[157] The Mongols were turning to Islam instead of joining forces with the Christians, as Lull had earlier predicted. Others shared his revulsion against the "extravagant hopes of the previous thirty years"[158] and returned with him to much of the mutual suspicion and absurd characterizations of Islam that had occasioned the era prior to any academic investigation of it.

A study of the theological evaluation of non-Christian religions by medieval thinkers is incomplete without the contribution of Thomas Aquinas, the *Doctor Angelicus* (ca. 1225-1274). He, more than his contemporaries, tackled the immense problem of incorporating within Christian thought the vast learning and wisdom of Aristotle. His two Summae, the earlier *Summa Contra Gentiles* (ca. 1260), and the masterful *Summa Theologica* (1265-1272), stand as the apex of

---

[154]Southern, *Western Views*, 67.

[155]E.A. Peers, *Fool of Love: The Life of Ramon Lull* (London: SCM Press Ltd., 1946) 28.

[156]Daniel, *Islam and the West*, 118.

[157]Southern, *Western Views*, 68.

[158]Ibid.

medieval scholasticism. The latter work remains the accepted basis of modern Roman Catholic theology.[159]

In *Summa Contra Gentiles*, a manual of Christian doctrine written for the use of missionaries, Thomas begins his explication of the fate of the virtuous heathen. One's natural capacity for reason enables certain knowledge of God, he writes, but one's "ultimate end is fixed in a certain knowledge of truth which surpasses his natural capacity."[160] Thomas suggests that since a person is ordered to the goal of God's designation, he or she must be divinely assisted by grace to attain it.[161] It is necessary for salvation for a person to believe certain things not accessible to the natural reason;[162] since the attainments of reason are inadequate, they must be augmented by revelation. The revelation is contained in the Scriptures, as understood by the councils and the Fathers, which is the tradition of the Church.

Thomas granted that all would not have the same degree of explicit faith, because aptitudes and opportunities for learning the articles of faith differ; however, he affirms that "belief of some kind in the mystery of Christ's

---

[159]*Oxford Dictionary*, 1371.

[160]*Summa Contra Gentiles*, Book III, ch. 147, Vernon J. Bourke, trans. (New York: Image Books, 1956) 223-24.

[161]Normally grace was thought to come to a person through the channels of the sacraments, the vehicles of the kinds of grace peculiar to the visible church. Thomas insisted on the sacraments as instrumental causes of grace and salvation. However, he did make exceptions for the virtuous heathen. See David Knowles, "The Middle Ages 604-1350," *A History of Christian Doctrine*, Hubert Cunliffe-Jones, ed. (Philadelphia: Fortress, 1978) 275, and Steven Ozment, *The Age of Reform 1250-1550* (New Haven: Yale University Press, 1980) 35.

[162]*Summa Theologica*, II-II, Q r, art. 3, *Basic Writings of Saint Thomas Aquinas*, vol. II, Anton C. Pegis, ed. (New York: Random House, 1945). In his delineation of natural and supernatural capacities, Thomas deliberately flies in the face of Anselm who believed that all the truths of Christianity are philosophically demonstrable.

Incarnation was necessary at all times and for all persons. . . ."[163] Thomas
qualified this assertion for "gentiles" who had not received the revelation of
Christ; they too could inherit the blessedness promised to those who have explicit
faith:

> If, however, some were saved without receiving any revelation, they were
> not saved without faith in a Mediator, for though they did not believe in
> Him explicitly, they did, nevertheless, have implicit faith through
> believing in divine providence, since they believed that God would
> deliver mankind in whatever way was pleasing to him. . . .[164]

In a different context, Thomas also affirms that "the reason why someone
does not have grace is that he refused to accept it, and not that God refused to
grant it."[165] This would imply that God had universally prepared men and
women to receive grace. God indeed wishes the salvation of all, and Christ died
for all; but, a person can freely refuse the gift of God, and God permits this
failure which is foreseen, but not decreed.

That the scholastics of the twelfth and thirteenth centuries were little
concerned about the nature of the church *per se* has been observed.[166] Aquinas,
as well as many other medieval theologians, affirmed *extra ecclesiam nulla salus*
while at the same time allowing that outside the church there *was* salvation—if
certain conditions were met. One must have faith, but there was implicit and
explicit faith. Virtuous pagans could win salvation if they believed in God's

---

[163]*Summa Theologica*, Z. 2, art. 7. Cf. W.J. Hankey, *God in Himself: Aquinas' Doctrine of God as expounded in the Summa Theologica* (Oxford: Oxford University Press, 1987).

[164]Ibid. Here Thomas has posited another means of grace than the sacraments of the church.

[165]Thos. Aq. Sent. 1.40, as quoted by Pelikan, *The Christian Tradition*, 3:273.

[166]Pelikan, *The Christian Tradition*, 3:298, notes: "During these two centuries we must look not primarily to the systematic theologians and summists, nor to the canonists and lawyer-popes, but to the monastic exegetes and expository preachers for a comprehensive doctrine of the church."

providence and had implicit faith in God's provision for redemption through the incarnation. They could learn of God through a special revelation, or from the Scriptures, or tradition. Thus the axiom was held in a paradoxical sense. Thomas dealt with the issue of *salus extra ecclesiam* in terms of election (those who respond to God's grace are the elect) and *fides implicita*.

The medieval synthesis which Thomas had achieved was not to endure for long. Two subsequent scholars of considerable influence, Duns Scotus and William of Ockham, did not share Thomas's confidence in the capacity of human reason to fathom at least some of the divine truths. They no longer saw reason as a supplement to faith; rather, they separated the functions of reason and faith. Divine revelation was obtainable only by faith, which is the essence of the Nominalist position.[167]

The thirteenth century and early fourteenth century witnessed a further concretization of the Catholic church's position over against other religions.[168] The papal tenure of Boniface VIII (ca. 1234-1303) was fraught with power struggles, both internal and external.[169] Two goals shaped his leadership: the liberation of the Holy Land and the consolidation of the power of the Bishop of Rome. In the papal Bull *Unam Sanctam*, promulgated 18 November 1302, these two concerns are intertwined. *Unam Sanctam* declared:

> With Faith urging us we are forced to believe and hold the one, holy,
> Catholic Church and that, apostolic, and we firmly believe and simply

---

[167]Matthew Spinka, *Advocates of Reform: From Wyclif to Erasmus*, vol. 14, The Library of Christian Classics (Philadelphia: The Westminster Press, 1953) XIV, describes the basic Nominalist position as "the distrust of reason in matters of religion and the acceptance of revealed truth by faith alone. . . ."

[168]The first chapter of the doctrinal declarations of the Fourth Lateran Council (1215), sounds the Cyprianic theme: "One indeed is the universal church of the faithful, outside which no one at all is saved. . . ." H. Denzinger, *Enchiridion Symbolorum Definitionum et Declarationum Rebus Fidei et Morum* (Freiburg, 1952²⁹) 167.

[169]*Oxford Dictionary*, 188.

confess this (Church), outside which there is no salvation nor remission of sin. . . .[170]

The Bull later strongly emphasized the position of the Pope as the Supreme Head of the Church; to reject his authority was to cease to belong to the church. In short, this declaration claimed for the Pope jurisdiction over all creatures.[171]

Another classic utterance of the church's denial of any hope of salvation for non-Christians is the oft-quoted Bull of Eugenius IV at the Council of Florence (1438-1445):

> Those not living within the Catholic Church, not only pagans, but also Jews and heretics and schismatics cannot become participants in eternal life, but will depart "into everlasting fire which was prepared for the devil and his angels" [Matt 25:41], unless before the end of this life the same have been added to the flock. . . .[172]

Assessment of the Medieval Period

The exclusivist position thus had representative expressions in the church in ancient and medieval times, and now on the eve of the Reformation. Cyprian's thesis had remained a dictum whose truth was unquestioned, although many sought more constructive ways to utilize the doctrine. Those who endeavored to deal theologically with the ultimate destiny of those outside the fold did so without doing violence to this fundamental expression of orthodoxy.

The centuries of the late Middle Ages were not without persons, however, who quietly dissented from the sharp exclusivism of these pronouncements.[173]

---

[170]Denzinger, *Enchiridion*, 186.

[171]*Oxford Dictionary*, 1405-1406.

[172]Denzinger, *Enchiridion*, 230.

[173]See T.P. Dunning, "Langland and the Salvation of the Heathen," *Medium Aevum* 12 (1943): 45-54, and M.D. Knowles, "The Censured Opinions of Uthred of Boldon," *Proceedings of the British Academy* 37 (1951): 305-42.

Because of the dissolution of the unity of medieval Christian civilization, these persons questioned the church's denial of eternal blessedness to anyone outside it.[174] Many theologians did manage to have it both ways: they constructed a *via media* through which one

> could accept the Christian assumption of the exclusiveness and finality of the Christian religion and at the same time find room within this exclusiveness for the large company of good men who lived before Christ but who . . . would have believed in Christ if they had had a chance to learn of him.[175]

Although many medieval theologians had no hope for the salvation of the heathen and rationalized or explained their positions in terms of predestination, others had a more hopeful way of regarding the dilemma. These acknowledged that (1) God wills the salvation of all persons without universalistic predetermination, and (2) no one is damned except through one's own fault.

Naive Christian exclusivism—which ignored the destiny of non-Christians, or glibly assigned them to eternal damnation—began to recede in the fifteenth century. The discoveries of other religious traditions through expanding travel and the fresh scrutiny of classical texts, revealing the virtues of the ancients, stretched all the categories and solutions of the patristic and scholastics.

REFORMATION

The age of Reformation occupies a relatively short time span[176] in the history of the Western Church, but its issues and implications continue to

---

[174]Southern, *Western Views*, 75-76.

[175]Craig R. Thompson, ed., *Inquisitio de Fide: A Colloquy by Desiderius Erasmus Roterodamus 1524* (New Haven: Yale University Press, 1950) 110.

[176]See Eric W. Gritsch's fresh new treatment of many of the pivotal events of the Reformation in *Martin—God's Court Jester* (Philadelphia: Fortress Press, 1983), and Alister E. McGrath, *Reformation Thought: An Introduction* (Oxford: Blackwell, 1988).

reverberate within the varied cathedrals of Christendom. The import of the Reformation may be viewed from many different perspectives: sociological, political, theological, and historiographical, for example, whether it is a medieval or modern phenomenon. Modern scholarship gives witness to all of these approaches. The focus of this investigation will necessarily be a narrow strand within the complexities associated with the Age of Reformation. Although the interrelated theological problems of non-Christian religions and *salus extra ecclesiam* were not the encompassing concerns they had been during the patristic and medieval eras, they did receive further attention in light of the new theological positions being developed.[177] This study will examine three streams which flow into the wide river called the Reformation: the Humanists, Protestant Reformers, and Radical Reformers.

Humanists

A significant tempering effect on the more extreme Protestant and Radical Reformers was wielded by the Humanists. Among the humanists of the fifteenth and sixteenth centuries who discussed intensely the theological problems posed by non-Christians, Desiderius Erasmus (1469-1536), New Testament Greek and patristic scholar, church satirist, and anti-scholastic thinker, provided the key influence.

Two of his works, *Antibarbarorum liber* (ca. 1489) and *Inquisitio de Fide* (1524), are noteworthy because of their commentary on the virtuous pagans and *salus extra ecclesiam*. The first colloquy depicts a discussion between humanist thinkers, among them Erasmus, who for literary discretion, speaks as Jacob Batt. The discussants investigate the relative merits of classical figures, seeking to discern which of their contributions were consonant with Christianity. Since the central thrust of Erasmus's theology was the *philosophi Christi* with its emphasis on virtue and wisdom, it was natural that he should question the church's refusal

---

[177]G.H. Williams, "Erasmus and the Reformers," 319.

of salvation to those ancients, who, in his estimation, had many attributes that appeared to be the way of Christ.[178] He commended their virtues and insisted:

> Whatever of the Gentiles has been bravely done, well said, ingeniously thought out, and diligently transmitted, Christ had prepared for his Kingdom (*Republicae*).[179]

Like Abelard, Erasmus attributed importance to the natural law; one's adherence to it could eventuate in real virtues, though not a means of meriting grace. This idea would be addressed again when he and Luther debated the freedom or bondage of the will. Erasmus's esteem for the virtuous pre-Christians seemingly cannot be gainsaid. Nonetheless, another colloquy balances the unequivocal praise of *Antibarbarorum liber*.

Inquisitio de Fide[180] moves toward a more explicit discussion of the "outer limits of the Holy Catholic Church"[181] and *salus extra ecclesiam*. Barbatius, representing Luther or a Lutheran, enunciates the classic Cyprianic theme when discussing the "Holy Church";

> outside this fellowship not even a man's good deeds bring him to salvation unless he is reunited with the holy congregation, and therefore follows "the remission of sins," because outside the Church there is no remission of sins, however much a man may torment himself with

---

[178]G. H. Williams, ibid., 325, characterizes Erasmus's *philosophi Christi* as being more interested in charity and peace than faith or hope; the focus was right *acting* more than orthodox belief.

[179]Albert Hyma, *The Youth of Erasmus* (Ann Arbor: University of Michigan Press, 1930) 283f.

[180]See *The Colloquies of Erasmus*, Craig R. Thompson, trans. (Chicago: The University of Chicago Press, 1965) 177-78, for a discussion of the relationship between Erasmus and Luther at the time of the writing of this colloquy. Erasmus's desire for rapprochement is apparent: he is illustrating that if they could agree on the fundamentals of the Apostles' Creed concerning salvation, they would realize the foolishness of schism.

[181]Williams, "Erasmus and the Reformers," 330.

penance or perform works of mercy. Not in the Church of heretics, I say,
but in the Holy Church, gathered by the spirit of Christ, is the remission
of sins through baptism. . . .[182]

With this strict interpretation Erasmus agrees. In this instance, he seems to have
limited "the membership in the church . . . to those within the range of its
sacramental ministry."[183]

Erasmus drew ample authority from the Fathers, for example, Clement, in
his belief that God accepted those without the Law who lived "as a law unto
themselves" (Rom 2:14-15). This position is counterpoint to his theme of
Inquisitio de Fide, and the interplay between the two is a striking features of his
writings. Indeed, Erasmus shared the ambiguity of the great medieval theologians
when he affirmed *extra ecclesiam nulla salus* and concomitantly held that a
Socrates could be saved.[184] His views were slightly more favorable to the godly
heathen than the main stream of scholasticism and considerably more flexible than
the Protestant Reformers, with the exception of Zwingli.

Erasmus's tolerant attitude toward virtuous pre-Christians did not extend
to the Turks; although he was an avowed pacifist, he believed Christendom should
defend itself without resorting to a crusade.[185] The goal was to convert the
Muslims, not to destroy them utterly. Adherents of other religions
contemporaneous with Christianity must experience rebirth in Christ and baptism,
Erasmus declared, because their situation was different from that of the godly
heathen before Christ, for whom implicit faith had been sufficient.

---

[182]Thompson, *Colloquies*, 187.

[183]Williams, "Erasmus and the Reformers," 331.

[184]*Convivium Religiosum*, Thompson, *Colloquies*, 68.

[185]Williams, "Erasmus and the Reformers," 332.

Protestant Reformers

The overriding concern for the sixteenth-century Reformers was the problem of salvation.[186] As theologians committed to the traditions of the Fathers,[187] they assumed the truth of *extra ecclesiam nulla salus*; however, their more pressing question was how to distinguish between the true church and the false church. The evaluation of non-Christian religions was a less insistent issue for them although it did receive mention in their writings, especially those of Luther.

The Reformation received its primary impetus from Martin Luther (1483-1546), a religious genius of rare stature. As a learned professor and *Doctor in Biblia* of the church, he felt bound to criticize those areas in which it had ceased to be the church as created by the Word of God. It was Luther's intention to prick and instruct the consciences of Christians on the basis of a study of Scripture.

From his intensive study of the book of Romans, Luther had heard the gospel afresh and realized the utter blasphemy of a person presuming his or her righteousness apart from the imputed righteousness of God. Hence Luther would not brook Erasmus's attitude toward the "virtuous pagans" and thus argued in his *De Servo Arbitrio* (1524) that *all* are ungodly and wicked.[188] Moreover, no one could become a new creature without the deepest experience of one's own sinfulness.[189] Another reason Luther rejected Erasmus's tolerant approach was

---

[186]Paul D.L. Avis, *The Church in the Theology of the Reformers* (Atlanta: John Knox Press, 1981) 1.

[187]Jaroslav Pelikan, "Form and Tradition in Worship: A Theological Interpretation," *Essays Presented at the First Liturgical Institute 1949* (Valparaiso IN: Valparaiso University Press, 1950) 22-23.

[188]See Luther's "Disputation Against Scholastic Theology," James Atkinson, ed. *Luther: Early Theological Works*, The Library of Christian Classics (Philadelphia: The Westminster Press, 1962) 268-69. Here he eschews the possibility that unregenerate humanity can perform any good work.

[189]See Heinz Bluhm, "Luther's View of Man in His First Published Work," *Harvard Theological Review* 41 (1948): 103-22. Cf. Benjamin Drewery, "Luther's Matured

that it would be "foolish of God to reveal righteousness to men if they either knew it already or possessed the seeds of it."[190] Whereas Erasmus allowed for the possibility of eternal salvation for the godly pre-Christians, Luther vehemently excludes them:

> [F]rom the beginning of the world there has always been more outstanding talent, greater learning, and more earnest application among the heathen than among Christians or the People of God. . . . For as Christ himself confesses, the children of this world are wiser than the children of light [Luke 16:8]. . . . What, then, are we to say impeded such men, so that none of them was able to attain to grace? For they certainly exercised free choice to the utmost of their powers, and who will care to say there was none among them who sought after truth with the utmost application? Yet we cannot but assert that none of them found it.[191]

Throughout his voluminous literary production, Luther did waver from this posture toward all those outside the church. In his *Large Catechism*, Luther kept faith with the patristic heritage in affirming Cyprian's position:

> [O]utside the Christian church that is, where the Gospel is not, there is no forgiveness, and hence no holiness. Therefore, all who seek to merit holiness through their works rather than through the Gospel and forgiveness of sin have expelled and separated themselves from the church.[192]

Later in the same article of the *Large Catechism* he more explicitly spells out what the fate is of those outside the true church:

---

[190]E. Gordon Rupp and Philip S. Watson, *Luther and Erasmus: Free Will and Salvation*, The Library of Christian Classics (Philadelphia: Westminster Press, 1969) 295.

[191]*De Servo Arbitrio*, Atkison, ed., *Luther*, 156.

[192]Phillip E. Pederson, ed. *What Does This Mean? Luther's Catechisms Today* (Minneapolis MN: Augsburg Publishing House, 1979) 124.

> All who are outside the Christian church, whether heathen, Turks, Jews,
> or false Christians and hypocrites, even though they believe in and
> worship only the one, true God, nevertheless do not know what his
> attitude is toward them. They cannot be confident of his love and
> blessing. Therefore they remain in eternal wrath and damnation, for they
> do not have the Lord Christ, and, besides, they are not illuminated and
> blessed by the gifts of the Holy Spirit.[193]

Only those who were within the church could experience salvation; membership
in the church presupposed election and one's utter faith in the sufficiency of the
proffer of Christ's righteousness. The church always has a christological center in
Luther's theology: it is defined in terms of the preached word, the simple gospel
of sins forgiven, and unmerited grace—all afforded by Christ.[194] Luther directs
those who seek Christ to come to the church.[195]

Luther's doctrine of the church as the community of the saints is linked
inseparably with his doctrine of salvation. A sinful person can never meet God
face to face in the world; only through encountering the "creative Presence of
Christ in his Church"[196] through faith does one become a part of the people of
God. Moreover, the church in the world is always *sola fide perceptibilis*, to be
recognized by faith alone.

Luther moved within the medieval apocalyptic interpretation of Islam. He
believed that Scripture designated the Turks as a rod of God's punishment on

---

[193]*Large Catechism*, art. III, ibid., 125.

[194]See E.G. Rupp, "Luther and the Doctrine of the Church," *Scottish Journal of Theology* 9 (1956): 384-92.

[195]Paul Althaus, *The Theology of Martin Luther*, Robert C. Schultz, trans. (Philadelphia: Fortress Press, 1966) 287.

[196]Rupp, "Luther and the Doctrine of the Church," 387.

Christendom for its contempt of the gospel.[197] With prophetic insight he insisted that Christians should not resist this judgment by sanctioning a war against the Turks.[198]

In Luther's view, Islam had only a very limited usefulness in God's providence. It was not a *preparatio evangelica* or a means of grace, even though the morality of the Muslims might far surpass that of the "papists." Rather, the menacing Turks simply served as a blunt tool in the disciplining hand of God. Luther generally believed that the Muslims were too hard-hearted to be converted, but the Christians should proclaim the gospel to them nonetheless, if only to exhibit their own faithfulness.[199] The apparent upright morality of the Muslims could never suffice for righteousness; only faith in Christ affords that.

A contemporary of Luther (1484-1531) and a kindred spirit in many respects,[200] Ulrich Zwingli sparked the Swiss Reformation with his 1522 treatise, *Concerning Freedom and the Choice of Food*. A passionate student of the Scriptures[201] and an eloquent proclaimer of the gospel, Zwingli was a theologian of Erasmian hue rather than Lutheran. Indeed, for anyone to suggest

---

[197]Unlike the Reformers and precedents in the medieval period, Luther did not identify the Anti-Christ with Islam. In Luther's theology, the papal office was unrivalled for that dubious honor.

[198]Martin Luther, *On War Against the Turks*, C.M. Jacob, trans., *Works of Martin Luther*, vol. 5 (1931) 79-123.

[199]Williams, "Erasmus and the Reformers," 351, describes Melanchthon as being more generous to the virtuous pagans than Luther, but on Islam was "much harsher and even less concerned to get at the theological and religious reality of the opposing religion."

[200]Most notable among their differences was their respective understanding of the sacramental teaching of the church. Jacques Courvoisier, *Zwingli, A Reformed Theologian* (Richmond: John Knox Press, 1963), offers an excellent description of the contours of Zwingli's theology.

[201]G.W. Bromiley, ed., *Zwingli and Bullinger*, The Library of Christian Classics (Philadelphia: The Westminster Press, 1953) 242. Cf. Courvoisier, *Zwingli*, 17.

that he significantly depended on Luther's innovations for his own seemed to Zwingli a horrible disservice to his theological creativity.[202]

Zwingli's humanistic leanings allowed him to include all the great and pious heathen in the number of the elect, a mark of his own infidelity, in Luther's opinion.[203] In *Exposition of the Faith* (1531) Zwingli broadly claims the salvation of all these persons as he describes eternal life in heaven:

> [Y]ou may expect to see the communion and fellowship of all the saints and sages and believers and the steadfast and the brave and the good who have ever lived since the world began. . . . In short there has not lived a single good man, there has not been a single pious heart or believing soul from the beginning of the world to the end, which you will not see there in the presence of God.[204]

Zwingli does not argue this position on the basis of the scholastic synthesis, which allowed natural law to be discernible by natural reason, but because of his conception of the divine sovereignty and election of grace.[205] The decree of election was a universal decree and it embraced all persons both before and after the time of Christ.[206] It was not, then, on the basis of personal piety that Zwingli saw these persons participating in salvation, but because "of the

---

[202]*Auslegen und Gründe der Schlussreden*, 1523: *Zwingli's Sämtliche Werke*, II, 144-48, quoted in Hans J. Hillerbrand, *The Reformation* (London: SCM Press, 1964) 126. See Ozment, *The Age of Reform*, 322.

[203]See Avis, *The Church in the Theology of the Reformers*, 173, and L. Capèran, *Le Problème du Salut des infideles: Essai historique*, 2 vols. (Toulouse: Grand Seminaire, 1934) 1:242-46.

[204]Bromiley, *Zwingli and Bullinger*, 275-76.

[205]Ibid., 242-43.

[206]Ibid.

eternal activity of God in election and atonement."[207] Zwingli interpreted their virtue as *signa electionis*. "For where there are works done worthy of God, there surely has long since been a pious covenant *(religio)* with God."[208] One could not be excluded simply because he or she was outside the temporal reach of the Gospel; the eternal Christ could effect salvation for anyone he desired because of the primordial election.

Zwingli found any doctrine of election incomprehensible apart from the church. The church is grounded in God's election, that is, the elect are identified with the members of the church. Faith is the consequence of election and, by it, one makes his or her election sure. Zwingli defines the church as the "whole community of those who, in one faith, are grounded upon and built up in the Lord Jesus Christ."[209]

Implicit in Zwingli's writings is the concept that no one outside the church can be saved. He did not have to resort to visible and invisible categories,[210] however, in order to include virtuous pre-Christians, Jews, and those who had not yet responded to their election with faith. He gives the church a cosmic dimension,[211] uniting all persons from Adam until the present.[212] The one church has both visible and invisible components, though the pure spiritual church

---

[207]Ibid., 243. Williams, "Erasmus and the Reformers," 357, believes Zwingli was willing to include these virtuous pagans because "he did not share Luther's view of the gravity and totality of the original sin of the first Adam." See also Althaus, *The Theology of Martin Luther*, 157-60.

[208]*De peccato originali declaratio* (1526), *Sämtliche Werke*, 5:359-96.

[209]Quoted in Courvoisier, *Zwingli*, 52.

[210]See Thompson, *Inquisitio De Fide*, 110-11. See also "A Reply to Emser which Zwingli incorporated into *Commentary On True and False Religion*, S.M. Jackson, ed. (Durham: The Labyrinth Press, 1981) 366f.

[211]Avis, *The Church in the Theology of the Reformers*, 5, and Courviosier, *Zwingli*, 52.

[212]In this Zwingli was influenced significantly by the Greek Fathers, who were now accessible to him in Greek.

is hidden in Christ. The church that is seen in the world is a mixed society, yet it is grasped by the movement of faith in Christ. Because it is not yet pure and undefiled, "it must repent and be reconciled to Christ again and again,"[213] *semper reformanda.* Zwingli's impulse toward a universalistic message is much more clearly developed in the Radical Reformation; the inclusiveness of his basic concepts, surprisingly, did not engender concern for overseas missions in his further writing, or in his immediate followers.[214]

John Calvin, the Genevan Reformer (1509-1564), was much more concerned about correct doctrine and proper church order than were the other Protestant Reformers. Calvin was consciously dependent on the teaching of the early church and takes seriously the testimony of the church fathers. Calvin's use of *extra ecclesiam nulla salus* hearkens to Cyprian's assertions, referring to the true church as the Mother of all the godly.[215] Just as a baby cannot enter life without the conception and nourishment of the mother, so it is with the life of the Christian in the church. Not only does the church give birth to believers, but she also nurtures them all the earthly life. "Furthermore, away from her bosom one cannot hope for any forgiveness of sins or any salvation. . . ."[216] It is disastrous to leave the church, for "God's fatherly favor and the especial witness of spiritual life are limited to his flock. . . ."[217] The church is God's chosen means of educating the elect people and they are foolish to disdain the holy plan. God has

---

[213]Courviosier, *Zwingli,* 50.

[214]See William R. Hogg, "The Rise of Protestant Missionary Concern, 1517-1914," *The Theology of the Christian Mission,* Gerald H. Anderson, ed. (New York: Abingdon Press, 1961) 96.

[215]John Calvin, *Institutes of the Christian Religion,* IV, ch. 1. 1. The edition of the *Institutes* used here is edited by John T. McNeill, The Library of Christian Classics, 2 vols. (Philadelphia: The Westminster Press, 1960), hereafter cited as *Institutes* with appropriate book, chapter, and article numbers.

[216]Ibid., IV, 1.4.

[217]Ibid.

entrusted the Gospel to the church; it is the place of encounter between God and humanity.

The church as the "communion of saints" stands inviolably by God's election and, thus, is as sure as eternal providence.[218] The *notae ecclesiae* are the right preaching of the Word of God and the sacraments "administered according to Christ's institution."[219]

Calvin employs Augustine's visible and invisible categories; all the elect constitute the invisible church, and it is known only to God. The visible church is comprised of all baptized persons who profess to worship the one God and Christ through the vehicle of the church. Of course, many hypocrites are intermingled with the saints; these persons "have nothing of Christ but the name and outward appearance."[220] The elect cannot discern wheat and tares within this visible church, and so they must hold a charitable judgment toward all.[221]

Calvin is decidedly negative about any natural theology in Islam or the pre-Christian religions (evidenced by religious or moral inclinations) that could effect a true knowledge of God. Even though the "unity of God has been engraved upon the hearts of all,"[222] making the worship of idols inexcusable,[223] unaided knowledge of God was sheer perversity. The universally-corrupting effects of sin result in the refusal of human beings to follow the rational processes to their logical conclusion (God), and they can only contemplate the creation, not the Creator. Calvin bluntly states: "religion was commonly adulterated throughout

---

[218]Ibid., IV, 1.3.

[219]Ibid., IV, 1.9.

[220]Ibid., IV, 1.7.

[221]Ibid., IV, 1.8.

[222]Ibid., I, 10.3.

[223]See T.H.L. Parker's discussion of Calvin's conception of the knowledge of God, "Calvin," *A History of Christian Doctrine*, H. Cunliffe-Jones, ed. (Philadelphia: Fortress Press, 1978) 388-89.

almost all ages."[224] In light of this general denouncement, it is not surprising that Calvin was little interested in the current phenomenon of Islam.

Williams judges the most restrictive aspect of Calvin's soteriology to be his consideration that the Holy Spirit was "limited to the things of Christ and the visible Church. . . ."[225] There is no working of the Spirit in the "cults contrived by men," Calvin asserted, "nor did any divine presence remain except on Mt. Zion. . . ."[226] Hence, salvation is not possible through general revelation, given Calvin's presuppositions.

Radical Reformation

The radicals of the sixteenth century, the Anabaptists and Spiritualists and others, primarily rejected the territorial Protestantism of Luther and Zwingli.[227] Among the writers of these traditions, there was a wide diversity, yet they fundamentally agreed that they must return to the root of faith and the church and free themselves from the "suffocating growth of ecclesiastical tradition and magisterial prerogative."[228] This study will pick up one thread developed in a certain strain of the radicals, the Anabaptists, that will further the investigation of *salus extra ecclesiam* and the non-Christian religions.

Whereas the writings of Luther and Calvin (dependent on Augustine's doctrine of election) had narrowed the scope of salvation through their exclusion of ancient worthies and their demand for conscious faith in Jesus Christ (*sola fide*) as the *sine qua non* of the true church, certain formulations among the Anabaptists of the extensive implications of the atonement and the solidarity of all humankind

---

[224]*Institutes*, I, 10.3.

[225]Williams, "Erasmus and the Reformers," 362.

[226]*Institutes*, I, 5.13.

[227]G.H. Williams and Angel M. Mergal, eds., *Spiritual and Anabaptist Writers*, The Library of Christian Classics (Philadelphia: The Westminster Press, 1957) 20.

[228]Ibid., 22.

demonstrated their greater concern for the salvation of those outside the church.[229] Following the speculation of Zwingli about the universal implications of the atonement, the Anabaptists saw in Christ's work as the Second Adam that which took from humanity the burden of the First Adam's guilt, and because of the essential unity of humanity with these two prototypes, Christ's removal of guilt applied to all.[230] Accordingly, more than any of the other Reformers, the Anabaptists had an impetus to preach the Gospel to all,[231] for all had the opportunity to respond. Christ had provided them with the prelapsarian capacity to choose freely. The radicals' views of the Turkish challenge and pre-Christian and praeter-Christian religions were slanted more positively than the Magisterial Reformers.[232] Indeed, because they had cut themselves loose from the territorial and political aspects of the magisterial reformation, they could deal primarily with the theological problems involved.[233]

The Anabaptists, for the most part, rejected the doctrine of absolute predestinarianism and the doctrine of the invisible church,[234] and also tacitly dropped the doctrine of original sin.[235] They pressed for the establishment of a true Christian church, completely reconstituted according to what they interpreted its apostolic pattern to be. The voluntary baptism of committed adults

---

[229]G.H. Williams, *The Radical Reformation* (Philadelphia: The Westminster Press, 1961) 836.

[230]G.H. Williams, "Sectarian Ecumenicity: Reflections on a Little Noticed Aspect of the Radical Reformation," *Review and Expositor* 64 (1967): 141-60.

[231]See Franklin H. Littell, *The Anabaptist View of the Church* (Hartford CT: American Society of Church History, 1952) 94f.

[232]Avis, *The Church in the Theology of the Reformers*, 206.

[233]Williams, *Radical Reformation*, 835.

[234]Ibid., xxxviii, and Avis, *The Church in the Theology of the Reformers*, 206.

[235]Williams, "Sectarian Ecumenicity," 146, and *Radical Reformation*, 839.

was its foundation. They resisted coercion and advocated total separation from the world; a distinctive, purified, visible church was their goal.

Among the Anabaptists, Melchior Hofmann most clearly expressed the universalizing accents of an inclusive theory of atonement and the essential unity of all persons with the two Adams. An early Lutheran, Hofmann (1495-ca. 1543) converted to Anabaptism while a sojourner in Strassburg. He stressed the irrevocable nature of the work of the Second Adam and its universal import and, on that basis, ascribed moral accountability to every person.[236]

Analogous to God's action in liberating the elect from Egypt was the action through Christ on the cross, affording liberation for all—whether or not they are yet cognitive of the redemptive act. Christ's sacrifice has already been completed on their behalf:

> For Jesus Christ has given himself up for all peoples, yea, each
> individual, and he has paid for the sin of the whole world, taken it away,
> done away with it, and achieved an eternal salvation.[237]

Because of this momentous event, Christians are instructed in their task of sharing the good news:

> [A]nd the proclamation of God's word shall go out to all peoples as a
> witness and absolutely none shall be excepted. But rather to all tribes,
> pagans, tongues, and nations the gospel shall be revealed to their
> enlightenment, yea, the whole world shall be brought into clarity of
> enlightenment and into a knowledge of the right understanding, taught,
> called and drawn by God's Spirit and Word.[238]

---

[236]See Hofmann's *On the Will in Bondage and Free*, Bibliotheca Reformatoria Neerlandica 5 (The Hague: 1909) 188, 194. His antithesis to Luther on this point could not be more profound.

[237]Melchior Hofmann, "The Ordinance of God," *Spiritual and Anabaptist Writers*, 186. See W.R. Estep's analysis of this treatise in *The Anabaptist Story* (Nashville: Broadman Press, 1963) 105-106.

[238]Ibid.

Later, in the same treatise, Hofmann mitigates what appears to be a thorough-going universalism:

> All those who hear this and do not stop up their ears but rather attend
> with alertness will inherit their salvation and will not despise it.[239]

The freedom of the will must be exercised in terms of a resolution to accept believer's baptism through which one is betrothed to Christ. The baptism gives evidence of the covenant made.[240] The inevitable next step is the struggle through the "wilderness"; if the believer is faithful, the struggle leads to victory.[241]

Hofmann reaffirms the universality of what Christ has done,[242] yet he stresses its contingent nature due to the failure of some persons to repent and freely choose to live as the "Bride of Christ," in chaste and obedient service. It is not because of a limiting concept of election that some do not turn to God:

> O how much God would like to have all people saved, if only they
> would! And it was impossible that he could condemn anybody who did
> his will, which people could always very well do. Surely it is not to be
> inferred that one cannot and may not choose to do the will of God as
> could Adam.[243]

---

[239]Ibid.

[240]Hofmann's description of the believer's relationship to Christ is laced with the language of matrimony throughout this treatise.

[241]Hofmann, *Ordinance*, 190-92. See also his "Truthful Witness," 1533 in *Anabaptism in Outline: Selected Primary Sources*, Walter Klassen, ed. (Scottsdale PA: Herald Press, 1981) 27-28.

[242]Two other Anabaptists, Denck and Hubmaier, are very similar in their views on the possibility of universal salvation.

[243]Hofmann, *Ordinance*, 198.

Assessment of the Reformation Period

Erasmus's classical interests and his understanding of Christian faith as *philosophi Christi* allowed him to hold open the possibility of salvation *extra ecclesiam*, while assenting to the catholic doctrine. Erasmus had a greater missionary impulse towards the Turks than did the Protestant Reformers; later the Radical Reformers extrapolate from his stance in their wide-ranging views.

Luther's understanding of human will put him in conflict with Erasmus's more humanistic method for attaining righteousness: for Luther, no virtue existed outside the imputed righteousness of Christ. Consequently, Luther draws the circle of membership in the church tighter.

Luther's view of the Turks places him squarely in the biblicist, apocalyptic stream that swirled throughout the Middle Ages. He unequivocally assumed the truth of Cyprian's axiom; however, it must pertain to the true church. Holding fiercely to *sola Scriptura* and his task as a reformer of the church, the question of the fate of the non-Christians was of little concern to him.

Calvin reiterated Cyprian almost verbatim in his perception of the relationship of salvation through Christ and his church. Calvin showed even less interest in the Turks and relegated to a bare minimum the possibility of a natural depravity of all persons precluded proper response to God's revelation through the creation; the darkened minds of humanity needed the "spectacles" of Scripture and the nurture of the church to participate in God's salvation through Christ.

Zwingli sounded a more hopeful note than Luther or Calvin, for he included the pious pre-Christians in the universal decree of election and intimated that all godly persons manifest a covenant with God. Personal piety simply evidenced their election. One must respond to election with faith, expressed through church membership.

The Radicals took their cue from Zwingli's concepts,[244] avowing that Christ died for the salvation of all and thus all are elected to salvation.[245] These Reformers greatly increased the potential number of persons who could experience salvation and, hence, keenly felt the apostolic task to be theirs.

THE MODERN PERIOD

The consideration of the historical and theological development of *extra ecclesiam nulla salus* and its shifting impact on the evaluation of non-Christian religions has revealed two primary impulses thus far. The first is the exclusive answer which denies salvation outside Christ and the church, which was the predominant view during the patristic, medieval, and reformation periods. It upholds the uniqueness of Christianity: the supremacy of its morality; the authenticity of its revelation alone; and its role as the fulfillment and centerpiece of salvation history. The church is regarded as constitutive of salvation, because Christ and his benefits are encountered and sustained only in the fellowship of believers. As the *sine qua non* of orthodoxy, both Roman Catholic and Protestant traditions stressed this position's veracity in terms of its faithfulness to the biblical witness and the historic teaching of the church. The church as the ark has been its durable symbol; those outside the sanctity and security of the church are without hope.

The second impulse, the inclusive response, accords an architectonic function to the axiom, yet permits the lens of significant qualifications to refract

---

[244]Many scholars have tried to link the intellectual origins of the Anabaptists to Erasmus rather than Zwingli. See Ozment, *The Age of Reform*, 346n21.

[245]Williams, *The Radical Reformation*, 838-39, notes that in the Radical Reformers' ideas about the "Friends of God" (the people of faith who are said to have experienced the revelation of God outside the covenants), and the concept of the "Gospel of all creatures" (a natural theology of the "universally suffering creation" that is able to illuminate the redemptive ways of God), the Radicals indirectly suggested avenues of salvation for other people and through other religions.

its strictness. A minority report, to be sure, it has been an undercurrent throughout Christian theology's attempt rightly to articulate the particularistic and universalistic themes in Scripture.[246] Certain presuppositions have allowed the broader attitude to take root: the degree and efficacy ascribed to natural theology; the concept of the solidarity of humankind and Christ's assumption of it; the obvious piety of many outside the Christian faith; the enduring phenomena of Judaism, Islam, and older religions; and questions of God's providence in Christianity's inability to convert or conquer these other religious bodies, to name just a few. Ambiguity has colored this viewpoint and, in the thinking of many, rendered it logically incomprehensible. Obviously, the church has played a lesser role in this scheme; it has been retained as the normative means, but not the necessary means in every case.

A third impulse develops in the modern period of critical interpreters following the Reformation. Beginning in the seventeenth century, scientific critical methodology began to be introduced into the fields of dogmatic theology and biblical study. The result was the development of the phenomenological[247] and historical approaches in the study of religions, which profoundly expanded the parameters of the discussion.

The increased awareness of many world religions with age-long traditions troubled Christian thinkers of *die Aufklärung*; in addition, the multiple divisions within Christianity raised questions about how to asses the validity of the claim of any doctrine to be based on a divine revelation.[248]

---

[246]Cf. H. de Lubac, *Histoire et Espirit. L'intelligence de l'Écriture d'après Origène* (Paris: [Aubier, 1950) and G. Mensching, *Tolerance and Truth in Religion*, H.-J. Klimkeit, trans. (Birmingham AL: University of Alabama Press, 1971) 35-38. See also the recent article by Peggy Starkey, "Biblical Faith and the Challenge of Religious Pluralism," *International Review of Missions* 71 (Jan 1982): 66-77, and Schlette, *Towards a Theology of Religions*, 25-26.

[247]See Rudolf Otto's critique of the phenomenological approach in *The Idea of the Holy* (Oxford: Oxford University Press, 1962) 4, 8.

[248]Epistemological questions moved to the forefront of theological discourse in light of the percipient contributions of Descartes (1596-1650), Hobbes (1588-1679), and Kant (1724-1804).

These trends and others fashioned the relativist[249] position of the modern period with regard to the role and significance of the non-Christian religions in the history of redemption. The relativist response calls into question any historically conditioned religion purporting to be the "ultimate" or "absolute." To continue to declare "no salvation outside the church" was to ignore the conflicting evidence of the modern world, so the argument went. The universality of religious experience was acknowledged, and one's subjective experience became the ultimate canon of truth instead of the church's dogma or the Bible's witness. As a consequence, qualitative judgments about Christianity's superiority to the world's religions on the basis of its ability to engender the greatest degree of "utter dependence" (as in Schleiermacher), or some other desired good, faltered.

Early in the modern period there were intimations of a relaxation of the incontrovertible Roman Catholic position as the church rejected the proposal of the Jansenist Paschasius Quesnel (1634-1719) who maintained *extra ecclesiam nulla conceditur gratia*, "outside the Church, no grace is granted."[250] His errors were officially condemned in the dogmatic constitution, "Unigenitus," 8 September 1713, which opened the door to a more careful elucidation of how the traditional doctrine should be interpreted and moved the Roman Catholic Church to a more inclusive attitude.[251]

The relativist position did not dominate the centuries following the Reformation, although it rapidly gained support. That period witnessed the ascendancy of the Protestant missionary campaign with its exclusivistic theological

---

[249]The term "relativist" is preferred over against "pluralist" because one who concedes salvific efficacy for non-Christian religions relativizes Christianity's historic claim of the necessity of confessing Christ for personal redemption. Incarnational Christology requires retaining this particularist stance, I believe.

[250]"Errors of Paschasius Quesnesl," Denzinger, *Enchiridion*, 1379.

[251]The Roman Catholic Church retreated from this position as Pius IX (1864) asserted that "the Catholic Church and the Papacy were the essential element in western (and by implication, all human) society. . . ." Pius could not "voluntarily accept the reduction of Christianity to one among several religious options. . . ." Cited in Cunliffe-Jones, *Christian Doctrine*, 515.

accoutrements. Further endeavors to formulate an inclusive theological position tried to keep pace. Not only did the missionary wing affirm Christianity's ultimacy, but theologians in the liberal tradition—Schleiermacher and Hegel, for example—postulated an *a priori* philosophical scheme to determine the "essence" of religion and then attempted to demonstrate why Christianity contains the *most* of the essence and is thus the apex of all religions.

Whereas, the salvation of individual pious non-Christians had been the primary goal of the inclusive formulations, in the hands of the relativists, the questions shifted to the status of the non-Christian religions in God's redemptive purposes.[252] The final section of this chapter will give attention to that inquiry as it examines the contributions of selected theologians in outlining the relativist position.

Revelation and Historical Relativism: Gotthold Ephraim Lessing

A prominent poet, dramatist, and religious thinker of the German Enlightenment, Lessing (1729-1781) raised issues concerning revelation and history which have profoundly affected modern theology. The very first of his published theological works, *Vindication of Hieronymous Cardanus*, in 1754, revealed his questioning of Christianity's claim to unique, unsurpassed status in the face of Judaism, Islam, and paganism.[253]

Lessing's formidable gifts as a playwright and insightful theologian are wedded in his play, *Nathan the Wise*, which is a plea for mutual respect among the religions—because all are attuned to the same God—and a rejection of dogma that leads to anti-Semitism or other forms of intolerance.[254] Lessing places on the lips of Nathan, in the now famous parable of the three rings, his thesis that the "truth" of a particular historical religion is secondary to the morality evidenced by

---

[252]See Schlette, *Towards a Theology of Religions*, 16-18.

[253]Henry Chadwick, *Lessing's Theological Writings* (London: Adam and Charles Black, 1956) 9-10.

[254]Ibid., 26-27.

its adherents;[255] loving, tolerant attitudes, and sincerity of heart are the marks of the universal "natural religion."[256]

Lessing's fascination with "natural religion" and his denigration of "positive" or "revealed religions" is a constant refrain in his theological writings. His maxim, "necessary truths of revelation" are not contingent upon accidental truths of history, was the linch-pin of his argument. Lessing sharpens this contention further by saying that "even if it were possible to prove the truth of the stories of Christ's resurrection, the contingent event in itself offered no proper basis for eternal truth."[257]

He insists that through the individual person's reason the essential elements of any religion, that is, humanitarian morality, are "immediately derived from God."[258] God's attempt to educate the whole human race through revelation, as Lessing put it, is simply a short-cut to give one "quicker and more easily" that which one could get from within oneself.[259] From this thought, Lessing explicated his understanding of a "progressive revelation." God did not impart everything at once but maintained "a certain order and a certain measure in his revelation,"[260] which had the purpose of assisting human reason.[261]

---

[255]Ibid., 44.

[256]G.C. Lessing, *On the Origin of Revealed Religion*, Henry Chadwick, ed., *Lessing's Theological Writings*, 104-105. Cf. Schlette, *Towards a Theology of Religions*, 24.

[257]Cited by John H.S. Kent, "Christian Theology in the Eighteenth to Twentieth Centuries" in Cunliffe-Jones, *Christian Doctrine*, 472.

[258]*On the Origin of Revealed Religion*, 104.

[259]G.E. Lessing, *The Education of the Human Race*, Henry Chadwick, ed., *Lessing's Theological Writings*, 83.

[260]Ibid. In the introductory material, Chadwick, ibid., 43, questions whether Lessing really believed in any transcendent revelation. As a theologian of the Enlightenment, Lessing did not reject the Bible; however, his anti-supernaturalistic presuppositions eclipse appeals to miracle and prophecy. He sees God immanent in nature and history.

Lessing adumbrates the relativist and evolutionary tendencies of the nineteenth and twentieth centuries in his efforts to base theology on the history of religion. The unsolved problem of uniting history and revelation emanates from his speculations[262] and makes dubious the certainty of any dogmatic formulation. The implications of his pioneering thought continue to plague those who attempt to ground doctrine in the events of history, and his indifference to the content of religious affirmations disturbs those who desire to say more about the significance of Christian theology when compared to other religions.

The Absoluteness of Christianity? Ernst Troeltsch

The problem of historicism was the all-inclusive theme of Troeltsch's life (1865-1923). More than any other theologian and philosopher of the era of Liberal Protestantism, he realized the implications and monumental challenge of the modern historical approach to Christianity's traditional claims of uniqueness and absoluteness. Troeltsch is unquestionably more significant for his creative contributions to theological method than for his achievement as a systematic theologian.[263] His principal academic quest was to construct a theology based on the historical method and, in his words, "to make at least some progress

---

[261]Chadwick, ibid., 40, credits the Alexandrian Fathers, Clement and Origen, as the chief influence on Lessing's understanding of the slow process of divine education.

[262]In many respects Bultmann is Lessing's heir; the Marburg scholar's radical historical scepticism does not mitigate the truth of the kerygma with its call to authentic Christian living, in his thinking. Like Lessing he does not wish to depend on the accidental truths of history for his theological base. This issue continues to generate considerable interest in the various theological specializations. See the new work by Charles E. Garrison, *Two Different Worlds: Christian Absolutes and the Relativism of Social Science* (Newark: University of Delaware Press, 1988).

[263]See A.O. Dyson, "Ernst Troeltsch and the Possibility of a Systematic Theology," *Ernst Troeltsch and the Future of Theology*, J.P. Clayton, ed. (Cambridge: Cambridge University Press, 1976) 81-99.

towards solving this basic problem of dogmatics in a manner which corresponds to our modern needs."[264]

True to his legacy of Enlightenment theology, in his book *Die Absolutheit des Christentums und die Religionsgeschichte*, first published in 1901, he rejected the miraculous, as for example, the incarnation and the resurrection, as the special buttress of classical Christian theology, especially when Christian theologians refused to countenance similar claims adduced by other world religions.[265] Troeltsch advocated that all religions should be analyzed as part of the overall spiritual and religious development of humankind and with identical criteria; Christianity should not be protected from such scrutiny by *a priori* supremacy claims. When religions are studied historically, he contended, the traditional isolation of Christianity (as miraculous divine revelation) from other religions (which are considered to be patently false) is dissolved.[266]

Troeltsch broke with what he termed the "mediating" theologies of Schleiermacher, Ritschl, and Herrmann, because of a "lingering absolutism that continued to regard Jesus and the church as the sole redemptive spheres, outside of which the whole of mankind is shut up in total inability."[267] He deemed the

---

[264]Cited in *Ernst Troeltsch: Writings on Theology and Religion*, Robert Morgan and Michael Pye, trans. and eds. (Atlanta: John Knox Press, 1977) 7.

[265]Ernst Troeltsch, *The Absoluteness of Christianity and the History of Religions*, David Reid, trans. (London: SCM Press, 1972) 48, 52, 58-60, 132.

[266]Ibid., 154. The American philosopher, William Hocking, shared many of Troeltsch's views of the historical and cultural relativism of Christianity. No longer could Christianity claim a special status among the world religions, but should be seen as one path to salvation amidst many others. His two key contributions to the discussion are *Rethinking Missions* (New York: Harper and Row, 1932) and *Living Religions and a World Faith* (New York: Macmillan, 1940).

[267]B.A. Gerrish, "Jesus, Myth, and History: Troeltsch's Stand in the 'Christ-Myth' Debate," *The Journal of Religion* 55 (1975): 23. Troeltsch rejects religious individualism, however, believing in the necessity of the *Christus-kult*; only there could one stay attuned to Christianity's center, Christ. Sarah Coakley seeks to dispel many of the misunderstandings of Troeltsch's Christology in her fine study, *Christ Without Absolutes: A Study of the Christology of Ernst Troeltsch* (Oxford: Clarendon Press, 1988). She

historic *extra ecclesiam nulla salus* parochial and methodologically inconsistent. The *most* a European Christian can claim is that Christianity is the supreme form of religion for him or her, he insisted. Troeltsch would not extrapolate Christianity's significance for all of humanity as Schleiermacher had done.[268] Moreover, the fact that western Christians can claim "supreme validity" for Christianity in their experience

> does not preclude that other racial groups, living under entirely different cultural conditions, may experience their contact with the Divine Life in quite a different way, and may themselves also possess a religion which has grown up with them, and from which they cannot sever themselves so long as they remain what they are.[269]

In light of this assertion, Troeltsch believed that the missionary task was superfluous; Christianity must recognize these other religions (and itself) as culturally and historically bounded expressions of the general religious consciousness. Conversion, as the goal of Christian witness to the world's religions, presupposes the claim of absolute validity[270] and, therefore, must cease.

---

carefully assesses Troeltsch's case against traditional incarnationalism, concluding that it was not possible for him to maintain "any 'incarnational christology' which asserts a *full, final,* or *exclusive* revelation of God in Christ . . ." (135).

[268]Friederich Schleiermacher, *The Christian Faith,* H.R. Mackintosh, ed., from 2nd Ger. ed., 1830 (Philadelphia: Fortress Press, 1976) 38, elevates Christianity to the "most perfect of the most highly developed forms of religion." In fairness to Schleiermacher it must be noted that he is much more generous than his forebears in admitting that all the world's religions possess some measure of truth; however, Christianity was distinguished by its relation in everything to the redemption offered in Jesus Christ.

[269]Ernst Troeltsch, *Christian Thought* (London: University of London Press, 1923) 26. Coakley, *Christ Without Absolutes,* offers a chronological bibliography of Troeltsch's works in German and English.

[270]Ibid., 28.

Assessment of the Modern Period

Lessing and Troeltsch's influence on a major theological problem of the twentieth century, namely, Christian theology's evaluation of the salvific efficacy of the world's religions, has been enormous. The enlarged understanding of human history which their thinking fostered challenged Christians with a view of the relative position of Christianity in the continuum of religious experience and reduced their confidence in its validity.[271] For fifteen centuries at least the Christian position was that all persons regardless of their culture must become Christians if they are to be saved; during the modern period, the questions which had been germinating came to fruition. The consensus no longer held.

The three impulses, exclusive, inclusive, and relative, considered in this chapter, have representative expressions in contemporary theology: Emil Brunner, Karl Rahner, and John Hick, respectively. The next three chapters will analyze the adequacy of these paradigmatic responses to the question "is there salvation outside Christ and the church?"

---

[271]Lessing and Troeltsch did not agree, however, on the means of connecting faith to contingent historical facts. Troeltsch avoided Lessing's more radical scepticism by affirming the "correct view of the relationship of the universally valid to what is historical" will not preclude the premise that "the highest and purest religious forces" may "breakthrough, receive embodiment, and are visibly guaranteed," even in and through "historical conditionedness and relativity. . . ." "Glaube und Geschichte," *Die Religion in Geschichte und Gegenwart*, F.M. Schiele and L. Zgcharnack, eds. (Tübingen: [Mohr, 1909-1914) 1453.

CHAPTER 3

EMIL BRUNNER:
CHRISTIAN EXCLUSIVISM

The classic Christian position over against other religious expressions of humankind has been Christian Exclusivism. Theologians who hold this position have argued consistently that one finds the salvation offered by God only through Christ and his church, the visible instrument of salvation. Based on seemingly irrefutable New Testament witnesses such as Acts 4:12 and John 14:6, many Christians have adjudged those who equivocate on this fundamental belief to have abdicated the Christian faith.

Early in the twentieth century Emil Brunner began to formulate his distinctive contribution to this historic theological posture. His well-reasoned argument has commended him to the mainstream of theological thinking, particularly those with a strong missionary commitment.

Brunner's life was inextricably intertwined with Zürich, Switzerland: he was born in Winterthur, near Zürich, in 1889. He received his academic preparation primarily in Zürich, where he occupied the Chair of Systematic and Practical Theology at the University of Zürich from 1924 to 1955; and, not least, he was an active minister in the Reformed Church of Zürich throughout his life. (It is reported that a bust of Zwingli stood just outside the door of his study at home.)

In an intellectual autobiography[1] Brunner discussed key influences in his theological pilgrimage. Rooted in the faith from earliest childhood in a home under the sway of the Religious Socialist Movement, Brunner encountered another theological stream in the then-in-vogue theological liberalism of the University of Zürich, where he delighted in the study of Kant and Husserl. Thoroughly immersed in the historical-critical methodologies, Brunner felt these tools necessary for preaching to a critical, scientifically-minded era and retained them even though his theological position shifted radically. He credited the solid christological foundation that he had gleaned in the Religious Socialist Movement (a legacy of Christoph Blumhardt) with the strength he found to resist the currently reigning agnostic humanism and materialism, which was identified with Darwinism."[2]

Early in his university study, Brunner began to search for a scientifically satisfying formulation" of his faith,[3] a task which occupied him all his days. His doctoral dissertation, *Das Symbolische in der Religiösen Erkenntis (The Symbolic Element in Religious Knowledge)*,[4] was his first attempt in that direction as he questioned the prevailing liberal system's views concerning experience and knowledge.[5]

---

[1]Emil Brunner, "Intellectual Autobiography," Keith Chamberlain, trans., *The Theology of Emil Brunner*, Charles W. Kegley, ed., *The Library of Living Theology*, vol. 3 (New York: Macmillan, 1962).

[2]Ibid., 6. The concern for social ethics that Brunner gained from this movement was to shape his theological and ethical posture and to prompt his stance as a loyal critic to his confessing community, the Reformed Church of Zürich. He felt the emphasis of the movement chiefly through the influence of Hermann Kutter, who was his pastor at one time.

[3]Ibid., 5. The American theological context was particularly receptive to this neoorthodox *via media* See I. John Hesselink's recent assessment, "Emil Brunner: A Centennial Perspective," *The Christian Century* 106:38 (1989): 1171-74.

[4]Emil Brunner, *Das Symbolische in der Religiösen Erkenntis* (Tübingen: J.C.B. Mohr, 1914).

[5]J. Edward Humphreys, *Emil Brunner: Makers of the Modern Theological Mind*, Bob E. Patterson (Waco: Word Books, 1976) 21. Like Barth, Brunner started as a theological liberal shaped by the thought of Troeltsch, Albrecht, and Ritschl.

Brunner's literary contributions were never aimed exclusively at the academic sphere (although *Die Mystik und Das Wort*,[6] his scathing critique of Schleiermacher could be the exception). The Zürich professor envisioned his calling to be a proclaimer of the gospel, and he never lost his primary commitment to make theology that which engaged secular humankind at the deepest level. Brunner served happily as a pastor in Obstalten in the Canton of Glarus and, in his words, "was a pastor with my whole heart and am still today."[7]

HISTORICAL AND THEOLOGICAL CONTEXT

A proper assessment of the contours of Emil Brunner's theology must include an understanding of the historical and theological context in which he worked. Brunner stands firmly in the stream of Reformed Theology and was an avid interpreter of Calvin; he may have been even more indebted to Luther. Luther's great stress on the gospel of forgiveness through faith as a personal encounter with the Word of God is clearly reflected in Brunner's conception of this Word and truth as encounter. Reformation research made great strides forward in the early twentieth century, and Brunner utilized its fruit in his theological formulations.[8] His *Dogmatik* is laced with quotations from Calvin, as he evidenced his theological kinship with the Geneva Reformer, though balanced by references to the passionate proclamations of Luther.

Break With Liberalism

The catastrophe of the First World War profoundly shaped the direction of Brunner's thinking, calling into question many of the presuppositions of

---

[6]Emil Brunner, *Die Mystik und Das Wort* (Tübingen: J.C.B. Mohr, 1928).

[7]Brunner, "Intellectual Autobiography," 7.

[8]Wilhelm Pauck, "The Church-Historical Setting of Brunner's Theology," *The Theology of Emil Brunner*, C.W. Kegley, ed., 35f. Cf. Heiko A. Oberman's useful study, *The Dawn of the Reformation* (Edinburgh: T. & T. Clark, 1986).

religious socialism[9] and theological liberalism. As a soldier he had observed the massive evil wreaked by humans upon one another which gravely challenged the cheerful optimism of nineteenth-century liberal theology. The rise of the totalitarian state dimmed his enthusiasm further and led him to examine the anthropology underlying such a social system.[10] All of this formed a matrix in which he clarified his understanding of what the *ekklēsia* should be.

Brunner had become dissatisfied with the tenets of Liberalism as early as 1918 when he welcomed Karl Barth's *Römerbrief*, in which he saw a confirmation of his own developing position. The" new theology" Barth and Brunner and others advocated was sharply critical of the Schleiermacher-dominated theology of the past century with its attempts to substitute religious experience for revelation.[11] From a measure of initial unanimity in theological perceptions, Brunner and Barth soon began to travel divergent paths in their reaction to Liberalism. The story of Brunner's great divide with Barth over the issue of general revelation in creation is well known and does not need retelling.[12]

Several points at issue in the controversy, however, have bearing on the present study: (1) whether there is revelation outside the Bible; (2) whether persons can come to know God apart from the biblical revelation; and(3) whether there is a point of contact (*Anknüpfungspunkt*) in a man or woman which can

---

[9]Brunner, "Intellectual Autobiography," 7.

[10]Brunner's significant anthropological study, *Der Mensch im Widerspruch*, published in 1935, is thought by many to be his chief theological contribution.

[11]Brunner's basic disagreement with Schleiermacher was over the latter's conception of revelation as simply relating to the higher self-consciousness of an individual. Such a scheme removed all need for the Word of God, in Brunner's opinion. See Friedrich Schleiermacher, *Brief Outline on the Study of Theology*, T. Tice, trans. (Richmond: John Knox Press, 1966), and Günter Scholtz, *Die Philosophie Schleiermachers* (Darmstadt: Wissenschaftliche Buchgesellschaft, 1984).

[12]See *Natural Theology: Comprising "Nature and Grace" by Professor Dr. Emil Brunner and the Reply "No!" by Karl Barth*, Peter Fraenkel, trans. (London: Geoffrey Bles, The Centenary Press, 1946).

receive God's revelation in Christ. Barth exclaimed a vehement *Nein!* to these proposals while Brunner acknowledged their truth and made them foundational to his theological position.[13]

The Task of Theology

Brunner believes that the tasks of theologians are multiple, but the most essential is biblical theology. The second task (*Die Andere Aufgabe der Theologie*)[14] is polemical. The Word of God accosts men and women and calls for *metanoia*, hence a well-defined Christian anthropology is an essential aspect of the polemical task. It is the second task that claims Brunner's attention, though his writing always presupposes the first task.

Brunner described his theological task as "eristic" because he was doing battle *for* something. He chose this word, derived from *erizein* which means "wrangle" or "quarrel"[15] rather than the word *apologia* ("defense"), because he viewed the theological task to be less concerned with the defense of the Christian faith than with its advancement.[16] Thus eristic theology at heart is a "missionary theology,"[17] because of the secularistic situation in which the church finds

---

[13]These proposals will be explored further in the context of Brunner's soteriology and ecclesiology.

[14]An article written for *Zwischen den Zeiten* in 1929.

[15]*A Greek-English Lexicon of the New Testament and Other Early Christian Literature*, W.F. Arndt and F.W. Gingrich, trans. and ed. (Chicago: University of Chicago Press, 1957) 309. Brunner's article "Secularism as a Problem for the Church," *International Review of Missions* 19 (1930): 507, illustrates how this word affected his method for doing theology: "As men of today we can only apprehend the divine Word through conflict with the thought of our time."

[16]Emil Brunner, *The Christian Doctrine of God: Dogmatics* I, Olive Wyon, trans. (Philadelphia: Westminster Press, 1950) 98-99. See P.G. Schrotenboer's *A New Apologetics: An Analysis and Appraisal of the Eristic Theology of Emil Brunner* (J.H. Kok N.V. Kampen: 1955). See also *Revelation and Reason: The Christian Doctrine of Faith and Knowledge*, Olive Wyon, trans. (Philadelphia: Westminster Press, 1946) 14 for further explication of this task of theology.

[17]*Dogmatics*, 1:101. Hugh Verson White, "Brunner's Missionary Theology," *The Theology of Emil Brunner*, C.W. Kegley, ed., 56, observes that in his evangelical concern Brunner "embodies the basic emphasis of the Reformation and, indeed, of Western

herself. Eristics connotes a theology in which the church seeks to hold forth Christianity to a world that has lost confidence in the church.

Brunner was acutely aware of the problems secularism posed for the church and devoted his efforts to enabling the church to transcend the sacral/secular antithesis. From the perspective of world history, Brunner argued, the "face of a culture and a civilization the orientation of which is purely secular is seen to be something new and unique."[18] The second fact of secularism (which is not new) is the "exclusive attention to the world that now is, the intramundane quality of thought. . . ."[19]

Brunner argued that the church was at fault in this because its lack of a clear word for its *Zeitgeist* forced persons to look elsewhere for leadership,[20] and hence secularism grew up on Christian soil. The theology of the nineteenth century, crafted by Schleiermacher, Hegel, Ritschl, and Troeltsch, was, in Brunner's words, a "dissolution of the Gospel into individualistic rational religion, of mystical or social-ethical hue."[21] In contradistinction to the stultifying ebb of modern theology, Brunner articulated the central task of theology to be the recovery of the church's understanding of the truth of the Word of God. That

---

Christianity upon Redemption." See Brunner's article "Toward a Missionary Theology," *Christian Century* 66 (1949): 816-18.

[18]Brunner, "Secularism," 495.

[19]Ibid., 496ff. Brunner admits the causative factor of "false sacralism" in the rise of secularism over the past 300 years. In the realm of modern science, secularism has provided a healthy corrective, compelling faith to "replace forms of belief which have become untenable and untrue, and can only be clung to against better knowledge." Many contemporary thinkers share Brunner's balanced view. Among them are: Ian Barbour, *Issues of Science and Religion* (London: SCM Press, 1966); S.L. Jaki, *The Road of Science and the Ways to God* (Chicago: University of Chicago Press, 1978); and A.R. Peacocke, *Creation and the World of Science* (Oxford: Clarendon Press, 1979).

[20]"Secularism," 504.

[21]Ibid., 505.

alone is what she must offer to the world—in a manner that engages rather than offends contemporary humanity.

A missionary concern certainly is not tangential to Brunner's theology, but arises out of the basic principles and concepts in his comprehensive theological system.[22] His Christian anthropology, for example, views humanity both as *imago dei* and *im Widerspruch*—a contradiction which necessitates a resolution.[23] This doctrine demonstrates that all persons need salvation and that all should be made aware of this need and the possibility of the need being met through the gift of salvation in Christ. Furthermore, the very nature of historical revelation implies the missionary task of Christianity, in Brunner's thinking,[24] for it can only be known through the witness of those who have received it. It will not be spread by a natural historic movement, as Schleiermacher suggested.

SOTERIOLOGICAL PERSPECTIVE

Redemption is the central theme in Brunner's theology. The architectonic function it serves for him reveals how tightly he clung to his Reformation heritage. The content of each doctrine in his dogmatic theology advances the centrality of what God has done and is doing through the revelation of the Word, Christ Jesus, for the reconciliation of humanity "curved in upon itself." Moreover, Brunner's soteriology illumines his focus on personalism.[25] He uses the language

---

[22]Schrotenboer, 17, describes the missionary concern as the "characterization of his whole theological method."

[23]Emil Brunner, *Man in Revolt: A Christian Anthropology*, Olive Wyon, trans. (London: Lutterworth Press, 1939) 168ff.

[24]H.V. White, "Brunner's Missionary Theology," 56.

[25]The debt Brunner owes to the thinking of Ebner, Buber, and especially Gogarten (all influenced by Kierkegaard) can be seen clearly throughout his writings. His theology is profoundly shaped by the implications of their attempts to transcend the objective-subjective dichotomy in knowing; personalism emerged as the fruit of their labors, and Brunner appropriated it as his primary theological method from about 1937 on. See *The*

of encounter rather than of transaction and presupposes all soteriological issues with his understanding of *imago dei* as *relation*.[26]

Anthropology

Brunner developed his distinctive Christian anthropology in the face of what he considered a pervasive misunderstanding of human personhood, self-knowledge being the most distorted.[27] He thought that sin perverts proper self-understanding and that only the Word of God could cut through the self's mirage to reveal the true self. To put it methodologically, "a Christian doctrine of man must be beaten out on the anvil of continual argument with man's own view of himself,"[28] and is, thus, a dialectical enterprise. Brunner's anthropology has two great components: his understanding of humanity as the image of God, and the situation of contradiction in which all regenerate persons reside.

Imago Dei. Drawing from a wide range of sources, and displaying a profound philosophical and biblical comprehension, Brunner structured his understanding of the image of God by shifting from a "faculty" approach to a relational approach. This revolution in understanding of the image is one of the key contributions of Neo-Orthodox theology, and of Brunner in particular.

Luther and Calvin had regarded the *imago dei* as "original righteousness" which was lost in the Fall and recovered only in Christ.[29] Both, however,

---

Divine Human Encounter, Amandus W. Loos, trans. (Philadelphia: Westminster Press, 1943) 7.

[26]Emil Brunner, *The Christian Doctrine of Creation and Redemption: Dogmatics* II, Olive Wyon, trans. (Philadelphia: Westminster Press, 1952) 69.

[27]Brunner reacts against Liberalism's anthropocentrism which did not, in his opinion, reflect sufficiently the Reformers' stress on the fallenness of all human strivings; he accused Kant, Hegel, Schleiermacher, Troeltsch, and Ritschl of drinking too deeply of the wells of modern Humanism.

[28]*Man in Revolt*, 9.

[29]See the analysis of Luther and Calvin in David Cairns, *The Image of God in Man* (London: Fontana Library of Theology and Philosophy, 1973[2]) 127-51.

emphasized the negative aspect of the image in fallen humanity. Calvin nuanced his position more than Luther, maintaining the relationship of fallen humankind to God, even though his stress was on the depravity of the image. With Luther he affirmed that a person's supernatural gifts were lost in the Fall, but one did retain natural gifts ("relics"), albeit corrupted.[30]

Whereas the "relational" theme was subordinated to the "relics" theme in Calvin, Brunner elevated the relational aspect to preeminence. The faculties of reason and will are involved in relationship, to be sure, but do not constitute the image. "Fallen" humanity has experienced a rupture in the personal relationship to God. Humankind remains *humanitas*, however. Yet a person is meant to be a being in relationship just as the Holy Trinity is Be-ing in loving relationship.[31]

Brunner posits a universal relationship of humanity to the Logos through general revelation in creation. The soteriological significance of Brunner's understanding is that this relationship makes possible a "point of contact" (*Anknüpfungspunkt*) in all persons for the gospel.[32] Because of this encounter with the Logos, each person is thereby responsible and guilty—a necessary prerequisite to hearing the gospel call of repentance. Accordingly, Brunner insisted that this was the source of the universal sense in which "all have sinned" and are guilty before God even though they may not have heard the gospel of Jesus Christ

---

[30]John Calvin, *Institutes of the Christian Religion*, John T. McNeill, ed., The Library of Christian Classics (Philadelphia: Westminster Press, 1960) II, 2.12. See Calvin's *Commentary* on John 3:6, and also Cairns, 142-44. John H. Leith's new work on Calvin is quite helpful in this area. See *John Calvin's Doctrine of the Christian Life* (Louisville: Westminster, 1989) 44-45.

[31]*Man in Revolt*, 74, 96. See appendix "On the Doctrine of the *Analogia Entis*," *Dogmatics*, 2:42-45; Brunner distinguishes his concept of a person "reflecting" God from the medieval Roman Catholic *analogia entis*, the foundation of a rational *theologia naturalis*.

[32]Barth vigorously attacked this conclusion of Brunner and largely structured his understanding of the image in opposition to it. See his response in *Natur und Gnade* and in *Church Dogmatics*, III, 2, 44.2.

proclaimed.[33] That persons have been created in the image of God is itself the "presupposition of sin."[34]

The humanity of the fallen person, that is, the capacity to understand a word addressed to him or her, and the sense of responsibility, comprise the "formal image"—a guilty, but responsible existence before God. As Brunner asserts:

> What we can say in clear terms is this, that the relationship to God which determines the whole being of man is not annihilated by sin, but perverted. Man does not cease to be a being responsible to God, but his responsibility is changed from a life in love to a life under the law, and life under the wrath of God.[35]

The "material image" is the person perfected in Christ. One must confess one's inability to remove the barrier erected by sin between oneself and God and accept in faith the renewal of the image.[36]

Im Widerspruch. Brunner contended that the situation whereby persons created in the image of God now stand in opposition to their origin eventuates a contradiction (*Widerspruch*) in human nature.[37] This contradiction is most readily manifested in the realm of human responsibility.[38] The primal rebellion

---

[33]*Man in Revolt*, 79f. Brunner maintained, as did Barth, that a Christian view of human beings could come only from the perspective of Christ, the Word, the Logos. Brunner proceeded from this starting point in a different way than Barth, emphasizing the continuity between the eternal Logos and the incarnate Christ.

[34]Ibid., 132.

[35]Ibid., 105.

[36]See appendix "On the History of the Doctrine of the *Imago Dei*," *Dogmatics*, 2:75-78, for further explication of the "formal" and "material" aspects of the image.

[37]*Man in Revolt*, 114

[38]Ibid., 115, 133. Brunner uses responsibility as the key to the contradiction. On p. 156 he writes: "Responsibility still remains the characteristic formula for the nature of man, for fallen man as well as for man in his origin." Cf. Leith's section on human responsibility, 138ff., to see Brunner's affinity for Calvin in this instance.

is that men and women think they can set themselves free from God, but, in truth, they remain in relation to God and responsible *coram deo* even though their existence is now turned away from God's intention. The deity alone should be the center of life for human beings. The self is now "bent back upon itself" (*cor incurvatum in se*),[39] and one stands perverted under the law of obligation—which is God's relation to those who refuse to live in responsible relationship with God and others. Thus, human beings have existence either in the love of God or in the wrath of God.

Sin is a "total act," because it neither relates simply to some aspect of one's "lower" nature nor to sin's individual manifestations, but to one's desire to be in a position that is not utterly dependent upon God.[40] All persons participate in this turning away from God and organically share in Adam's sin, hence, the veracity of the biblical idea of the solidarity of sin.[41]

Only the biblical revelation deals realistically with the evil (*das Böse*) that is both characteristic of the acts of humanity, and, at the same time, is that which ineluctably thwarts a person's attempts to choose the good freely. Brunner contended that the Bible never reduces one's personal responsibility for sin, yet it speaks of the "sense of Fate in evil" as it calls people "slaves of sin" (John 8:34).[42] One knows that he or she is responsible, for "some knowledge of this, in some form, constitutes an essential part of human nature and one that can never

---

[39]Brunner uses Luther's classic phrase, believing it to be the most descriptive picture of life lived in opposition to God. See *Man in Revolt*, 136f.

[40]Brunner, *Dogmatics*, 2:94-95. Brunner rejects the optimism of idealism in a manner similar to Reinhold Niebuhr in his classic, *The Nature and Destiny of Man*, vol. 1 (New York: Charles Scribner's Sons, 1941) 112ff.

[41]Ibid., 96. In *Man in Revolt*, 142, Brunner approaches the problematic concept of original sin from the perspective of the New Testament—which is characteristic of his methodology. The Christian's experience of the solidarity of redeemed humanity in Christ gives the clue to the unity of the human race in sin.

[42]*Man in Revolt*, 115, 136. In this section Brunner reminds the reader that Scripture does not ignore the satanic element; evil forces were there before the "sin of Adam."

be lost."[43] God has chosen to reveal God's own self through Creation, through Scripture, and through the "One in whom all is fulfilled";[44] thus, no one has any excuse. Moreover, a sense of guilt or "bad conscience" pervades, and its removal poses the central problem of the Christian faith.[45]

Efficacy of human religious strivings. A sense of the Holy, the religious element, is common to all, and all bow in some form to its inner demand.[46] Whether agnostic, atheistic, or simply as a "godless disposition," the religious instinct expresses itself. Furthermore, the history of religion is "above all else: a witness—even if perverted—to the relation of man to God."[47] "Pagan religions" testify of this inescapable relationship; they would not exist if God did not "declare himself to everyone since the dawn of humanity in his works, in nature and history."[48]

Brunner calls this knowledge of God "original revelation"[49] and declares it to be the presupposition of the varied forms of seeking after God—which humans inevitably transform into human illusion.[50] These illusions, based on the egocentricity which is at its very core the failure to give glory to God (Rom

---

[43]Ibid., 156. See Brunner, *The Letter to the Romans*, H.A. Kennedy, trans. (Philadelphia: Westminster Press, 1959) 17.

[44]Emil Brunner, *Revelation and Reason: The Christian Doctrine of Faith and Knowledge*, Olive Wyon, trans. (Philadelphia: Westminster Press, 1946) 58.

[45]*Man in Revolt*, 135. On p. 178, Brunner asserts: "there is nothing more profoundly human than the sense of guilt; nothing in which the lost image of God manifests its presence more clearly." Wolfhart Pannenberg, *Christian Spirituality* (Philadelphia: Westminster Press, 1983) 13ff., analyzes the role of guilt consciousness in Protestant piety. He shares Brunner's view of the integral part guilt plays vis-à-vis genuine faith.

[46]Ibid., 178-79.

[47]Ibid., 180.

[48]*Letter to the Romans*, 17.

[49]*Revelation and Reason*, 262.

[50]Ibid., 264.

1:12f.), issue in religions which are a morass of "wonderful and terrible, sublime and gruesome elements."[51]

Bound to frustrate and deceive, these other religions fail to deal with the nature of human beings as the image of God which has been perverted from God's intention for them. Indeed, Brunner believes the distinctive mark of non-biblical religions (*falsa religio*) to be the "lack of realism" that refuses to see God without false projections, and thus cannot appropriately interpret the posture of humanity.[52] It is only from the standpoint of the Word of God that these religions can be seen for what they really are. What they lack is precisely what is foundational to Christianity, namely, revelation. The efforts of these religions are futile because "nothing whatever that man may undertake, neither sacrifices nor mystical practices, in short no human work, can obtain for him salvation and fellowship with God."[53]

In his writings Brunner expresses a dialectical attitude toward other religions.[54] He affirms the fact that they are a response to God, yet he rejects them as a distorted response. He proposes a relation of judgment and fulfillment between the Christian gospel and the other religions—a judgment upon their sin and a fulfillment of their hidden origin in divine revelation.

Uniqueness of Christianity

The uniqueness of Christianity is that it alone lives by the Word of God, the "revelation in which God imparts himself."[55] Others make claims about the

---

[51]Ibid., 265.

[52]Ibid., 266.

[53]Emil Brunner, *The Christian Doctrine of the Church, Faith and the Consummation*, vol. 3, David Cairns, trans. (Philadelphia: Westminster Press, 1962) 194.

[54]Cf. Hendrik Kraemer, *The Christian Message in a Non-Christian World* (Grand Rapids: Kregel Publications, 1938). Kraemer's perspective is very similar to Brunner's dialectic approach.

[55]*Revelation and Reason*, 258.

efficacy of their revelations, yet none can assert anything comparable to the incarnation. Consequently, faith in the God revealed by Jesus is "not *one* of the religions of the world."[56]

Brunner clearly recognizes the difficulty many have in believing that Christianity transcends the categories by which other religions are characterized. He admits the seeming intolerance of Christianity, but argues that Christianity's exclusive claim rises out of the very nature of the Christian revelation, and thus he cannot set it aside as he accuses the "relativizing" Lessing and Schleiermacher of doing. He suggests that they confused attitudes with the question of truth.[57] Brunner unabashedly maintains that "the uncompromising attitude toward the world religions is the natural and inevitable consequence of the Christian faith itself."[58] To do battle with the idolatry (*Abgötterei*) of the other religions is not a detached, academic exercise, but the very heart of the faith. It is a matter of life and death, as it was when Elijah faced the priests of Baal.[59]

Revelation, as Brunner defines it, is always a gift whereby God manifests God's personal reality and the desire to create community between Godself as personal Being and human beings, and, subsequently, to create community within humanity.[60] Revelation is never what a person can decipher or postulate through reasoning skills; it is always what comes to him or her as a "disclosure" of the two sides of a person's relation to God—who God is, and whom God intends human beings to be.

Brunner strives to keep the objective (what God reveals) and the subjective (what one receives) as interrelated and indivisible components of revelation as the

---

[56]Ibid.

[57]Ibid., 219. See *Die Mystik und das Wort*.

[58]Ibid., 220-21.

[59]Emil Brunner, *Die Christusbotschaft im Kampf mit den Religionen* (Stuttgart: Evang. Missionsverlag, 1931) 1.

[60]*Revelation and Reason*, 27.

Bible depicts it. Revelation "only reaches its goal"[61] when one responds positively to it:

> The fact of the illumination is therefore an integral part of the process of revelation; without this an event is no more a revelation than light is light without the seeing, illuminated eye.[62]

Thus revelation occurs in the meeting of two subjects; truth is apprehended in the personal encounter between divine and human, and the reception of revelation is faith. One abdicates isolated self-reliance in the revelation-event as one recognizes God's sovereignty, the divine rule (*basileia tou theou*) over all humankind.[63]

The Mediator. The Christian understanding of revelation unequivocally affirms the continuum of promise and fulfillment found in the Scriptures. It is a history of the "coming God" who makes the divine self known through word and deed among the covenant people: Israel in the Old Testament, and, in the New Testament, all who would respond to the fullest disclosure, Jesus Christ. The Old Testament constantly points beyond itself and the New Testament gathers up the prophecies of the Old Testament as it proclaims the Christ, the goal and fulfillment of God's self-revealing.[64] This revelatory activity differs from the general revelation that comes to all through the creation; it is a special (*Einmaligkeit*) revelation that reaches its profound height in Jesus Christ, to whom

---

[61]Ibid., 33.

[62]Ibid. Brunner's personalist approach to the doctrine of revelation anticipated contemporary American theology's concern with the subject-object polarization of "foundationalist" theologies. See Ronald Thiemann's constructive proposal in *Revelation and Theology: The Gospel as Narrated Promise* (South Bend: University of Notre Dame Press, 1985).

[63]Ibid.

[64]Ibid., 87-101. In *The Mediator*, Olive Wyon, trans. (London: Lutterworth Press, 1934) 286, Brunner describes the relation of the Testaments thus: "the whole of the Old Testament and its revelation is Advent; the New Testament is the Christmas message."

the apostolic *ephapax* was applied.[65] General revelation is, however, presuppositional to the message of God's renewing grace in Jesus Christ. One could not be a sinner and in need of God's provision if one had not "held down in unrighteousness" (Rom 1:18) the truth of God which had come through creation.

One cannot traverse the distance between self and God created by the perverting power of sin; he or she requires one whom God "throws like a bridge across to us, over which God comes to us." Thus in his very nature, Jesus Christ, the incarnate Word, "the gulf between God and man has been bridged."[66] Christianity differs from the "religions" by tying itself to this one historic, unrepeatable event of revelation and atonement; if it really happened, it can take place only once for all through this Mediator:

> If Jesus Christ really be the Redeemer, then it is evident that "in no other is there salvation," that "in His name every knee shall bow." Only this unconditionally personal event, the fact that God the Creator came to man, can be the absolute and unique event; all other happenings are by their very nature repeatable, capable of intensification and variation; but this is not.[67]

In his well-known sermon, "In None Other is Salvation," the echo of this controlling *Geist* in Brunner's soteriology is heard again:

> [U]nconditioned forgiving and atoning love is disclosed to us and bestowed upon us in Jesus Christ the Crucified and nowhere else, and

---

[65]*The Mediator*, 25n2. The controlling concept of personalism in Brunner's theology is most evident when he moves into the realm of special revelation. God as Subject meets the creation, i.e., the human being, as subject in personal relation, rather than standing over against the person as Object. Revelation, then, is to be found in personal encounter rather than propositions.

[66]Ibid., 490-91.

[67]*Revelation and Reason*, 31.

thus He alone is our Savior and His Name alone is the Name whereby we must be saved.[68]

Brunner clearly makes Christianity's claim to exclusive saving truth an essential part of the Christian faith. "A real Christian faith is impossible apart from the conviction that here and here alone is salvation,"[69] Brunner baldly asserts. He refuses to equivocate on this point.

Appropriating the saving work of Christ. Although Brunner stresses the universality of what Christ has done as Mediator, he nowhere allows it the exclusively objective framework characteristic of Barth.[70] Instead, Brunner chooses to make the personal (subjective) the keystone of his soteriological structure.

To understand Brunner's *ordo salutis*, one must thoroughly understand the "I-Thou" epistemological framework that underlies his concept of faith. Indeed, Brunner would argue, the event of reconciliation between God and humanity can *only* be spoken of in "I-Thou" language.[71] Just as revelation only comes to its

---

[68]Emil Brunner, *The Great Invitation and Other Sermons*, Harold Knight, trans. (Philadelphia: Westminster Press, 1955) 111. This collection was originally published as *Fraumünster Predigten* (Zürich: Zwingli-Verlag, 1953).

[69]*The Mediator*, 210.

[70]Karl Barth, *Church Dogmatics: The Doctrine of Reconciliation* IV, 2, G.W. Bromiley, trans., and G.W. Bromiley and T.F. Torrance, eds. (Edinburgh: T. & T. Clark, 1958) 502-503. See Brunner's analysis and critique of this aspect of Barth's thought in *Dogmatics*, 1:346-53. On p. 349 he notes that "objectivism" has always been characteristic of all his teaching and constitutes the "forcible severance of revelation and faith." The contrast which Brunner sees between his position and that of Barth is clearly summarized in Brunner's article "Der Neue Barth: Bemerkungen zu Karl Barth's Lehre vom Menschen," *Zeitschrift für Theologie und Kirche* 48 (1951): esp. 97-100. Brunner criticizes Barth's view that all participate in God's salvation because of their creation in Christ. Brunner insists, however, that one is reconciled "in so far as he believes" (99).

[71]*Dogmatics*, 3:107.

goal in the positive response of one subject to another, so only in faith does God's righteousness come to its goal.[72]

The locus of God's ultimate self-revealing is the cross of Christ; there a person gains knowledge of who God is—namely loving, redeeming, and righteous—and knowledge of oneself—"how it stands" with himself or herself.[73] In the event of the cross one can see God's judgment on all moral and religious attempts at self-justification; for the one who refuses to be judged as the guilty one, deserving the death Christ died, the cross is the stone of stumbling.[74] But for those who regard the cross as *pro nobis*, a word of assurance can be heard; identification with the cursed blasphemer constitutes the "radical self-knowledge of the sinner" and is transformed into identification with the Son of God who gains God's approval.[75] In the Crucified One a person encounters God who judges and acquits; "justification is God's verdict which faith bears and accepts."[76]

Brunner describes faith as "believing in a person" (an act) rather than cognitive assent to facts.[77] One's whole being is summoned by the Word and the Spirit to become, by faith, the person that God purposes[78]—one who depends entirely upon God. Only by the operation of the Holy Spirit can the self-communication of God and the self-understanding of the person coincide.[79] One

---

[72]Ibid., 204.

[73]Ibid., 194.

[74]Ibid., 195. George Rupp, *Christologies and Cultures: Toward a Typology of Religious Worldviews* (Paris: Mouton, 1974) 61, analyzes Brunner's "Anselmic" tendencies in atonement theory.

[75]Ibid., 195-98.

[76]Ibid., 204.

[77]Ibid., 197.

[78]Ibid., 200-205.

[79]Ibid., 205.

cannot hear and respond to God's convicting and assuring word without the Spirit's help. Faith or conversion occurs as the Spirit confirms from within one the reality of being called God's child.[80]

Brunner's soteriology is not, strictly speaking, an *ordo salutis* which implies a temporal sequence;[81] instead, repentance and regeneration, conversion and sanctification are "different steps of this one happening."[82] One's participation, the change of heart or *shub*, is not incidental to this process. Brunner seeks to balance post-Reformation theology which denied the presence of the human partner and reduced it to "the pure passivity of an object."[83] He wants to transcend the "one sidedness of objectivism" which confesses *sola gratia* without the accompanying *sola fide*,[84] for faith in Christ demands the active participation of the person.[85]

Decree of universal salvation. Brunner staunchly repudiates any doctrine of the "double decree"[86] as a "shocking caricature of the Christian message";[87] conversely, he also rejects universalism as a twisting of Scripture.[88] The biblical message is the unconditional love of God for all and the indisputable fact that God

---

[80]Ibid., 285. Cf. 11.

[81]Ibid., 281.

[82]Ibid.

[83]Ibid., 280.

[84]Ibid., 224, 285.

[85]Ibid., 281.

[86]Calvin, *Institutes* III, 5.21. Cf. *Man in Revolt*, 76.

[87]*Dogmatics*, 3:416. See *Dogmatics*, 1:303-20, "The Eternal Divine Decrees and the Doctrine of Election." Brunner follows Luther and faults Calvin in adjudging the doctrine of Predestination to be speculative theology which does not create a real knowledge of God.

[88]*Dogmatics*, 1:348-49.

wills to give salvation to all.[89] One can choose to be with God, a choice that issues in life, or against God, a choice that ends in perdition.[90] God's self-revelation in the Bible is always the call to decision about one's foundational and ultimate relationship to God.

Judgment results from a person's refusal to act with responsibility before the One who judges—not because of contrived schemes of election. Moreover, it is the reality of judgment which gives responsibility its ultimate seriousness and, thus, clarifies the relationship between God and humanity.[91] A person speaks to God from the posture of having already been addressed; it is a position that permits no neutrality because one must decide whether or not to endorse God's prior decision made about him or her, namely, that God has elected each person to belong to God.[92]

Brunner teaches both the Last Judgment and universal salvation because both stand paradoxically alongside one another in the Bible. When one attempts to overcome this paradox, inevitably one side is elevated and the other is slighted. The logical contradiction does not yield to the rules of logic, for its intent is not smooth harmonization; it stands in stark, discordant antithesis as a word of challenge more than a word of doctrine.[93] There can be no detached, theoretical deciding of this juxtaposition of logically exclusive concepts; the message of the Word draws each into the struggle to decide the content of one's relationship with

---

[89]*Dogmatics*, 3:415-22.

[90]Ibid., 419.

[91]Emil Brunner, *Eternal Hope*, Harold Knight, trans. (Philadelphia: Westminster Press, 1954) 178. Cf. *Dogmatics*, 3:419.

[92]Ibid., 177.

[93]Ibid., 183. Brunner both avoided and incurred many criticisms through this approach; his unwillingness to find a constructive synthesis or resolution left many unsatisfied.

God[94] and the contradiction is resolved in existential participation—not in seeking to give a final answer to the dilemma.[95] This much can be said:

> The Word of Christ is for us the word of decision, which, so far as we believe, gives us salvation, and precisely because it summons us to this decision, forbids us to believe in a deliverance which awaits us, or anyone else, outside the sphere of faith.[96]

ECCLESIOLOGICAL PERSPECTIVE

As in the soteriological section, this treatment does not purport to be a comprehensive summary of Brunner's ecclesiology, but is an analysis of those features that contribute to the exclusive position he posits for Christianity over against the religions.[97] The number and variety of monographs,[98] articles,[99]

---

[94]Ibid., 183-84.

[95]*Dogmatics*, 3:423.

[96]*Dogmatics*, 1:353. See George S. Hendry's positive evaluation of Brunner's approach to this issue in the article "An Appraisal of Brunner's Theology," *Theology Today* 19 (1963): 529.

[97]Brunner never refers to Christianity as a "religion" because it is not, in his opinion, just one more example of the species religion, but the unique, revealed, personal Word of God to humanity. See *Revelation and Reason*, 258.

[98]Works in English are: *The Church and the Oxford Group* (London: Hodder and Stoughton, 1937); *The Predicament of the Church Today* (London: Lutterworth Press, 1940); *The Church in the New Social Order* (London: SCM Press, 1952); and *The Misunderstanding of the Church*, Harold Knight, trans. (London: Lutterworth Press, 1952).
Untranslated monographs include: *Der Staat als Problem der Kirche* (Bern: Gotthelf-Verlag, 1933); *Die Kirche unserer Tage*. Schweizer Buch (Zürich: Schweizer Druck-und-Verlaghaus, 1938). For a full listing of the writings of Emil Brunner to 1962, see *The Theology of Emil Brunner*, C.W. Kegley, ed., 355-84.

[99]Significant articles include: "Was ist Kirche?" Zwinglikalender 1953, Basel, Reinhardt; "Secularism and the Church," *International Review of Missions* 19 (1930): 495-511; "Ecclesia and Evangelism," *Japan Christian Quarterly* 21 (1955): 154-59; "Theologie und Kirche," *Zwischen den Zeiten* 8 (1930): Heft. 5.

sermons,[100] and lectures[101] devoted to the doctrine of the church (in addition to his thorough treatment in his *Dogmatik*) demonstrate Brunner's vital concern for this aspect of Christian theology. Brunner readily admits that the question of the church is *"the* unsolved problem of Protestant theology,"[102] and his extensive study seeks to redress the problem.

The Misunderstanding of the Church

Almost from the beginning, Brunner contends, the understanding of the church has rested on a misconception: the identification of the *ekklesia* with the church as an *institution.*[103] Basic to Brunner's ecclesiology is his distinction between the Spirit-filled community of the New Testament and the juridical institutional form that historically has perverted its true intent. The tendency

> towards a false ecclesiasticism began in the first century and grew from century to century. The simple and unique conception of the church as the community of believers, which can have no Head save Christ himself, whose Divine authority is not based upon some numinous force confronting the individual believer, but simply and solely upon the Word and Spirit of God, indwelling the Christian community as a whole, gradually disappeared.[104]

---

[100]The notable sermon on this topic is "The Rock on Which the Church is Built," Reformation Sunday sermon, Matt 16:13-19, 7 Nov 1948, printed in *The Great Invitation and Other Sermons*, 26-33.

[101]"The Church Between East and West," printed in *The Congregational Quarterly* 27 (1949): No. 3; and "The Church as Gift and Task," *The Japan Christian Quarterly* 20 (1954): No. 3.

[102]Emil Brunner, *The Divine Imperative*, Olive Wyon, trans. (Philadelphia: Westminster Press, 1947) 523.

[103]This is the thesis of Brunner's book *The Misunderstanding of the Church.* Cf. *Dogmatics* III, chap. 4. See also Dale Moody, "The Church in Theology," *The Theology of Emil Brunner*, C.W. Kegley, ed., 227, which gives a helpful analysis of Brunner's tendency to identify the institutional church with the "Es-Welt" (the "it-world" or the impersonal sphere), while the *Gemeinde* is the community of personal relations.

[104]*The Divine Imperative*, 562.

The Zürich professor regards the *ekklesia* of Paul as the norm and the more hierarchically structured ecclesiology of the Pastoral Epistles as the corruption of the Pauline communities, and the first step towards institutionalization.[105] The church must be regarded pneumatologically; when this basic criterion is neglected, the institutional model flourishes.

In light of this critique, Brunner harshly denounces the Roman Catholic Church as the history of aberration. He views two areas as primarily responsible for development of the *ekklesia* into the church: the sacramental view of salvation which works *ex opere operato* in the sacrifice of the Mass, and the assertion of formal legal authority.[106] In his opinion, the priest-bishop as the Vicar of Christ who alone administers the sacraments as channels of saving grace is fundamentally a corruption of the brotherhood/sisterhood who share a common life in Christ.[107]

The "Ekklesia": Essential to the Experience of Faith

Brunner rejects Calvin's consideration of the church as an external support of faith (*externum subsidium fidei*)[108] rather than essentially bound up with faith.[109] Like Calvin, Brunner regards faith as an individual encounter with God, issuing in obedience and love; but, unlike Calvin, he (in contradistinction to mainstream Reformed tradition) makes becoming a part of the community of faith the *conditio sine qua non* of encountering God in faith. The fellowship of faith is not added to it as "something which does not belong to its nature."[110]

---

[105]*Dogmatics*, 3:40-41, 47, 59.

[106]Ibid., 60f.

[107]*The Misunderstanding of the Church*, 83.

[108]*Institutes*, IV, 1.1.

[109]*Dogmatics*, 3:19.

[110]Ibid. Brunner depends heavily on K.L. Schmidt's article on *ekklesia* in *Theological Dictionary of the New Testament*, vol. 3, Gerhard Kittel, ed., Geoffrey W. Bromiley, trans. (Grand Rapids: Eerdmans, 1965) 502-36. Hereafter it will be abbreviated as *TDNT*.

Essential to the experience of faith is the realization of proper communion with God and others who experience the new life in Christ; the act of becoming a believer is the "event in which a human being becomes conscious of community. . . ."[111] As one finds one's brother or sister, he or she finds God. "Individual believers" do not exist at all![112] It is not an institution that the community shares, but Christ and the Holy Spirit.[113] Christ, the Spirit, the community, and the believer are inextricably bound. "When the Word of God kindles a flame of faith in the heart of a human being, he ceases to be an 'individual' and becomes a 'member' of the body."[114]

The Ekklesia as "Mother" of the faithful. In Brunner's reference to the church as "Mother," he echoes a prominent exclusive theme in church history. From his perspective, faith exists only in the church, and the church is the place where the decision of faith is made.[115] The revelation of Jesus Christ is a "living and present event, which takes place in and through the Church,"[116] because the church alone is the "historical connecting link between the Jesus of History and every period of time, and with every individual."[117] The Word is entrusted to the keeping of the Christian fellowship,[118] and no one becomes a Christian "without the Church having been his mother in the Faith; for through the Church alone he understands the message of Christ which makes him a

---

[111]*The Divine Imperative*, 525.

[112]*Revelation and Reason*, 137.

[113]*The Misunderstanding of the Church*, 11.

[114]*Revelation and Reason*, 137.

[115]*The Divine Imperative*, 523-24.

[116]*Revelation and Reason*, 137.

[117]*The Divine Imperative*, 537.

[118]*The Misunderstanding of the Church*, 11.

Christian."[119] The fellowship of Jesus precedes the individual believer as the *mater omnium priorum*[120] and is the means by which the same salvation is given to others.[121]

The ekklesia as the movement of salvation. For Brunner the *ekklesia* is not merely "a means of salvation" but the "reality of salvation itself."[122] Thus, *extra ecclesiam nulla salus* would imply, for him, the *locus* of salvation, that is to say, "where Christ is, there is the Church" (*ubi Christus, ibi ecclesia*), rather than the *ekklesia* as the sacramental bearer or dispenser of salvation. One should not assert the unconditional necessity of baptism and the Lord's Supper as the material means for salvation. The New Testament clearly witnesses that one can believe in Christ and in salvation through Him without sharing in these rites.[123] The *ekklesia* as the movement of salvation conveys two aspects of its reality: as a living fellowship it both proceeds out of union with Christ and leads to Christ.

The exclusive theme is the dominant thread in the tapestry of Brunner's ecclesiology. He unequivocally maintains

> that the individual human being cannot be united with God apart from an
> organic connection with the fellowship of the Church and its tradition. He
> has to receive that which unites him with God through Jesus Christ from
> men and women of his own day. The main point is that man comes into
> an immediate relation with God; but this personal fellowship with God
> is only possible through the historical Mediator, and only within the
> fellowship of the Church.[124]

---

[119]*The Divine Imperative*, 564.

[120]*The Misunderstanding of the Church*, 11. Cf. *Revelation and Reason*, 159-60.

[121]*Revelation and Reason*, 138.

[122]*The Misunderstanding of the Church*, 15. Another aspect of this reality is Brunner's assertion that the *ekklesia* belongs to the "substance of revelation and constitutes the true end of the latter" (14).

[123]Ibid., 71.

[124]*Revelation and Reason*, 147-48.

Christian faith without the church is an impossibility for Brunner.[125] It is through the preaching of the church, the spoken word of members of the Body, that persons come to know the revelation of God and are given salvation in Jesus Christ.[126]

Evangelism occurs where there is real *ekklesia*;[127] indeed, it is the main criterion by which to discern whether a church or group is *ekklesia*. "Sharing is the very center of the Gospel"[128] and demarcates the Body of Christ. The movement of the Holy Spirit within the Body (*koinonia*) is the key contagion for those outside even though they do not yet understand Christ, who is the source of this fellowship.[129] Thus the church must always be visible, "a fact, a reality in which one lives."[130]

As the "movement of salvation" the church is *universal*. Other cultures do not need to be stamped with the trappings of European or American churches in order to witness faithfully to the gospel of Jesus Christ. One of the marks of the church universal is its diversity; Brunner welcomes a spectrum of expressions as long as the churches have a common testimony to Christ and do not succumb to a sectarian spirit.

EVALUATION

Having set forth an exposition of Brunner's soteriology and ecclesiology, it now remains to offer an evaluation of the perspective his views afford on the

---

[125]Ibid., 161.

[126]See Emil Brunner, *God and Man: Four Essays on the Nature of Personality*, David Cairns, trans. (London: SCM Press, 1936) 106f.

[127]Emil Brunner, "Ecclesia and Evangelism," *Japan Christian Quarterly* 21 (1955): 155.

[128]Ibid., 155.

[129]Ibid., 156.

[130]Emil Brunner, "One Holy Catholic Church," *Theology Today* 4 (1947): 318.

problem of religious pluralism and the uniqueness of Christianity. First, however, several general observations of theological method need to be considered.

View and Role of Scripture

Brunner's style of thinking is predominantly biblical, and he self-consciously strives to shape his theology in accordance with Scripture. Nevertheless, it is fair to ask to what extent he ascribes authority to the Bible. He inveighs against investing absolute authority in Scripture (in the manner of orthodox Protestantism) as he vehemently criticizes the identification of the Word of God with the inspired words of the Bible. To do so assumes an objective knowledge of God, for example, that the Bible has infallible truths about God. Conversely, Brunner desires to illumine the biblical *intention*, which, sadly, has been distorted in the objectifying reflection of theology.

Brunner grants that Scripture is the primary witness to the revelation of God in Jesus Christ and is, therefore, normative. Although the apostolic witness is preeminent because of its proximity to the personal revelation in the Son of God, all Scripture functions for Brunner as the "cradle of Christ"—to use Luther's beloved phrase. Yet, the authority of the Bible is always a conditional authority because its historical reports and theological doctrine of the apostles depend upon critical evaluation.[131] Indeed, Jesus Christ alone has unconditional authority, for in him God has encountered humanity at the most profound level and thus sweeps all Scripture's normativity aside to the position of relativity. Scripture speaks about Christ and points persons to him, Brunner maintains, but believing the word of Scripture about him can never usurp personally hearing his address. Brunner's bifocal view of Scripture disturbs those who maintain an infallible, inerrant text: he argues that when Scripture speaks about the world, it is subject to

---

[131]Paul G. Schrotenboer, "Emil Brunner," *Creative Minds in Contemporary Theology*, Phillip E. Hughes, ed. (Grand Rapids: Eerdmans, 1966) 106. Cf. E.L. Allen's analysis in *Creation and Grace: A Guide to the Thought of Emil Brunner* (London: Hodder and Stoughton) 12.

demythologization; when it speaks about Christ, it is the source that can introduce him who is the focus of faith.

To be sure, Brunner operates with a Bible of uneven terrain. The New Testament nearly eclipses the Old, because he believes the Old Testament only witnesses to the refracted, less-than-personal disclosure of God and thus is secondary and provisional, whereas the New Testament witnesses to the fullness of self-revelation in the Incarnation. Brunner also discriminates within the New Testament writings: the Pastoral Epistles are greatly inferior, in his opinion, to the earlier apostolic testimony.

Brunner claims that he is unwilling to do what he terms "exegetical gymnastics" in order to downplay paradox or problematic passages, namely, the teachings on judgment and universal salvation. Consequently, he has a fairly straightforward approach for the most part. It appears, however, in this particular case, he has inappropriately drawn the curtain of "paradox" on the seemingly antithetical strands in the New Testament. His exegesis is negligible and the literary contexts and historical setting are, for the most part, ignored. Perhaps it is fair to criticize the lack of detailed exegesis throughout his theological writings. He spends more time exegeting the writings of the Fathers, Schoolmen, Reformers, and modern theologians (especially his *bête noire*, Schleiermacher) than he does exegeting Scripture.

Because Brunner formulated his theology in dialogue with the disciplines of philosophy, psychology, sociology, and the natural sciences, his critical approach to Scripture seeks to make relevant the fruits of his biblical study to the critically-attuned mind. It is to his credit that he constantly sought to bring theology out of its isolated context into the sphere of public hearing and examination. Thus he refused to limit his thinking to biblical categories and modes of expression if he finds, for instance, that existentialist themes have greater resonance in contemporary minds. Further, he showed considerable sensitivity to the historical and cultural wrappings of Scripture because he wanted to remove the obstacles to faith. Demythologization, for him, was necessary for the "missionary situation of the church." This stance offers possibilities when dealing with issues raised by conflicting truth claims of different religions; accepting revealed truth on the authority of the Bible offers many fewer. Brunner does not hesitate, however, to use the *literal* words of Scripture such as "none other name" to underscore his stance on the finality of Christ. One can correctly question his hermeneutical consistency.

Biblical Personalism

In his theological methodology, Brunner started with the New Testament and read the Old Testament narratives in its light.[132] It was his conviction that the basis of *all* Christian articles of faith is the Incarnate Word, Jesus Christ,[133] and thus he consistently employed the methodology of interpreting all other areas of doctrine by the "personal correspondence" it manifests.

Brunner has been criticized for using the personalistic model to determine all of his theology. Some question whether it is a biblical construct, or an extra-biblical construct that when used exclusively compromises aspects of the biblical message.[134] Brunner, obviously, felt that his epistemological model, that is, the

---

[132]*Dogmatics*, 2:89. See the analysis of this method and others in the collection edited by Donald K. McKim, *A Guide to Contemporary Hermeneutics: Major Trends in Biblical Interpretation* (Grand Rapids: Eerdmans, 1986).

[133]Ibid., 6. Cf. Avery Dulles's similar contention in *The Resilient Church: The Necessity and Limits of Adaptation* (New York: Doubleday, 1977) 78: "Christian theology must keep the spotlight on the utter uniqueness and transcendence of what happened in the career of Jesus Christ. If this is obscured, the Christ event will not elicit the kind of worship and thanksgiving needed to sustain the Christian community in its vibrant relationship to God."

[134]See Schrotenboer, "Emil Brunner," 119-27. See also Paul Tillich's article, "Some Questions on Brunner's Epistemology," *The Theology of Emil Brunner*, C.W. Kegley, ed., 101-107. Here Tillich criticizes Brunner for assuming that "person-to-person" encounter is the only valid analogy of the Divine-human encounter. It is the writer's opinion that Brunner's "biblical personalism" is certainly a pivotal strand in the scriptural witness; however, it may not fully give credence to another strand, the mysterious, numinous theophanic disclosures which evidence the medium of nature more than the personal model. Brunner's accentuation of personalism contributed to a diminishment of revelation through creation.

priority of the personal over the impersonal, could be found within Scripture itself and is the very heart of what revelation means. Certainly, one must agree that Brunner's case *is* strong. Arguments can be made, however, for the inadequacy of the model for cultures where the influence of existentialist categories is not felt.

The charm of Brunner's "biblical personalism" is its rejection of any intellectualization of faith. Because one is always in either positive or negative relationship to God by the very fact of being human, one's reason cannot, in detached fashion, objectively assess revelation's plausibility. God does not reveal God's own self as an object for thought, but as the One who enters into personal relationship with men and women. Moreover, that one can be addressed by the Word of God because one bears the *imago dei* gives to all the possibility of sharing an "I-Thou" relationship with God—a much more universal note than many in the Reformed tradition would sound.

The "Point of Contact"

It is precisely this strand in Brunner's thinking that clashes so sharply with his total rejection of a natural theology. Obviously, his understanding of the nature of faith and revelation would disallow employing *analogia entis* as a means of rationally knowing the person and character of God, and rightly so. Perhaps the stringency with which he argues that the *Anknüpfungspunkt* is only a negative capacity—enabling one to feel guilty and responsible before God rather than a capacity for salvation—is due to his awareness that positing a universal divine encounter makes more tenuous believing there is "no salvation apart from Christ and his church." The idea that creation carries enough revelation to produce guilt but not enough for salvation is difficult to sustain from a scriptural perspective,[135] although Brunner reports accurately that Scripture is a clear

---

[135]In his commentary, *Letter to the Romans*, 21, Brunner's interpretation of Rom 2:12-16 seems to leave open the question of being able to respond positively to God on the basis of general revelation. Cf. Paul F. Knitter's analysis of Protestant theologians' arguments concerning the salvific efficacy of general revelation in *No Other Name? A Critical Survey of Christian Attitudes Toward the World Religions* (Maryknoll: Orbis Books, 1985) 98ff.

witness to the existence of revelation in creation. He needed to probe more fruitfully God's relation to all peoples in creation.

Further, he fails to clarify the relational content of this general revelation. Is it impersonal? He has insisted in all his writings that God moves personally toward God's creatures, and it is reasonable to assume God encounters human beings through the creation in the same personal-relation model. If in encountering God in this manner one becomes aware of his or her sinfulness, does this not establish the foundation of a relationship that Jesus called "justified" in the parable of the publican in Luke 18:9-14? Brunner cannot maintain general revelation as he does without the possibility of its establishing a saving-faith relationship to God. Otherwise he sacrifices his powerful personal-relation model of salvation.

A related issue is the correlation of the work of Christ in redemption and the work of Christ as the Logos. Brunner's analysis indicates a major dichotomy in that no possibility of salvation exists on the basis of the latter. Is this necessary in order to uphold the ontological necessity of Jesus Christ's redemptive act as the basis for all salvation? Perhaps Tillich's notion that all revelation is special and transforming[136] needs to supplement the lack of positive value Brunner sees in the universal encounter with the Logos. Brunner maintains that the corruption of the formal image[137] by sin clearly precludes valid knowledge of God apart from the redeeming grace of the gospel of Jesus Christ; this conclusion has extremely negative implications for any hope of salvation through the efficacy of non-Christian religions.

The Finality of Christ

Brunner correctly argues that Christianity cannot dispense with its claims to uniqueness and still remain authentic because it is founded on the unrepeatable

---

[136]Paul Tillich, *Systematic Theology*, vol. 1 (Chicago: University of Chicago Press, 1951) 139. Cf. Paul Althaus, *Die Christliche Wahrheit* (Gütersloh: Gütersloher Verlagshaus, 1966) 37-94.

[137]See above, note 36.

event of revelation and atonement accomplished by the Incarnate Word, Jesus Christ. Bound up with this claim is the exclusion from the pale of salvation of the "other religions," whose response to God is considered to be perverted. Only the Word of God enables the response of repentance and faith on the part of the subjects addressed. Thus, Brunner declares, only in Christ is fellowship with God possible.

One senses that Brunner would like to avoid the logical conclusions of this exclusivism as he concomitantly holds the doctrines of judgment and universal salvation. Nevertheless, he did not lessen the obvious exclusivism when talking about Jesus Christ as the "fulfillment of revelation." At first blush, this claim has a very parochial tone. It seems to grow more out of doctrinal assertions than sensitive interaction with devoted members of non-Christian religions. Given Brunner's teaching experience in Japan and the inevitable engagement with other faiths, maintaining his exclusivist posture only sharpened the conflict between truth claims.

Brunner characterized his theology as a "missionary theology" and focused his writings on aiding the church in combating the secularism this century takes for granted.[138] The direction of his theological message (particularly his anthropology) was toward post-Christian Europeans and was not so intimately concerned with the issues posed by his exclusivism vis-à-vis a religiously pluralistic world. His writing lacks the pathos of one struggling with the fate of those who by geographical or cultural accident have not been afforded the opportunity for personal encounter with Christ; further, it reflects little of the impact of inter-faith dialogue.

Absoluteness of Christianity?

Maintaining the finality of Christ is not to claim the finality or absoluteness of Christianity as a religion. Sounding a major theme of dialectical

---

[138]See Langdon Gilkey's percipient study, *Society and the Sacred: Toward a Theology of Culture in Decline* (New York: Crossroad, 1981).

theology, Brunner designates Christ as the judge of all religions, including Christianity. Brunner is justifiably critical of those who presume to correlate the finality of Christ with that of Christianity. Indeed, there is a disjunction present between Christ and Christianity; Christ's followers continue to strive after his vision of living under the rule of God. With this concept Brunner has made a signal contribution in moving toward a Christian theology of non-Christian religions. Christianity must affirm that it shares the same limits of creatureliness as other ways of faith, and it must faithfully point to the One who transcends all human piety.

It is regrettable that this commendable distinction is not consistently carried out in Brunner's varied writings. Sometimes his descriptions of the characteristics of the "other religions" are less than charitable.[139] He observes and critiques them as if from an unbiased pinnacle, seeming to forget (when he asserts "Christianity is not *one* of the religions") that he, too, is a part of a particular historical tradition. His repudiation of Troeltsch's historical relativism as well as the approach of the *Religions-geschichtliche Schule* is most evident. Appropriately, he retains the historical particularity of the ministry of the Incarnate Word but, at times, fails to acknowledge Christianity's relativity.

Soteriological Perspective

Brunner has persuasively argued that encounter with God is fundamental to the revelatory event and, consequently, has made the *personal* response of the individual the crucial feature of salvation. Believing that the personal emphasis is the truest and most effective paradigm for transcultural communication of the gospel, he also insists that the truly human character of life in any culture can only be created by the address of the Word of God. This assertion effectively

---

[139]*Revelation and Reason*, 218-36. In contrast, W.C. Smith provides a constructive way to view the faith of others in *Religious Diversity* (New York: Crossroad, 1976) and *Towards a World Theology* (Philadelphia: Westminster Press, 1981).

distinguishes Christianity from culture while affirming the significance of the inner relation of religion to culture.

Another positive aspect of his utilization of the personal model is the bridging effect between the perennial subjective-objective chasm for the doctrine of salvation. Brunner emphasizes the significance of the objective components of Christ's redemptive ministry without eclipsing a person's responsibility for corresponding answer. The gospel for Brunner is always an urgent summons to personal decision for Jesus Christ. And faith is the total response of the individual to the One who speaks to him or her.

Because all human piety is suspect for Brunner, "walking in the light one has been given" is never adequate for salvation. Although human religious strivings may witness to the original revelation, they progress blindly toward destruction because of their ignorance of Christ.

Ecclesiological Perspective

Brunner's constructive suggestions point in the direction of a viable Protestant ecclesiology. His emphasis is that in salvation one becomes a part of the body. By underlining communal Christian life rather than privatized experience, he seeks to bring a measure of balance to the hyper-individualism characteristic of much of Protestantism. Further, his description of the *ekklēsia* as "Mother of the Faithful" gives it more than a peripheral role; indeed, the church is the medium of salvation which connects all persons with the work and person of Jesus Christ.

Recognizing the small Spirit-filled community as the norm, Brunner avoids the Roman Catholic dilemma when asserting "no salvation outside the church"—meaning the Roman Catholic Church.[140] Brunner allows small pockets of believers to be *ekklēsia*, which is the usual model in a missions context and is easily translated into indigenous modes. He can use Cyprian's phrase, but adapts it in such a way that "church" can refer to any of these spiritual organisms.

---

[140]This idea will be treated more in depth in chapter four.

The emphasis thus becomes the fellowship of Christ—not sacramental dispensing of salvation—which is a different accent from the traditional Roman Catholic interpretation.

SUMMARY

Brunner has attempted a theology of the "other religions" in his work, albeit from a limited perspective, and thus has offered an exclusivist answer to the question "is there salvation outside Christ and his church?" His preoccupation with the church's failure to engage secularist society blunts his concern for the issues related to the finality of Christ in a world of decidedly pluralistic religious contours.

Brunner submits a consistent ecclesiological and soteriological perspective that deals with many of the New Testament materials. However, the universal motifs are touched only slightly; they do not modify his position noticeably. His approach is indicative of a significant, but shrinking, sphere of contemporary Christianity.[141]

---

[141]S. Mark Heim, *Is Christ the Only Way? Christian Faith in a Pluralistic World* (Valley Forge: Judson Press, 1985), offers a significant nuanced explication of the exclusivist position. Cf. his "Thinking about Theocentric Christology," *Journal of Ecumenical Studies* 24 (1987): 1-52.

CHAPTER 4

KARL RAHNER:
CHRISTIAN INCLUSIVISM

A second response to the soteriological problem posed by religious pluralism can aptly be called Christian Inclusivism. Its roots go as far back as Justin the Martyr and Gregory of Nyssa, who argued for the inclusive nature of the redemption provided in Jesus Christ.[1] For these Greek Fathers, ignorance of Jesus Christ was not a sufficient reason to exclude pious followers of other ways of faith. The Roman Catholic Church has, throughout its history, struggled with the soteriological implications for the faithful outside the Church,[2] both Christian and non-Christian. Karl Rahner, a prolific German Jesuit, whom many consider to be the most influential Catholic theologian in the second half of the twentieth century, has given sustained attention to this particular issue, producing a creative and highly controversial solution.

---

[1]T.F. Torrance, *The Doctrine of Grace in the Apostolic Fathers* (Edinburgh: Oliver and Boyd, 1948) offers considerable insight.

[2]Due to the many different translators of Rahner, there is no consistency in the capitalization of "church." In this chapter, when referring explicitly to the Roman Catholic Church, the term will be capitalized, except of course, if a direct quotation does otherwise. Often Rahner refers to "church" in a general sense and thus the lower-case will be appropriate.

HISTORICAL AND THEOLOGICAL CONTEXT

Karl Rahner was born 5 March 1904, in Freiburg, Germany, into a traditionally pious Catholic family. A thoroughly average student in school, Karl surprised his family by entering the Society of Jesus in 1922; he was ordained in 1932.[3] His graduate studies in philosophy took him to the University of Freiburg where he was privileged to hear the great Martin Heidegger lecture. Rahner's doctoral dissertation, later published as *Spirit in the World*,[4] was a critique of St. Thomas's metaphysics of knowledge and had the ignominious distinction of being rejected because of its contemporary overtones.[5] Rahner then moved to the University of Innsbruck where, happily for the theological world, he completed a theological doctorate in 1936.

The war years in Vienna and Munich, where he ministered through teaching and parish work, left their stamp on Rahner's pastoral concerns and the tone of his theological and devotional writings. As he wrestled with the ambiguities of modern life, he became cognizant of the suffering and nihilism of the war and post-war generations. The perceived absence of God from the world and the spectre of death are prominent themes in the Rahnerian literature.

Since 1948, his teaching career as a professor of dogmatic theology has taken him to the universities of Innsbruck, Munich, and Münster. Professor Rahner is unique in having made important contributions in almost every field of

---

[3]Robert Kress, *A Rahner Handbook* (Atlanta: John Knox Press, 1982) 1-2; Herbert Vorgrimler, *Karl Rahner: His Life, Thought, and Work*, Edward Quinn, trans. (London: Burns & Oates, 1965) 16-17; and, Herbert Vorgrimler, *Understanding Karl Rahner: An Introduction to His Life and Thought*, John Bowden, trans. (New York: Crossroad, 1986) 46ff.

[4]*Spirit in the World*, William Dych, S.J., trans. (New York: Herder and Herder, 1968). For a chronology and systematic listing of Rahner's writings, see Roman Bleistein and Elmar Klinger, *Bibliographie Karl Rahner 1924-1969* (Freiburg: Herder, 1969) and Roman Bleistein, *Bibliographie 1969-1974* (Freiburg: Herder, 1974).

[5]For a recent critique of this seminal publication, see Denis J.M. Bradley, "Rahner's *Spirit in the World*: Aquinas or Hegel?" *The Thomist* 41 (April, 1977): 167-99.

contemporary theological inquiry: the philosophy of religion, dogmatics, ecclesiology, pneumatology, Christology, hermeneutics, and moral and pastoral theology. Further, his devotional writings reflect one who is thoroughly immersed in the spirituality and discipline of Ignatius—a key influence in his theology. Rahner retired in 1971 from the Chair of Dogmatic Theology in the University of Münster, but continued his prodigious contributions to a wide scope of theological topics until the end of his life. When he died on 30 March 1984, he departed with the sure confession: "I will know as I am known."

Setting in Roman Catholic Theology

Two trends are discernible in twentieth-century Catholic theology which had their genesis in the late nineteenth century.[6] One reactionary trend has clung to scholastic methodology as the true Catholic orthodoxy. This trend has viewed modern historical thinking as an enemy rather than an ally. The "modernist" movement of the early twentieth century caused the Church to react with a defensive ecclesiasticism that echoed the timbre of the Council of Trent.[7] The second trend, evidencing greater openness, has shown considerable interest in an *ad fontes* approach which generated biblical and historical studies in the data of the Christian past. A concomitant of this trend was a revival of Thomistic thought[8] and a desire to foster dialogue between the insights of Aquinas and contemporary philosophy. As a philosophical theologian, Rahner stands firmly in this stream of Catholic theology; he walks in the tracks of Aquinas, in conversation with Kant, German Idealism, and Heidegger.

---

[6]Anne Carr, *The Theological Method of Karl Rahner*, American Academy of Religions Dissertation Series, H. Ganse Little, Jr., ed. (Missoula MT: Scholars Press, 1977) 7-8.

[7]Alec R. Vidler, *The Modernist Movement in the Roman Church* (Cambridge: Cambridge University Press, 1934).

[8]See Helen James John, *The Thomist Spectrum* (New York: Fordham University Press, 1966), on the Thomistic revival. See also Johannes B. Metz's analysis of Rahner's place in Thomistic thought in his Foreword to *Spirit in the World* (xii-xviii).

Rahner has been both in and out of favor in the Roman Catholic Church, for he has had to contend with extremes throughout his teaching career. In the company of other creative Catholic theologians, he was put under Roman pre-censorship during the era of particularly censorious Church policies (1950-1962). Only because of the support of influential persons such as Konrad Adenauer was he allowed to function as a *peritus* (expert) at the Second Vatican Council, 1962-1965.[9]

Rahner's contribution to Vatican II was enormous; indeed, the significance of his leadership and theological creativity is hard to estimate. With the aid of other progressive theologians, he was able to set much of the agenda to be taken up by the Council, and thus it was possible to "rescue the Council from the preparatory commissions' restrictive approach and content."[10]   Rahner's distinctive contributions to contemporary Roman Catholic theology have been respected increasingly in the *aggiornamento* of thought since the Council.

The Task of Theology

One of the reasons for Rahner's pervasive influence on the post-conciliar renaissance in Catholic theology and the larger Christian communion is his unfailing commitment as a priest, mystic, and theologian to the basic confessions of the Christian faith and his intense involvement in the practical life of the church.[11]   Further, his quest to "find God in all things" has endeared him to contemporary believers who struggle for truth in a world that often presents more

---

[9]Kress, 8-9.

[10]Ibid., 9. See George Bull, *Vatican Politics at the Second Vatican Council 1962-65* (London: Oxford University Press, 1966).

[11]Ibid., 63. Kress notes that one of Rahner's great feats has been to "rescue the inner meaning of traditional doctrines from the obscurity of . . . scholastic formulations." His theological method has been to respond to significant issues and concerns as they emerge in the ongoing life of the Church. See Karl Rahner, "Reflections on Methodology in Theology," *Theological Investigations*, vol. 11, David Bourke, trans. (London: Darton, Longman & Todd, 1974) 68-114.

questions than answers. In his *Selbstporträt*, Rahner describes his theology as being preoccupied with

> the answers to the many individual questions which my
> responsibility to the man of today required of me, so that
> he might be soberly critical and a Christian at the same
> time.[12]

Rahner relentlessly questions the Church's traditional teaching over against the modern person's experience of herself or himself. He is well attuned to the present-day crisis of faith and has the facility necessary to engage the questions of modern life confronting the secular humanist as well as the devout layperson or sceptical priest, whether Protestant or Catholic.

Two influences on Rahner's theology implicitly shape his work: Kant (especially Maréchal's interpretation of him) and Heidegger.[13] Rahner adopts Heidegger's starting point: the human person who raises the question of being.[14] He draws from Kant's epistemology, which shapes the transcendental limits of human knowledge and the viability of metaphysics. In addition, Rahner works out all his ideas and distinctions in direct relationship to the theology of Thomas Aquinas, and his own positions share many of Thomas's presuppositions.

The Transcendental Method

Understanding Rahner's use of the transcendental method[15] is the necessary presupposition to understanding his profound theological insights into

---

[12]Karl Rahner, "Selbstporträt," *Forscher und Gelehrte*, W. Ernst Böhm, ed. (Stuttgart: Battenberg, 1966) 21.

[13]Francis P. Fiorenza, "Introduction: Karl Rahner and the Kantian Problematic," *Spirit in the World*, xix-xlv, offers an excellent discussion of Rahner's relationship to Kant, Thomistic theology, Heidegger, and Maréchal, the key components in Rahner's theological thought.

[14]Heidegger's profound treatment of this subject is the monumental *Being and Time*, John Macquarrie and Edward Robinson, trans. (London: SCM Press, 1962).

[15]See Joseph F. Donceel, S.J., *The Searching Mind: An Introduction to a Philosophy of God* (Notre Dame: University of Notre Dame Press, 1979).

the problem of a Christian theology of the non-Christian religions. The goal of this method for Rahner is to ascertain the conditions in a person which allow the possibility of revelation by indicating the necessary relationship between Christian faith and the essential structures of the human spirit. Appropriately for this method, he sketched the characteristics of modern mentality which render it less open to the affirmation of God.[16]

The human being has a transcendental capacity; this capability is such that it must question its own constitution, Rahner says, and, thus, it can investigate the conditions presupposed by or necessary for any knowledge.[17] One's questioning inevitably leads to the basic metaphysical question because

> it is the reflexive articulation of that question which pervades the ground of human existence itself, the question about being. For in fact, to put it first of all quite formally, the metaphysical question is that question which in a final and radical sharpening of man's questioning turns upon itself as such and thereby turns upon the presuppositions which are operative in itself; it is the question turned consciously upon itself, the *transcendental* question, which does not merely place something asked about in question, but the one questioning and his question itself, and thereby absolutely everything.[18]

Because human being has a transcendental capacity (*potentia obedientialis*) which can ask questions about being, and this capacity is the minimal knowledge of God,

---

[16]Vorgrimler, *Understanding Karl Rahner*, 111ff., details Rahner's preoccupation with carrying on a dialogue with representatives of the natural sciences, Marxists, and non-Christians—all shapers of modernity. He was convinced that the Church must find a language in which to communicate its message to the contemporary "cultured despisers" who placed their trust in inevitable evolutionary progress, economic reform, and variegated forms of "spirituality." Cf. Langdon Gilkey's assessment in *Naming the Whirlwind: The Renewal of God Language* (Indianapolis: Bobbs-Merrill, 1969); he has discerned these characteristics to be the modern conviction that all reality is contingent, relative, and temporal, and that the human being is autonomous.

[17]*Spirit in the World*, 57-58.

[18]Ibid., 58.

it is "able to receive a higher, greater communication of being from God than it has already received in creation, if God chooses to grant it."[19] Rahner insists that the knowledge of the *a priori* conditions of the possibility of knowledge in the subject are of necessity also an aspect of our knowledge of the object itself—even a metaphysical knowledge of God. This capacity defines humanity as spirit, for "spirit is the potentiality for the reception of all being and the active desire for it."[20]

Rahner's appropriation of the transcendental method makes necessary a primarily anthropocentric approach to theology. He is concerned with the religious basis of the human situation; consequently, the person is the prior concern for him, not the Church's statement of faith. Only this methodology can enable the theologian to overcome the process of incrustation and ossification of Christian teaching, Rahner maintains.[21]

SOTERIOLOGICAL PERSPECTIVE

Rahner takes as a given these fundamental tenets of Catholic theology: God wills the salvation of all[22] and offers supernatural grace to each through Jesus Christ (this grace may be accepted or rejected); further, he affirms the necessity

---

[19]Kress, 29. See Karl Rahner, "Transcendental Theology," *Encyclopedia of Theology: The Concise Sacramentum Mundi*, Karl Rahner, ed. (New York: Crossroad, 1982) 1748-751.

[20]*Spirit in the World*, 283. God is not known as an object; rather, God is perceived as the principle of human knowing and reality.

[21]His methodology has an affinity with Schleiermacher who also began with the self-consciousness of the individual. Keith W. Clements clarifies this aspect of Schleiermacher's thought in his new study, *Friedrich Schleiermacher: Pioneer of Modern Theology* (London: Collins, 1987) 66ff. Cf. Stephen Sykes, *The Identity of Christianity* (Philadelphia: Fortress Press, 1984) 81ff.

[22]See Karl Rahner, "Universal Salvific Will," *Encyclopedia of Theology: The Concise Sacramentum Mundi* (New York: Crossroad, 1982) 1499-504.

of Christian faith for salvation.[23] It is clear that the "salvation willed by God is the salvation won by Christ."[24] This salvation he defines as the "strictly supernatural and direct presence of God in himself [the person] afforded by grace."[25]

Ever since God acted decisively through Christ's death and resurrection, Christianity is "*the* religion which binds man to God,"[26] he asserts. Accordingly, Rahner seeks to delineate how all persons must in some dimension have the opportunity to encounter Christ's saving gospel.[27] He vehemently rejects any suggestion that persons outside the Church are condemned to eternal meaninglessness[28] yet upholds the old theological formula that there is no salvation outside the Church:

> If on the one hand, we conceive salvation as something specifically
> *Christian*, if there is no salvation apart from Christ . . . ; and if, on the
> other hand, God has really and truly intended this salvation for all

---

[23]Rahner frequently reminds his readers of the definitive word of the Second Vatican Council of the truth of the universal salvific will of God. He cites two texts regularly to support this position: 1 Tim 2:4-6 and Acts 17:23. See Karl Rahner, *The Christian of the Future* (New York: Herder and Herder, 1967) 94ff., and *Karl Rahner in Dialogue: Conversations and Interviews 1965-1982*, Paul Imhof and Hubert Biallowons, eds. (New York: Crossroads, 1986). Here he notes his understanding of the council's declaration: ". . . the Second Vatican Council teaches expressly that very many people (one might even perhaps say hopefully, all people) find grace-filled, supernatural salvation—even when they are not Christians . . ." (121).

[24]Karl Rahner, "Christianity and the Non-Christian Religions," *Theological Investigations*, vol. 5, Karl-H. Kruger, trans. (Baltimore: Helicon Press, 1966) 122.

[25]Karl Rahner, "The One Christ and the Universality of Salvation," *Theological Investigations*, vol. 16, David Morland, O.S.B., trans. (London: Darton, Longman & Todd, 1979) 200.

[26]Rahner, "Christianity and the Non-Christian Religions," 5:118.

[27]Karl Rahner, "Anonymous Christians," *Theological Investigations*, vol. 6, Karl-H. Kruger and Boniface Kruger, trans. (Baltimore: Helicon Press, 1969) 391.

[28]Ibid.

men—then these two aspects cannot be reconciled in any other way then [sic] by stating that every human being is really and truly exposed to the influence of divine supernatural grace.[29]

The urgent problems of vast secularism and the many non-Christian ways of faith sets Rahner on a course of attempting to reconcile these disparate tenets of his thought.

Christianity as the Absolute Religion

Basic to Christianity's understanding of itself, Rahner maintains, is the belief that it is the one absolute religion, intended for all humanity. The understanding of itself "as the true and lawful religion for all" is valid only "where and when it enters with existential power and demanding force into the realm of another religion—and judging it by itself—puts it in question."[30]

Historically mediated. Rahner willingly confronts the issues raised by declaring that Christianity as a historically contingent religion has an absolute claim which is universal. Though absolute, this claim must be mediated historically.[31] It must enter into the historical continuum of other religions, setting itself over against each at an appropriate time. The nexus moment of the absolute claim of Christianity and a non-Christian religion cannot be predicted, for this moment has itself a history in a particular individual or culture. Therefore, Rahner leaves the question open as to what exact point in time Christianity becomes the existential demand for each person in his or her historical and cultural setting.[32]

---

[29]Rahner, "Christianity and the Non-Christian Religions," 123.

[30]Ibid., 118.

[31]Ibid., 119.

[32]Ibid., 119-20. In one of his last interviews in 1982 with Leonard Reinisch for Radio Bayern (BR#2), Munich, he reiterated his understanding of the encompassing salvation of the one, eternal God, which is at work beyond the institutional sphere of the Christian Church. See *Karl Rahner in Dialogue 1965-1982*, 340.

All religions grace-filled. A religion retains its validity until this nexus with Christianity, even though it surely has elements of depravity in it. It is not a religion devoid of grace, however, but simply a previous stage in sacred history, "produced by God's action in historical revelation but now superseded."[33] Indeed, "it is *a priori* quite possible to suppose that there are supernatural grace-filled elements in the non-Christian religions."[34] God in grace is seeking each person through the religion or faith that one confesses.

The Supernatural Existential

An overarching concern of Rahner is the necessary condition for the human encounter with the mystery of divine love, or how nature is related to grace. What in being human allows receiving God's communication? Rahner assumes that the human being is by nature oriented towards God and describes this nature as the "supernatural existential." This is the guiding presupposition of his theological anthropology. As a relation to God, it is the result of God's historical act in Jesus Christ through which men and women are called to intimacy with God. Each has the potentiality to respond to divine grace, but there is no guarantee that all will respond.

Rahner's "supernatural existential" consists in the fact that every human is invited by God to be saved. The divine will manifests itself in each person's nature. In this contention, he rejects the Roman Catholic Church's teaching, following the Council of Trent, that grace is a supernatural structure above the human's conscious, spiritual and moral life. Hence, there is no "natural" man or woman who does not yearn for the supernatural (God); this yearning is precisely the effect of the "supernatural existential."[35] It is through this dynamic benefit

---

[33]Karl Rahner, "Christianity," *Encyclopedia of Theology: The Concise Sacramentum Mundi*, Karl Rahner, ed. (New York: Crossroad, 1982) 193.

[34]Rahner, "Christianity and the Non-Christian Religions," 118ff.

[35]Karl Rahner, *Foundations of Christian Faith: An Introduction to the Idea of Christianity*, William V. Dych (New York: Seabury Press, 1978) 126-33; Karl Rahner, "Atheism and Implicit Christianity," *Theological Investigations*, vol. 9, Graham Harrison, trans. (London: Darton, Longman & Todd, 1972) 146; and Karl Rahner, "Relationship

to humankind that God offers God's own self-communication.[36] God then is the source of the transcending drive common to all humanity.[37]

Created for grace, each human is included in the universal salvific will, and God reveals this purpose through the enduring offer (*Angebot*) of grace. Only a graced person has a prepared capacity, a transcendent supernatural horizon towards God, to receive God's communication. In order for one to choose freely to accept this proferred grace, its reality must be consciously (thematically) realized by the subject; however, this is not the only way one can appropriate God's offer of grace. Rahner's thesis is that

> because the universal and supernatural will of God is working for human
> salvation, the unlimited transcendence of man, itself directed of necessity
> towards God, is raised up consciously by grace, although possibly without

---

Between Nature and Grace: The Supernatural Existential," *Theological Investigations*, vol. 1, (London: Darton, Longman & Todd, 1961) 300-302, 310-15.

[36]Ibid., 126. Cf. Klaus Riesenhuber, S.J., "Der anonyme Christ nach Karl Rahner," *Zeitschrift für katholische Theologie* 86 (1964): 286-303. Ernst Troeltsch anticipated the work of Rahner through his metaphysics of immanent transcendence. He argued that the human being gave testimony to the immanence of God within. The human's self-awareness, constant questioning, and need to trust "seem to point to an active presence of the Absolute Spirit in finite things, to an activity of the universe, as Schleiermacher says, in individual souls." See his *Gesammelte Werke*, vol. 2 (Tübingen: 1913) 764. Using language similar to Rahner, Troeltsch calls this the *religious a priori* within the human spirit, which is the innate orientation toward and the experience of the divine built into human nature. See his "Die Selbständigkeit der Religion," *Zeitschrift für Theologie und Kirche* 5 (1895): 367-436.

[37]Ibid., 127, 129. Cf. Gerald A. McCool's analysis in the collection he edited, *A Rahner Reader* (London: Darton, Longman & Todd, 1975) 185. The idea of the "supernatural existential" supplies for Rahner, according to McCool ". . . the indispensable grounding for Rahner's theology of the anonymous Christian and of the salvific character of the non-Christian religions" (xxvi). James A. Carpenter, *Nature and Grace: Toward An Integral Perspective* (New York: Crossroad, 1988) 57ff. notes the unresolved tensions in Rahner's attempts to relate nature and grace, the natural and the supernatural. In the opinion of Hans Küng, *Does God Exist?* Edward Quinn, trans. (London: Collins, 1980) 520ff., this aspect of Rahner's thought incurred the most hostility from the Roman Magisterium, leading to Rahner being placed directly under his order's Roman censorship for a time.

explicit thematic reflection, in such a way that the possibility of faith in revelation is thereby made available.[38]

Human nature, then, is constituted only by virtue of God's prevenient intent.

Jesus Christ: God's Self-Communication of Grace

Jesus Christ is the presupposition of the "supernatural existential." The bestowal of grace and incarnation are the two basic modes of God's self-communication,[39] Rahner believes. That the Word became flesh is the ultimate expression of God's self-giving,[40] thereby endowing the creature with the possibility of being assumed, of "becoming the material of a possible history of God."[41] Viewed in this manner, "the incarnation of God is the uniquely supreme case of the actualisation of man's nature in general."[42] Christology is constitutive of anthropology; moreover, only through Christology—the human in freest, purest form—can persons find God.

Further, Rahner boldly suggests, "anyone who accepts his own humanity in full . . . has accepted the Son of Man, because God has accepted man in him."[43] Rahner is attempting to demonstrate an inner relatedness between the

---

[38]Karl Rahner, "Anonymous and Explicit Faith," *Theological Investigations*, vol. 16, David Morland, trans. (New York: Seabury, 1979) 55.

[39]Rahner, "Anonymous Christians," 393. The personal self-communication of God is not at the same level as the grace and favor of God in creation; the latter is a "lower grace."

[40]Rahner does not take this fundamental dogma of Christianity in a mythological way. See *Foundations of Christian Faith*, 180.

[41]Karl Rahner, "On the Theology of the Incarnation," *Theological Investigations*, vol. 4, Kevin Smyth, trans. (London: Darton, Longman & Todd, 1966) 115. Human nature as such is the possible self-expression of the self-emptying God, in Rahner's scheme.

[42]Rahner, "Anonymous Christians," 393.

[43]Rahner, "Theology of the Incarnation," 119.

historical man, Jesus of Nazareth, and the transcendental constitution of the human being in order to show the absolute importance of Christ to all human beings.[44]

In Rahner's formulations, Christology is essentially soteriology. Jesus is the mediator of God's universal saving will; the Incarnate One is an intrinsic moment within the whole process, that is, the evolution of creation, by which grace is bestowed upon all spiritual creatures.[45] Rahner never seeks to deny or to obfuscate the unique status of Jesus as Savior, and he examines carefully the connection that exists between the cross of Christ and the potential salvation of all persons.

He correctly views the cross as the *consequence*, not the *cause* of the salvific will of God.[46] This cross does not transform God, as Anselmian theories suggest, nor does the fact of the incarnation by itself construe redemption in the Eastern sense of divinization through assumption.[47]

Cross as sacramental sign and grace. Finding notions of "blood sacrifice" or "ransom" inadequate for contemporary minds,[48] Rahner suggests the cross and resurrection have

> a primary sacramental causality for the salvation of all men, in so far as it mediates salvation to man by means of salvific grace which is universally operative in the world.[49]

---

[44]Kress, *A Rahner Handbook*, 37. Jesus is the unique instance of the total self-fulfillment of human reality, actualized through giving himself away. See Rahner's article, "Grace," *Sacramentum Mundi*, 2:416-17.

[45]Rahner, *Foundations of Christian Faith*, 201.

[46]Rahner, "The One Christ and the Universality of Salvation," 207.

[47]Ibid., 210-11. Cf. Paul Tillich, *A History of Christian Thought*, Carl E. Braaten, ed. (New York: Simon & Schuster, 1967) 37ff., and James A. Carpenter, *Nature and Grace*, 18ff.

[48]Ibid., 211. Rahner believes that Pauline notions which framed Christ's death in the context of sacrifice "do not reflect the original understanding of the saving significance of the Cross of Jesus for all men. . . ." See Wilhelm Thüsing's counter-argument in Karl Rahner and Wilhelm Thüsing, *A New Christology* (New York: Seabury Press, 1980) 82f.

[49]Rahner, "The One Christ and the Universality of Salvation," 212.

Through Christ's death, God's self-giving love and freedom find an irreducible historical expression. Because of the solidarity of humankind in salvation, the cross and resurrection of Jesus Christ, as the paradigmatic *anthropos,* signify to the world the logical possibility of its salvation through the confluence of human and divine freedom. God communicated God's personal being to this one in such a unique manner that Christ became "the definitive and irreversible self-gift of God to the world."[50]

Individual freedom as the instrument of salvation. Rahner stresses that all real salvation depends upon the exercise of an individual's freedom;[51] the soteriological significance of Christ's death and resurrection for all must be individually appropriated. The person's response to the grace given in Christ is not exacted; rather, one is invited to a "dialogue partnership."[52] There is no Barthian suprahistorical transaction in Rahner's thinking that predestines all to be saved; rather, salvation is through One who is within the flow of humanity, is God-filled and established as the Christ by God's grace, One who freely turns to God and thus gives to all the same opportunity.[53]

God's grace revealed in the death of Christ liberates the individual's freedom, enabling him or her to be similarly obedient. Jesus entered into death in free obedience, establishing God's offer and word of grace; the resurrection reveals God's acceptance of this response and thus institutes utter obedience to God in the world historically and irrevocably.[54] Rahner emphasizes Jesus' solidarity with all of humanity and insists that the movement of salvation history as a whole must be applied to the salvation of the individual, that is, "that the

---

[50]Ibid., 214. Cf. Rahner and Thüsing, *A New Christology*, 34-35.

[51]Rahner, *Foundations of Christian Faith*, 282.

[52]See Rahner's article, "Grace," *Sacramentum Mundi*, 2:416-17.

[53]Rahner, *Foundations of Christian Faith*, 283-84.

[54]Rahner, "The One Christ and the Universality of Salvation," 214-15.

grace of Christ . . . was temporally present throughout the whole of salvation history and was prior to its manifestation in the *Ursakrament* of history which is Christ himself. . . ."[55]

Jesus in the Non-Christian Religions

Rahner is concerned to determine what the non-Christian religions may contribute to the salvation experience of the non-Christians. He rejects the possibility of private revelations (an older theory that permitted divine revelation to the non-Christians, perhaps at the point of death) because of the historical and social character of Christianity.[56] Rahner suggests that the expanse of time between the revelation to Adam and the revelation to Moses was not devoid of divine revelation; rather, the many other religions, namely, those uncharted in the biblical chronology, awakened and kept alive for humanity the divine mystery.[57] It is proper, therefore, to count them as having a positive saving function during that interim, and, concomitantly, also those religions today that function where the message of Jesus has not yet reached.

The religions have a positive saving function because Jesus Christ is present in them through his Spirit.

> If there can be a faith which is creative for salvation among non-Christians, and if it may be hoped that in fact it is found on a large scale,

---

[55]Karl Rahner, "Anonymous Christianity and the Missionary Task of the Church," *Theological Investigations*, vol. 12, David Bourke, trans. (London: Darton, Longman & Todd, 1974) 171-72. George A. Lindbeck, *The Nature of Doctrine: Religion and Theology in a Postliberal Age* (Philadelphia: Westminster, 1984) 56ff., calls Rahner's attempt to reconcile *Christus solus* with the salvation of non-Christians an "experiential-expressivist" approach. He also believes Rahner's proposal diminishes the biblical insistence on *fides ex auditu* and must be corrected.

[56]Karl Rahner, "Jesus Christ in the Non-Christian Religions," *Theological Investigations*, vol. 17, Margaret Kohl, trans. (New York: Seabury Press, 1981) 42.

[57]Ibid., 42-43. Cf. Hans Küng, "The World Religions in God's Plan of Salvation," *Christian Revelation and World Religions*, J. Neuner, S.J., ed. (London: Burns and Oates, 1967) 25-66.

then it is to be taken for granted that this faith is made possible and is based upon the supernatural grace of the Spirit.[58]

The relation between the ubiquitous grace of the Spirit and the historical event of the cross becomes clear when one views the universal self-communication of God to the world, that is, the Holy Spirit, as the "*a priori* cause of the Incarnation and of the Cross of Christ."[59] Conversely, the event of Christ serves as the final cause of the communication of the Spirit to the world; therefore, the Spirit communicated is always the Spirit of Jesus.[60]

Present in the justifying faith of all persons is a "searching memory" which is directed towards the absolute savior, Jesus Christ. By "searching memory" Rahner means the transcendental orientation towards God, borne along by grace, which yearns for and anticipates an immediate self-communication of God. Although one's "searching memory" may not have an explicitly religious content, it is the *a priori* structure that allows one to perceive and retain that which one encounters in history.[61] It seeks for the one in history who is the absolute bringer of salvation, namely, the event in history "in which a free decision about the salvific outcome of history is made and becomes tangible."[62] Moreover, one already has a genuine existential relation with the thing or person sought. Through his Spirit, Jesus Christ is present in the non-Christians (and thus the non-Christian religions) as the cause of this *memoria*. It involves all persons in a "Christology of quest."[63]

---

[58]Rahner, *Foundations of Christian Faith*, 316.

[59]Ibid., 317.

[60]Ibid., 318.

[61]Ibid., 319-22. Rahner's reflection on this topic is sprinkled throughout many of his essays. See "Some Implications of the Scholastic Concept of Uncreated Grace," *Theological Investigations*, vol. 1 (Baltimore: Helicon, 1961) 319-46.

[62]Ibid., 320-21.

[63]Rahner, "The One Christ and the Universality of Salvation," 221.

Anonymous Christians

Two working assumptions in Rahner's theology have been clarified thus far: all persons achieve salvation only through Christ, and all persons have the transcendental capacity for the possibility and intelligibility of a supernatural faith in revelation. He brings these fundamental beliefs into dialogue with those who, by no fault of their own, have never really been touched by the explicit message of Christianity. In this number, Rahner includes all who lived before Christ, non-Christians since the time of Christ, and "all those who consciously and explicitly believe that they are required by their conscience to refuse the Gospel of Christ as this is presented to them."[64]

There are two possible ways, Rahner says, of resolving the conflict between (1) the possibility of supernatural salvation and of a corresponding faith that must be granted to non-Christians, and (2) the impossibility of salvation without reference to Christ. The first way is the position taken in the past that consigns non-Christians to hell or allows salvation on the grounds of righteous living. The second way is the more reasonable position of "anonymous Christians,"[65] that is, Rahner's own creative proposal. This concept is very important to Rahner and is the key to his treatment of religious pluralism. It is clear to him that every human being is exposed to the influence of divine grace that offers salvation to each through union with God.

---

[64]Ibid., 216.

[65]Ibid., 218. There is a rich theological background to Rahner's formulation. He notes some of the ingredients in the essay, "Anonymous Christianity and the Missionary Task of the Church," 167-68. Some of the precursors to Rahner's view are the New Testament recognition that God imparts the Spirit before baptism, in some cases; the medieval doctrine of the *votum baptismi* (baptism of desire); or, more recently, the idea that an implicit *votum ecclesiae* was sufficient for justification. Lindbeck, *The Nature of Doctrine*, 61, criticizes the notion of "anonymous Christianity" for its "religious pretentiousness" and "imperialism." He writes, "There is something arrogant about supposing that Christians know what non-believers experience and believe in the depths of their beings better than they know themselves. . . ." Similarly, Carpenter, *Nature and Grace*, 72, calls Rahner's idea of "anonymous Christianity" an updating of a strand of Logos Christology of the ancient church and, in the present context, sounds like "imperialist aggression" (73).

Simply put, the "anonymous Christian" is one who is, like all persons, oriented towards God, and thus, is a part of redeemed humankind, but has not yet entered into the visible Church through baptism. In each discussion of this concept, Rahner underscores the fact that the anonymous Christian's failure to embrace Christianity does not signify any serious personal fault in God's sight.[66] The anonymous Christian is one who has in his or her basic intentionality responded to the approach of the ever-seeking divine grace. Rahner distinguishes this basic intentionality, that is, "anonymous faith," from explicit faith.

Anonymous faith. By "anonymous faith" Rahner means a faith which salvation presupposes, that is, hope and love of God and neighbor, yet which occurs "without any explicit and conscious relationship . . . to the revelation of Jesus Christ contained in the Old and/or New Testament and without any explicit reference to God through an objective idea of God."[67] "Anonymous faith" means more than mere "good will" based wholly on a natural knowledge of God, contends Rahner—as many have read the Second Vatican Council's Pastoral Constitution on the Church in the Modern World, No. 22, and the Dogmatic Constitution on the Church, No. 16, to be saying.[68] "Anonymous faith" is, in a real sense, an act of faith, albeit rudimentary.

The self-communication of God to each human being constitutes the inner dynamism, goal, and entelechy (realization of form-giving cause) of life; it is an awareness of being oriented towards the immediacy of God which has not yet been objectively apprehended at the level of conscious thought in the "anonymous

---

[66]Karl Rahner, "Observations on the Problem of the 'Anonymous Christian,'" *Theological Investigations*, vol. 14, David Bourke, trans. (Boston: Darton, Longman & Todd, 1976) 282.

[67]Rahner, "Anonymous and Explicit Faith," 52.

[68]*The Documents of Vatican II*, W.M. Abbott, ed. (New York: Herder and Herder, 1966).

Christian."[69]   Rahner's construction gives theological form to what is said in *Lumen Gentium*, No. 16:

> Those also can attain to everlasting salvation who, through no fault of their own, do not know the gospel of Christ or his Church, yet sincerely seek God and, moved by his grace, strive by their deeds to do his will as it is known to them through the dictates of conscience.[70]

Grace has created faith through effecting an *a priori* transcendental change of awareness.[71]   Thus when one fully accepts himself or herself in his or her unlimited transcendence, without reflection, that one has accepted God, in Rahner's estimation.

Atheism and anonymous Christianity. Rahner not only deals with the "God-pleasing pagans" but with the atheist in his "anonymous Christian" framework, for both are in a Christ-determined situation. Because of the unlimited, transcendent nature in each person, the inner impetus of the spirit of the atheist directs him or her to the infinite Absolute being; however, for the atheist, this experience of transcendence towards God is mediated through non-religious categories or concepts.[72]   God's universal salvific will joins the person's acceptance of this unlimited transcendence, "raising it up by grace." One can speak of

> genuine faith on condition that a man freely accepts his own unlimited transcendence which is raised up by grace and directed to the immediate presence of God as its final goal.[73]

---

[69]Rahner, "Observations on the Problem of the 'Anonymous Christian,'" 290-91.

[70]*Dogmatic Constitution on the Church* (Boston: Daughters of St. Paul, 1964) 18.

[71]Rahner, "Observations on the Problem of the 'Anonymous Christian,'" 291.

[72]Rahner, "Anonymous and Explicit Faith," 54-55.

[73]Ibid., 55.

This in itself constitutes revelation. One cannot shrink back from this supernatural destination without becoming less than human—a truncation of a person created for the self-expression of God.

An atheist can, in Rahner's judgment, be justified and receive salvation if he or she acts in accordance with his or her conscience.[74] Such behavior can be considered an unreflective turning to God, or *metanoia*.[75] No moral blame is to be ascribed to such a person, Rahner asserts, pointing to the teaching of Vatican II.[76] Clearly, one can speak in a valid way of the "possibility of co-existence of a conceptually objectified atheism and a nonpropositional and existentially realised theism,"[77] evidenced by the presence of faith, hope, and love. It would be an error to speak of a greater possibility of salvation for a polytheistic heathen who evidenced these than for a modern atheist, Rahner concludes, since both are products of their cultural environments.[78]

The Universality of Salvation

Throughout his soteriological analysis, Rahner has demonstrated the possibility of supernatural salvation for all. That this salvation is actualized by all presents a more difficult issue theologically, for one is limited by the boundary of what has not yet occurred.

Progressive in his theological concepts as a key modern architect of Roman Catholicism, Rahner departs from previous theology's certainty about eternal damnation and hell—traditionally held to be as much a given as heaven and the

---

[74]Rahner, "Atheism and Implicit Christianity," 151, states the conviction that "not every individual atheist can be regarded as a gravely culpable sinner . . ." which implies that some *are* culpable. However, the fact that one acts in accordance with one's moral conscience implicitly affirms God because one posits an absolute moral demand. Cf. *Karl Rahner in Dialogue* (340), where he adds the proviso about "sinning mortally against one's conscience."

[75]Rahner, "The One Christ and the Universality of Salvation," 203.

[76]Rahner, "Atheism and Implicit Christianity," 147.

[77]Ibid.

[78]Ibid., 150.

eternal beatitude.[79]   Rahner believes that what is known of human freedom requires him to say something about the possibility that one might suffer the absolute loss that is hell;[80] however, because he lives in the eschaton of Jesus Christ and therefore has the hope that all will be saved through grace, he maintains "we are not obliged to declare that we know with certainty that in fact the history of salvation is going to end for certain people in absolute loss."[81] Further, Rahner says Christians must take seriously the biblical injunction against judging a person.[82]

One does not have the right, moreover, to hold unreservedly the doctrine of *apocatastasis*. As one who can incur guilt, a person must reckon up to the very end that it is possible to reach the point of an absolute rejection of God.[83] Were one to reckon otherwise, "the seriousness of free history would be abolished."[84] Because of Rahner's emphasis on the universal saving will of God, there is a note of optimism about salvation (*Heilsoptimismus*) throughout his writings.[85]

---

[79]Leo O'Donovan, "Living into Mystery: Karl Rahner's Reflections at 75," *America* 140 (March 10, 1979): 179. Cf. his *On the Theology of Death* (New York: Seabury Press, 1973) 38ff., for his reflection on the possibility of death as damnation. Whether death is an event of salvation or damnation depends upon "whether it is endured in faith or in godlessness . . ."

[80]Rahner, *Foundations of Christian Faith*, 435.

[81]Ibid. But cf. Rahner's "The One Christ and the Universality of Salvation," 200, ". . . a man can lose the possibility of salvation through serious personal sin of his own."

[82]Rahner, "The One Christ and the Universality of Salvation," 203.

[83]Rahner, *Foundations of Christian Faith*, 443. In his essay "The One Christ and the Universality of Salvation," 200, Rahner suggests that one's journey towards salvation, i.e., union with God, may not be terminated by death. It appears that Rahner is hinting that the Church's traditional teaching about purgatory needs reworking. Rahner's writings in this area are not entirely consistent.

[84]Ibid., 444.

[85]Rahner, "Christianity and the Non-Christian Religions," 5:124.

A doctrine of two parallel ways, one leading to heaven, the other to hell, does not really reflect the teaching of the Church and Scripture, in Rahner's opinion. He prefers to put primary emphasis on the doctrine that the whole world will enter into eternal life with God; however, the possibility that a person's freedom will end in eternal loss stands closely by—a negative side of eschatological teaching.[86]

ECCLESIOLOGICAL PERSPECTIVE

Resonating with the overtones of the documents of Vatican II, Rahner has argued for the absoluteness of Christianity and the necessity for every person to have a relationship to the self-giving God, revealed in Christ. Further, in order to maintain God's universal salvific will, he has found it necessary to argue that each person is being drawn by the Spirit towards Jesus Christ, either explicitly or implicitly. In that the church and its sacraments continue the decisive achievement and revelation of Christ in history, Rahner must show that all persons are, in some sense, members of the church.

Christians and "anonymous Christians" are directed towards the same goal: the culmination of God's salvific activity, which is, on earth, the church. Although the statements of the Second Vatican Council, reflecting the reality of religious pluralism, have prompted Rahner to offer his "anonymous Christian" hypothesis, he nevertheless wishes to safeguard the necessity of the church—its baptism, sacraments, and proclamation.[87] Thus, he connects the salvation offered to all through Christ with the church when he states: "It is only in Jesus Christ that this

---

[86]Ibid.

[87]Rahner, "Atheism and Implicit Christianity," 145. Rahner's approach to the ecclesiological issue is evidenced in his thorough analysis of the 1943 papal encyclical, *Mystici Corpus Christi*, in "Membership of the Church," *Theological Investigations*, vol. 2 (Baltimore: Helicon Press, 1963) 1-88.

salvation is conferred, and through Christianity and the Church that it must be mediated to all men."[88]

The Necessity of the Church for Salvation

Rahner is convinced that church is part of the real essence of what is Christian; indeed, Christianity is necessarily church, because faith cannot be a privatized and interior movement in an individual.[89] The religious existence of a person is "ecclesi"; it forms a community.[90] The fundamental relationship of a person to God must have a concrete and tangible history; otherwise, this relationship is trapped in transcendental subjectivity and has nothing to do with the reality of life.[91] The church functions in the salvation history of God's grace as "the necessary historical and social mediation of salvation."[92] It exists where the Eucharist is celebrated and baptism is administered, and "whenever the word of Christ which demands faith is proclaimed in the Spirit of Christ."[93]

So constituted, the church has an authoritative claim upon the whole person for his or her salvation,[94] and it mediates the concreteness of God's demands upon the person. There are degrees of membership in the church,

> not only in ascending order from fullness of the Christian faith and the recognition of the visible head of the Church, to the living community of the Eucharist, indeed to the realisation of holiness, but also in descending

---

[88]Karl Rahner, "The Church, Churches, and Religions," *Theological Investigations*, vol. 10, Graham Harrison, trans. (London: Darton, Longman & Todd, 1972-1973) 31.

[89]Rahner, *Foundations of Christian Faith*, 330, 342. He reminds the reader, however, that the doctrine of the Church is not the central truth of Christianity; Jesus Christ is.

[90]Ibid.

[91]Ibid., 345.

[92]Ibid.

[93]Ibid., 348.

[94]Ibid., 347.

order from the explicitness of baptism into a non-official and anonymous Christianity. . . .[95]

The proper end of each person is full membership in the church, becoming a Christian in a sense manifested at the historical level. "Anonymous Christianity" has an intrinsic dynamism which demands to be realized in the visible sacramental mode of the church.[96]

The church is founded by Jesus and, therefore, is greater than a human social organization of one's own making or projection. The church's authoritative claim must not be exercised as an unchristian religious dictatorship or an ecclesiastical totalitarianism. Rahner defends the rights and duties of the individual in the church.

Extra Ecclesiam Nulla Salus. As a theologian of the Roman Catholic Church, Rahner always seeks to affirm the truth of the church's dogma while, at the same time, giving it a broader interpretation. This is his tack when employing the traditional dictum *extra ecclesiam nulla salus*.[97]

Rahner professes that outside the Catholic Church, that is, in other Christian communions, there are things that validly bear the name Christian. In other words, in accordance with Vatican II, he asserts that the Body of Christ is not subsumed in the Roman Catholic Church. Moreover, while holding that the church is a necessary means of salvation as the visible society, he will also define "church" as "humanity consecrated by Christ" (a cosmic view of the church which includes all of humanity), which allows for the possibility of salvation for someone outside the church.[98] He writes:

---

[95]Rahner, "Anonymous Christians," 6:391.

[96]See Karl Rahner, "The Individual in the Church," *Nature and Grace* (New York: Sheed and Ward, 1963) 5-63.

[97]In *Hearers of the Word* (New York: Herder and Herder, 1969), 179, he uses the axiom in an oblique way, failing to correlate closely the salvation offered by the Church with that offered by Christ, yet holding to the uniqueness of Christian revelation.

[98]Leo O'Donovan, "A Changing Ecclesiology in a Changing Church: A Symposium on Development in the Ecclesiology of Karl Rahner," *Theological Studies* 38 (1977): 743.

The Church, as something visible and as a sign of the union with God by grace, must itself be composed of a further twofold reality, *viz.* Church as an established juridical organization in the sacred order and Church as humanity consecrated by the Incarnation.[99]

Being accepted into the Body of Christ is the necessary pre-condition for salvation. This occurs through the "supernatural existential" in the human being. With this caveat, Rahner can claim *extra ecclesiam nulla salus*.

The sacrament of the world's salvation. The church is the explicit visibility of the grace that is offered universally. Cyprian's maxim, through Rahner's reformulation, has been reinterpreted to mean "without the church no salvation." The world can experience salvation through the church even where the world has not in an historically demonstrable manner become part of the church.

Rahner does not regard the church primarily as the means through which grace is mediated; rather, his ecclesiology views the church as the *result*, not the *cause* of grace given to the world.[100] The offer of grace comes through transcendental means, namely, the "supernatural existential," and through the visible expression which is the church. Rahner articulates the "diaspora" situation of the church[101] as one in which the church will evidence to a preeminently non-Christian world the God who is close, full of grace, and inclusive of all humanity. Because of the solidarity of human history, the church is the promise of salvation to all—both before and after Christ. It is "leaven . . . at work in the rest of the meal."[102]

---

[99]Rahner, "Membership of the Church," 86. Cf. Karl Rahner, "Dogmatic Notes on 'Ecclesiological Piety,'" *Theological Investigations*, vol. 5 (Baltimore: Helicon, 1966) 336-65.

[100]Ibid., 746. Jerome P. Theisen, O.S.B., *The Ultimate Church and the Promise of Salvation* (Collegeville MN: St. John's University Press, 1976) 81ff., elucidates Rahner's understanding of the church in the modern world, concluding that it is both "traditional and forward looking" (102).

[101]Karl Rahner, *The Christian of the Future*, W.J. O'Hara, trans. (New York: Herder and Herder, 1967) 79.

[102]Ibid., 89.

The Mission of the Church

The many voices of the New Testament are in unison concerning the universal missionary task of the church. The concept of "anonymous Christianity" seems, at first blush, to be antithetical to this fundamental understanding of the church's mission, or at least to lessen its impetus.[103]

Rahner believes it to be a more constructive approach to view "anonymous Christianity" as the "enabling condition for a preaching of the faith."[104] The hearer of the gospel must have already experienced the offer of the grace of faith in order to understand the preaching. Indeed, the missionary task of the church and "anonymous Christianity" necessarily co-exist.[105] Though Rahner's position demands further clarification of what comprises "mission," the nuances of his theology cannot help but widen the aperture through which one views this task.

Formerly, the theological justification of missions was the need for each person to be converted. The church maintained that the only hope that individuals outside her flock had of escaping perdition rested upon the faithfulness of her missionaries. This traditional theology, prior to the modern age, had no knowledge of the length and breadth of non-Christian human history, Rahner explains.[106] Today, persons can more clearly consider how one can be justified through authentic faith without encountering the explicit preaching of Jesus Christ.[107]

The missionary task of the church consists primarily of extending the grace of God incarnationally throughout all the dimensions of human life;[108] however, it is not the church's *Sendung* (commission) to "humanize" the world through

---

[103]Karl Rahner, "Anonymous Christianity and the Missionary Task of the Church," 168.

[104]Ibid., 169.

[105]Ibid., 171.

[106]Ibid., 175.

[107]Ibid.

[108]Ibid., 176; *The Christian of the Future*, 85.

humanitarian means.[109] The church's task includes the salvation of the individual, but it also has as its goal the transformation of all specific histories and cultures through making Christ present in them. It cannot be gainsaid that the preaching of Christ's gospel and grace augments the possibility that one will respond to his salvation; the mission of the church renders a people more responsible because of its exposure to the message of Christ, according to Rahner's perception of the teaching of the New Testament.[110] One becomes more responsible to make one's Christianity explicit and is, himself or herself, entrusted with the missionary task of helping one's neighbor achieve the self-realization that grace facilitates.[111]

The attitude of the missionary. The missionary can "imitate God's forbearance"[112] because he or she knows one can hope for that which God has willed, the salvation of all persons.[113]   Going to those outside explicit Christianity in the church, the missionary can joyfully recognize in them Christ's work. He or she then helps the non-Christian make explicit what is already implicit. One does not testify of God's grace to non-Christians with the hope of converting them if it means turning them into radically different persons, but of "trying to bring them to their true selves."[114] Preaching the gospel does not

---

[109]Karl Rahner, "The Church's Commission to Bring Salvation and the Humanization of the World," *Theological Investigations*, vol. 14, David Bourke, trans. (London: Darton, Longman & Todd, 1976) 295-313.

[110]Ibid., 177.

[111]Ibid.

[112]Rahner, *The Christian of the Future*, 85.

[113]The missionary must come to grips with the fact, Rahner contends, that most people are saved and drawn into eternal life without the Church's institutionalized means.

[114]Rahner, *The Christian of the Future*, 88. Cf. Carpenter, *Nature and Grace*, 63. There is only a faint echo in Rahner's formulation of the Augustinian and Reformed tradition in which the concept of "depravity" is so central. His anthropocentric methodology is indebted to Thomas Aquinas, but particularly to the existentialism of Heidegger.

introduce the knowledge of God among "pagans"; it is the explication of what one already is by grace.

God's "yes" to the world. Rahner does not envision a crusader church standing poised to do battle with the evil world. The church is God's "Yes of consent" spoken to the world. Rahner expects the Christian of the future to come to regard the church as that which is consonant with the very depths of human affirmations rather than standing in contradiction to them. The church functions as God's promise to fulfill these yearnings, not to condemn them. The church will come to respect the world's institutions and strivings over against viewing them as a mass of decomposition and deterioration.[115]

EVALUATION

Through his formulation of the transcendental orientation of all men and women to God, Karl Rahner offers an inclusive Christian theology of the world's religions. He both gives them a useful function in the economy of salvation history and makes a plausible case for regarding their adherents as "anonymous Christians" because of the common "supernatural existential" they share with explicit or "thematized" Christians. His proposals call the Christian to a much more positive evaluation of the non-Christian, which is a healthy corrective. Rahner has provided a much needed alternative to exclusivist and thorough-going relativist positions. To his credit, he has retained his roots in traditional theology by arguing on the basis of the centrality of Jesus Christ and the necessity of the church;[116] clearly, however, his Christology is hardly traditional.

---

[115]Karl Rahner, *Mission and Grace*, Cecily Hastings, trans. (London: Sheed and Ward, 1963) 35.

[116]He has managed to do this apart from narrow sectarianism; he definitely includes all Christian communions in the Body of Christ although he sees a more direct continuity for the Roman Catholic Church with the church that Jesus founded.

As well as any theologian today, Rahner is attuned to the various problems posed by Christianity's traditional pronouncements vis-à-vis other ways of faith, be they one of the great world religions or a deliberate atheism. Further, he does not try to treat this particular soteriological problem in isolation from his whole theological system. It is not an after-thought. Perhaps it is fair to say that his theology has taken form precisely through its engagement with the present-day crisis of faith in post-Christian nations and the continuing expressions of faith in other cultures where the influence of the non-Christian religions is felt. In the pages that follow an attempt will be made to evaluate the several positive contributions of Rahner and then submit a critical analysis of those areas that appear problematic or in need of further clarification.

Theological Methodology

At every point, Rahner shows himself to be a theologian striving to be progressive yet faithful to the Roman Catholic Church. His general methodology takes its point of departure from the conciliar decrees of Vatican II, which is utterly authoritative for him. He builds his theology on the basis of the Council's dogma rather than criticizing the foundation of its pronouncements. This approach is useful to Roman Catholicism in that it fleshes out some unclear concepts in the decrees,[117] but it seems too uncritical of them at times. The sayings of Vatican II often lack substantial scriptural warrant, and Rahner does not seem to think it necessary to go behind the decrees to Scripture. There is a curious lack of attention to hermeneutical theory, especially as it impinges upon biblical hermeneutics. This approach makes less credible his position in certain areas; for example, the Council's accentuation of the universal salvific will of God plays down the hard sayings of the Synoptics about the dual destiny of the righteous and the unrighteous,[118] and Rahner follows its lead. He has used a couple of New

---

[117]The Council stressed that the possibility of salvation exists for non-Christians, but did not discuss in detail how the salvation might be achieved.

[118]See, for example, Matt 25:31-46 and Luke 13:22-30.

Testament texts as the umbrella for his position, namely, 1 Tim 2:4-6 and Acts 17:23, that speak of God's universal saving intention,[119] and has left many sayings of judgment unnoticed, as did Vatican II.

A strong catalyst to the formulation of "anonymous Christianity" is the world-wide militant atheism. Rahner is correct to see this phenomenon as a new theological datum around which to construct his theology, but his inclusion of explicit atheists in universal salvation history seems overly accommodating. Perhaps this phenomenon could be viewed more constructively as the burgeoning sinfulness of humanity rather than a justifiable atheism which Christians must hasten to include among the redeemed.

Scripture is an important source for Rahner's theology, yet is clearly secondary to synthesizing dogmatic pronouncements. Commenting on Rahner's expertise in biblical studies, Harvey Egan has remarked: "His exegetical mastery and overall *sense* of Scripture are awesome. . . ."[120] Egan's assessment may have been overly generous, but Scripture clearly functions as a constant norm of faith for Rahner even though explicit references are sometimes sparse in his essays or monographs. Rahner unswervingly affirms the inspiration of Scripture yet gives proper regard to the humanity of its historically-conditioned authors. He has shown a helpful way forward for Roman Catholics in the dogmatic appropriation of recent biblical scholarship.[121]

Rahner's ecclesiology is closely related to his attitude towards Scripture. The faith of the early church was objectified in its canon and, consequently, the apostolic church and the testimony of the Bible have remained the norm for the

---

[119]Among the many places where Rahner employs these texts, see the clear statement in his *The Christian of the Future*, 94-97.

[120]Harvey Egan, "Book Review of Rahner's *Foundations of Christian Faith*," *Theological Studies* 38 (1977): 555-56. Cf. Karl Rahner, "The Position of Christology in the Church Between Exegesis and Dogmatics," *Theological Investigations*, 11:185-214.

[121]See especially Karl Rahner and Wilhelm Thüsing, *A New Christology* (New York: Seabury Press, 1980).

church. The lived faith of the church continually interacts with Scripture; hence Rahner does not appeal to one over against the other. Developments in the church's conscious awareness of her faith color her interpretation of Scripture. Therefore, Rahner can lay a heavy emphasis on the universalistic passages because of a "breakthrough of . . . optimism in the Church concerning salvation for all men. . . ."[122] Moreover, the Old and New Testaments do not rule out such an optimistic interpretation, Rahner argues. He fails, however, to question the origin of this "astonishing phenomenon" in the development of the church's faith. Has the church capitulated to a false sense of the spiritual solidarity of humankind, thinking that all must share the same ultimate destiny?[123] The development of the church's awareness of her faith may not be a sufficient criterion if realized apart from the searching light of Scripture. Rahner tends to de-emphasize Scripture's normative role on this issue.

The Use of the Transcendental Method

The goal of Rahner's use of the transcendental method is noteworthy insofar as he tries to link all persons both before and after Christ with the salvation accomplished in his death and resurrection. He repeatedly affirms that "God desires the salvation of everyone; and this salvation willed by God is the salvation won by Christ."[124]

The subtleties and sheer power of Rahner's intellectual reasoning are to be commended as well as his desire to provide a christological foundation for universal salvation. To accomplish this goal, Rahner depends upon several assumptions. First, there is an optimistic conception of human nature which reflects his Aristotelian-Thomistic bent. Thus the non-Christian religions are viewed as a transitional state rather than a diabolical flowering of unrighteousness

---

[122]Rahner, "Observations on the Problem of the 'Anonymous Christian,'" 214.

[123]Ibid., 293-94. Cf. Joseph A. Bracken, S.J., "Salvation: A Matter of Personal Choice," *Theological Studies* 37 (1976): 410-24.

[124]Rahner, "Christianity and the Non-Christian Religions," 122.

in revolt against God.[125] It is fair for Rahner to assume that grace has touched these religions and that genuine revelation permeates them because of the Spirit's presence in them. However, his optimistic appraisal of "religious humanity" in general is applied to the individual as well. There are few hints in Rahner's theology that one will refuse to be drawn by the Spirit to the full acceptance of the gospel of Christ. Moreover, he guards against a privatization of salvation to the degree that he neglects the individual's responsibility for conscious participation. He has not sufficiently considered the freedom of those who do reject God in sin and whose consciences must be challenged and transformed by the mystery of the cross of Christ.

What constitutes the giving of the Spirit for Rahner? This concept needs further refining. He argues that the Spirit is present in the "anonymous Christian" because in Christ's death and resurrection the Spirit was communicated to the world. The way Rahner sketches this concept does not make necessary any conscious acceptance or rejection. In Rahner's thinking, one receives the Spirit because one is human.[126]

From the New Testament materials he justifies the possibility that one can receive the Spirit before baptism; however, he needs to deal more carefully with the fact that in the New Testament order (especially Acts) one did not receive the Spirit without confession of faith. Rahner is arguing that one has non-reflective experiences of the Spirit, which reflect the reality of God's grace at work everywhere. To argue thus, Rahner must abandon some aspects of the instrumentality of human freedom in salvation.

---

[125]Rahner shows his affinity to the affirmations of Schleiermacher and Hegel in this schematization.

[126]One of the major inconsistencies in Rahner's approach is the failure to correlate creation and redemption adequately. While one can applaud his desire to view the grace shown in Christ in the context of the on-going grace-filled bestowal of God upon the world (hence, an "evolutionary christology"), one is left to question whether the guidance of the Spirit is granted through the grace of the incarnation or from the divine grace active in the creative process as such.

Another problem is attached to Rahner's understanding of the Spirit's functioning. He argues that the Spirit gives revelation apart from the Christian proclamation of the gospel, which is a tenable assertion biblically. But does this weaken the link between the Spirit and the Word? If the Spirit is already leading to a goal that is analogous to the goal of the preaching of the Gospel, some would contend that the preaching of the Gospel may be rendered superfluous, and that a relativizing of Christian truth is underway.[127] Further, has he sundered the unified activity of the Trinity?[128] The New Testament consistently defines the Holy Spirit in light of the resurrection of Jesus as the "Spirit of the Risen Lord." Rahner's assertion does not necessitate such bifurcation, but he needs to clarify further the relationship of the Spirit to the proclamation of the gospel. In addition, sustained reflection on the role of Christ in creation would forge the link between creation and redemption more firmly.

Less problematic is Rahner's assumption that Christology defines anthropology. He believes the fullness of human nature culminates in Christ and that human nature is constituted by God calling persons to God's own self in Christ. He masterfully argues that the person is "situated" differently, that is, is in a grace-filled world, because of this historical expression of grace in Christ and the church.[129] Hence, he or she searches for God, and Rahner does not regard human seeking for God as an idolatrous action of unrighteousness (as does Barth), but as an evidence of the potentiality of responding to God's gracious call. This

[127]See Helmut Thielicke, *The Evangelical Faith*, vol. 3, Geoffrey W. Bromiley, trans. and ed. (Grand Rapids: Eerdmans, 1982) 305f. Cf. Paul Tillich, *Systematic Theology*, vol. 3 (Chicago: University of Chicago Press, 1963) 128, for his insights on the relationship of Spirit and the Word.

[128]James Carpenter, *Nature and Grace*, suggests it would be profitable for Rahner ". . . to regard creation, incarnation, and consummation as aspects of the divine self-communication . . . with the Trinity as disclosed in the incarnation and as operative in all three movements of the divine grace" (69).

[129]Rahner's analysis is very compatible with the profound study of a fellow Jesuit, Piet Schoonenberg, of the solidarity of human sin and thus salvation history. See *Man and Sin* (Notre Dame: University of Notre Dame Press, 1965).

appears to be a signal contribution to the task of developing a Christian theology of the non-Christian religions.

The "Supernatural Existential"

Rahner is correct to emphasize the reality that God is taking a gracious initiative towards all persons and has supplied all of them with the capacity to respond in some dimension. The expression of God's grace poured out on the world in Christ's life and death transforms each person's subjective horizon, orienting one toward God. On the basis of this reality, Rahner believes that following the dictates of one's conscience suffices for salvation. This is a facile concept; Rahner does not discuss if or how the conscience is transformed. It appears that he unquestioningly gives conscience an inherent positive moral value.[130] Moreover, the relationship between "supernatural existential" and "conscience" remains to be explored and clarified. Does it not seem too little to say that one can attain salvation because, despite his or her invincible error, that one has lived according to the dictates of conscience? Rahner's argument has made the conscience arbiter of righteousness, particularly when one's conscience requires one to refuse the gospel of Christ.[131] Perhaps Rahner needs to say more about the nature of one's worship and charity and their relationship

---

[130]A theologian of Rahner's stature and facility in understanding the nature of human being should have analyzed the biblical and psychological ramifications of conscience, but he does not seem to have done so. For the former, see Christian Maurer, *Theological Dictionary of the New Testament*, Gerhard Friedrich and G.W. Bromiley, eds. (Grand Rapids: Eerdmans, 1971) 7:899-919, for the article on syneidēsis. Paul first used the term in the Christian Church, giving it a sense altogether new. Paul talks about the conscience making a person more aware of how one is inwardly divided. It does not have the sense of a correct moral guide for the believer or the unbeliever. See Dale Moody, *The Word of Truth: A Summary of Christian Doctrine Based on Biblical Revelation* (Grand Rapids: Eerdmans, 1981) 241ff. Moody calls conscience a "sense of moral responsibility," but it does not give consent to right and wrong.

[131]Rahner grants to the atheist the right to refuse overtly the gospel if, thereby, he or she remains truer to conscience, i.e., accepts his or her humanity fully. Rahner concludes that an atheist is really seeking God, while verbally or cognitively denying that quest. In my thinking, he violates the intent of the *Dogmatic Constitution on the Church*.

toconscience. One can applaud Rahner's emphasis on the necessity of the individual's free involvement in salvation, but it appears he has denied any limits to subjectivity in this area. Like Schleiermacher, Rahner gives to one's religious experience a near *ex cathedra* autonomy. That Rahner is more a philosophical theologian than a biblical theologian is most apparent in the contours of his argument for the "supernatural existential."

The Destiny of Non-Christian Humanity

Rahner's "anonymous Christian" proposal is useful in that it allows a method of including non-Christians, who, by no fault of their own, have not responded explicitly to the message of Jesus. He has contended that the inner dynamism of the "Christology of quest" will impel one towards an explicit Christian life as a member of the church. He does not say enough, however, about the destiny of the "anonymous Christian" who dies without this actualization. Russell Aldwinckle faults Rahner at this point and argues that there is no consistent eschatology in his systematic treatment of the problem.[132]

How one dies is of utmost significance in Rahner's scheme. One who accepts the reality of death and abandons oneself to it can find it to be the fulfillment of the potentiality of the "supernatural existential," according to Rahner.

> The ultimate act of freedom, in which he decides his own fate totally and irrevocably, is the act in which he either *willingly accepts or definitively rebels against* his own utter impotence, in which he is utterly subject to the control of a mystery which cannot be expressed—that mystery which we call God.[133]

---

[132]Russell Aldwinckle, *Jesus—A Savior or the Savior?* (Macon GA: Mercer University Press, 1982) 179ff. In addition to Rahner's *On the Theology of Death*, see the articles "On Christian Dying," "The Life of the Dead," and "The Resurrection of the Body," republished in McCool's *A Rahner Reader*, 352-61. John Hick, *Death and Eternal Life* (London: Collins, 1979) 228ff., criticizes Rahner's insistence on the moment of physical death as the final determinant of one's ultimate destiny.

[133]McCool, *A Rahner Reader*, 355.

The problem with this assertion is that it seems one can consciously offer oneself to God at this point, but without reference to Jesus Christ. Rahner's argument for the Christian conception of salvation is greatly weakened at this point.

With the main stream of Catholic theology, Rahner views death as the point of final ratification of how one has been living life. An individual's death can prove to be a mortal sin "because of a rebellious refusal to acknowledge one's impotence and commit oneself wholly to God . . . , " as Aldwinckle paraphrases Rahner's construction.[134]   Rahner indicates no further possibility of salvation for one who has died in this way, a point rather inconsistent with his strong leanings towards universalism.

The Solidarity of Salvation History

Rahner is acutely aware of the social nature and unity of humanity. He derives his concept of the solidarity of salvation history from the shared history of all humanity and the inter-communicative nature of existence rather than from a monogenetical assumption. Indeed, the soteriological significance of Christ's death lies in his common humanity with all persons. Christ exemplifies God's gracious giving of self and paradigmatically actualizes the potential of men and women for response, a principle Rahner calls the "supernatural existential."

> Prior to any subjective appropriation of salvation, man is inwardly determined by a supernatural existential which consists of the fact that Christ in his death "justified" sinful man before the all-holy God. . . . This . . . can be simply called the supernatural existential of being (objectively) redeemed or of being (objectively) justified.[135]

Rahner simply believes that the death of Christ creates a new context in which faith can occur. Objectively, Christ's death transforms the hopes of all persons for salvation.

---

[134]Ibid., 181.

[135]Karl Rahner, "Controversial Theology on Justification," *Theological Investigations*, (Baltimore: Helicon, 1966) 4:200.

Like Christ, each person now can obediently accept death, realizing his or her impotence in the face of its power over humanity, and offer absolute trust in the gracious, beckoning God. By this, Rahner has proposed a method by which persons can identify with Christ's death and discover its personal significance, and, thus, share his life.

The way Rahner views the unity of human history allows him to stress appropriately Jesus Christ's significance for those before and after his definitive manifestation of God's care. He has rightly seen the organic nature of all of humanity and has been sensitive to the modern person's heightened sense of history which makes a common destiny a paramount concern. Rahner's emphasis on the unity of the whole of humanity mandates determining a means of salvation for the innumerable people who are not Christians (for whatever reason) because all of history is salvation history for him.[136]

Rahner is correct to devise a method to relate all persons to Christ's redemption, but has he said enough about the content of Christ's death "for the many?" It appears that he has offered little more than a variation of the moral-exemplar theme in his view of Christ's atoning death. Further, the stress Rahner places on incarnation threatens to eclipse the significance of atonement. He does not explicate what had entrapped human freedom; he simply asserts that Christ's death liberates that freedom so that human beings might embrace death in the same manner as he. Consequently, it seems that Rahner has trivialized the reality and power of sin and the unrepentant character of much of humanity in his view of the cross as "sacramental sign and grace."

Rahner has been criticized frequently for the paternalistic ring to the name "anonymous Christian." It has been seen as an unfair inclusion of other ways of

---

[136]Rahner flatly rejects the transhistorical tendencies of Karl Barth's thought and has affinity with the emphatically historical approach of Wolfhart Pannenberg. See George Rupp, "Religious Pluralism in the Context of an Emerging World Culture," *Harvard Theological Review* 66 (1973): 207-18.

faith into Christianity, an inclusion that they might denounce or resent.[137]
Rahner carefully stresses that the term is not created for apologetic purposes, but
for the Christian theologian as he or she comes to grips with the church's historic
faith and the phenomenon of religious pluralism. Because Christology defines
soteriology for Rahner, it is necessary to relate the salvation of all persons to
Christ's provision of redemption. "Anonymous Christians" as a discrete category
of persons provides a way to express this relationship. The principle depends on
the affirmation of the absolutely unique and universal efficacy of the historical
event of Christ.[138]   If Christian self-understanding is contemporary, it must
embrace the reality of a variety of religious systems. Rahner is never dogmatic
about this particular terminology and has challenged others to find something
more *a propos*. Problematic though the terminology and its implications may be,
at least Rahner has taken this concern out of the realm of vague syllogisms and
suggested a solution to the problem.

Ecclesiology

Rahner has enlarged the concept "church" while, at the same time, clinging
to the historical priority and significance of the Roman Catholic Church.[139] By
defining church in a more inclusive way, allowing "degrees of membership," he
can draw virtually every person into its circumference and still retain the idea that
the church functions as the primordial sacrament which is necessary because of
the historical nature of the Christian faith. He also retains the basic concept of the

---

[137]Hans Küng fears that this view fails to take the representatives of other religions
seriously and to do injury to the Christian cause. See his *On Being a Christian*, Edward
Quinn, trans. (New York: Doubleday and Co., 1976) 97-98. Cf. Paul F. Knitter's
assessment of the limits of "anonymous Christianity" in *No Other Name?*, 128ff.

[138]Curiously, Rahner never lets go of his overarching Christocentrism although central
aspects of his anthropology undermines its constitutive role.

[139]Karl Rahner, "On Conversions to the Church," *Theological Investigations*
(Baltimore: Helicon, 1967) 3:373-84.

church as the community in which Jesus Christ is proclaimed as Lord. And yet, *all* grace has an "ecclesial structure," he maintains.[140]

Rahner discredits any triumphalism on the part of the church; such arrogance has greatly mitigated the church's role as faithful witness, conformed to the humility of her Lord. He realistically looks at the "diaspora-Church" of the future and calls Christians to be the true servant church.

Does Rahner's inclusive position reduce missionary zeal? Before offering a response, it is important to remember that one must not presuppose a theology of missions when seeking to ascertain a theology of the religions; rather a theology of non-Christian religions must undergird any missiological attempt. Rahner does not make such a methodological misstep.

Rahner's proposals would greatly re-shape the contours of the missionary task. And, yes, they most likely would reduce zealous missionary efforts at conversion of those believed to be remote from God because of their devotion to God through another expression of faith. Rahner intends to re-shape the idea of missions, moving from the standpoint of utter denouncement of the non-Christian religions to affirmation of the good work of God visible in them. Certainly, this more positive approach could have constructive results in dialogue and in effectively communicating Christ's presence to them through a non-pejorative attitude. A keystone in Rahner's theology is the necessity of a non-judgmental attitude towards the faith of others. In this, he properly regards God's knowledge of one's salvation to be somewhat hidden from the scrutiny of another person. One must be careful, however, that in affirming the grace-filled elements in the other religions one does not neglect the need for explicit preaching of the gospel; neither should one fail to denounce the sinful elements in these religions,[141] as Rahner's program tends to do.

---

[140]Karl Rahner, "The Meaning of Frequent Confessions of Devotion," *Theological Investigations* (Baltimore: Helicon, 1967) 3:186ff.

[141]Rahner leaves no place for Barth's idea that revolt and human arrogance are *the* mark of religion, and he offers a more unqualified affirmation of them than does Brunner. George Lindbeck, *The Nature of Doctrine* (60), chides Rahner's inflated view of implicit faith, believing it is "far too glorious . . . and must rather be applied to ultimate completion when faith passes into the beatific vision."

To his credit, Rahner desires that the mission of the church not degenerate into a humanitarian movement. It must continue to be that organ through which Christ visibly mediates salvation. Still, his conception of the church as sacrament seems to be a somewhat passive construct; and the flexibility in his use of "church" leaves many unresolved questions.

SUMMARY

Karl Rahner has made a significant, positive contribution to a Christian theology of the non-Christian religions. His approach is sensitive both to the church's historic positions and to the contemporary religious scene. He has blended the insights of existential philosophy with the teaching of the church and offered a hopeful, inclusive personal eschatology, holistic christology, and practical ecclesiology.

He has given life and breath to the pronouncements of Vatican II and thereby performed an invaluable service to his tradition. Rahner has caught the spirit of much of the Bible's teaching in his caution about judging the fate of another (which only God knows), in his emphasis on the bedrock truth that God desires to include all persons in the redemptive history, and in the breadth of the efficacy of Christ's life, death, and resurrection.

Rahner has explored to some degree the anatomy of religious intention and the structures of human knowing; he has rightly reminded his readers that the human being was created for God and is oriented towards God even as God is seeking her or him. He has given a positive value to human yearnings, believing them to be grounded in God. However, through his affirming, inclusive approach, some of the sting and gravity of sin has been obscured, though some would consider this a positive gain. Rahner needed to probe further the human responsibility in both sin and salvation as well as the biblical conclusion about the dual destiny of the righteous and the unrighteous.

CHAPTER 5

JOHN HICK:
CHRISTIAN RELATIVISM

A third means of answering the question "is there salvation outside Christ and his church?" can be appropriately described as Christian relativism.[1] Stemming from the historical relativism and emphasis on religious consciousness of Lessing, Schleiermacher, and Troeltsch, the relativist position has found contemporary expression in the writings of John Hick, a British philosopher of religion. This position argues that Christianity is but one of a group of world faiths, each of which provides the principal path of salvation for a large section of the human race. Hick often sums up this view by quoting a passage from the

---

[1]In Hick's article, "Pluralism and the Reality of the Transcendent," *Theologians in Transition. The Christian Century* "How My Mind Has Changed" Series, James M. Wall, ed. (New York: Crossroad, 1981) 61, he states why he prefers the term "pluralism" to "relativism." He believes pluralism indicates more than one realm of genuine salvation and true awareness of the divine; relativism, on the other hand, suggests that each is only relatively true, and therefore, none is a truly adequate way of faith. The present study contends that relativism more accurately characterizes Hick's particular approach and will illustrate that contention in the evaluation of his position. Whether his approach can be called "Christian" is also a matter of debate in the minds of many; that issue will also be addressed.

Recently Francis X. Clooney, "Christianity and World Religions: Religion, Reason, and Pluralism," *Religious Studies Review* 15 (1989): 199, has noted two kinds of pluralism: the first only acknowledges the fact of pluralism, i.e., there are billions of non-Christians; the second rejects any claim to universal truth because all truth is local, contextualized, and partial. Cf. Tom F. Driver's article, "The Case for Pluralism," *The Myth of Christian Uniqueness*, John Hick and Paul F. Knitter, eds. (Maryknoll: Orbis Books, 1987) 203ff. For a survey of Christian attitudes toward religious pluralism, see Paul F. Knitter, *No Other Name? A Critical Survey of Christian Attitudes toward the World Religions* (Maryknoll: Orbis Books, 1985).

Bhagavad Gita: "Howsoever men may approach me, even so do I accept them; for, on all sides, whatever path they may choose is mine."[2]

Renowned as a percipient philosopher and an exceptionally lucid author, his writings have been, until about a decade ago, of a more purely philosophical nature,[3] utilizing creatively the fruits of linguistic analysis. More recently he has been absorbed in constructing a philosophical theology of religious pluralism.

In his academic career he has divided his time between his native England and the United States. He has taught philosophy at Cornell University, Princeton Theological Seminary, Cambridge University, the University of Birmingham, and is currently Danforth Professor of the Graduate School of Religion at Claremont, California. He is widely sought as a guest lecturer in the area of his most recent concentration, for he stands at the headwaters of the stream of issues related to a Christian theology of the other faiths.

HISTORICAL AND THEOLOGICAL CONTEXT

To understand Hick's formulation of Christian Relativism, it is important to note both his theological background and the contemporary influences on his thinking.

---

[2]Cited in Hick's article, "Whatever Path Men Choose is Mine," *The Modern Churchman* 18 (Winter, 1974): 17.

[3]*Philosophy of Religion* (Englewood Cliffs NJ: Prentice-Hall, 1963); *Classical and Contemporary Readings in the Philosophy of Religion*, John Hick, ed. (Englewood Cliffs NJ: Prentice-Hall, 1964); *Faith and Knowledge*, 2nd ed. (Ithaca: Cornell University Press, 1966); *Evil and the God of Love* (Norfolk, Great Britain: Fontana Library, 1968); John Hick and Arthur McGill, eds., *The Many-Faced Argument* (New York: Macmillan, 1967); John Hick, ed., *Faith and the Philosophers* (New York: St. Martin's Press, 1964); *Arguments for the Existence of God* (New York: Seabury Press, 1971); *Biology and the Soul* (Cambridge: Cambridge University Press, 1972); and, recently, *An Interpretation of Religion* (New Haven: Yale University Press, 1989), based upon Hick's 1986-87 Gifford Lectures. For a comprehensive bibliography of Hick's writings from 1952-1986, see Gavin D'Costa, *John Hick's Theology of Religions: A Critical Evaluation* (Lanham/New York/London: University Press of America, 1987) 215-31.

Personal Experience of Faith

Hick chronicles his spiritual pilgrimage in the introduction to a recent book, *God Has Many Names*.[4] He spent his early years disinterestedly attending the Anglican Church, he recalls, and, though infinitely boring, he remembers that he had a "rather strong sense of the reality of God as the personal and loving lord of the universe, and of life as having a meaning within God's purpose."[5] Influenced in college by conservative Christians, he had a spiritual conversion and embraced a fundamentalist brand of the faith in the Presbyterian Church of England. And, for several years, Hick was deeply rooted in the conservative-evangelical thought world—which he can still appreciate though he has moved beyond its narrow circumference.

Hick's questioning mind soon became uneasy with some of the theological presuppositions of evangelical theology, and he began to challenge and modify some of the contours of his faith. Further study at Edinburgh (M.A.), Cambridge, and Oxford (D.Phil.), helped to refine the parameters of his emerging philosophical theology.[6]

Almost from the outset of his theological education, theodicy became the central theological problem for Hick[7] and is a recurring theme in his books and articles. One facet of the problem which has claimed his primary attention in recent years is related to the diversity of religious expression and the exclusivism with which he believes traditional Christianity has consigned all non-Christians

---

[4]*God Has Many Names: Britain's New Religious Pluralism* (London: Macmillan Press, 1980) 1-9.

[5]Ibid.

[6]Two key influences on Hick's theology appear to have been F.D.E. Schleiermacher's writings and H.H. Farmer, his theology teacher at Westminster College in Cambridge; he is, perhaps, more indebted to the following Anglo-Saxon positivists and analytical philosophers: B. Russell, A.J. Ayer, D.Z. Phillips, R.B. Braithwaite, et al.

[7]His *Evil and the God of Love*, rev. ed. (New York: Harper and Row, 1978), and *An Interpretation of Religion*, in particular, reveal the methodological significance of theodicy for Hick.

into outer darkness. Retaining such an immoral belief poses insurmountable problems to a viable doctrine of God as personal and loving, in Hick's thinking.[8]

Historical Context: Living in a Multi-Faith Society

One reason Hick began to focus more intently on the questions posed for Christian theology by religious pluralism was his move in 1967 to Birmingham—a multi-cultural, multi-racial, and multi-faith city—to assume the H.G. Wood Chair at Birmingham University. Suddenly he was thrust into the very practical problems of living in a pluralistic society.[9] For him and others, the

> concrete religious question was whether British Christians would be able to see the presence among them of people of another colour, another culture, another faith, as challenging them, in God's providence, to a larger practice of human brotherhood and a larger awareness of divine Fatherhood.[10]

More specifically, the Birmingham professor confesses that living in this new situation demanded of him a more consistent view concerning the possibility of salvation for devoted followers of other ways of faith, in whom he could recognize the Spirit.[11] Heretofore, he had assumed the prevailing doctrine which proclaimed that outside the church, or outside Christianity, there is no salvation; though, he admits, he did not stress its negative implications.[12]

---

[8]John Hick, *Arguments for the Existence of God*, vii. See *Philosophy of Religion*, 2nd ed., 36f. Cf. "Is There Only One Way to God?" *Theology* 85 (1982): 4-7.

[9]John Hick, "Living in a Multi-cultural Society," XI. Practical Reflections of a Theologian, *The Expository Times* 89 (1978): 100-104. Cf. his reflection offered in the autobiographical chapter, "Three Controversies," in *Problems of Religious Pluralism* (New York: St. Martin's Press, 1985) 1-15.

[10]Ibid., 101.

[11]"Is There Only One Way to God?", 4.

[12]John Hick, *God and the Universe of Faiths: Essays in the Philosophy of Religion* (London: Macmillan Press, 1973) 121-22.

Face-to-face relationships with people of the world's great religions (those whom he had by implication believed to be eternally lost)—Muslims from Pakistan and Bangladesh; an old Jewish community; Sikhs from the Indian Punjab; Hindus from many parts of India; and fervent Pentecostal Christians from Jamaica, Trinidad, and other Caribbean islands—forced him to deal with a range of theological problems that he could no longer conveniently ignore. It was in this context that he began to formulate what he calls the "Copernican Revolution in Theology," which was a total re-shaping of his perspective on the non-Christian religions.

The Task of Theology

The theological task for Hick is to seek a viable theology for the late twentieth century "which will avoid the anachronisms while preserving the living reality of Christian faith."[13] He charts a middle way between the traditional and pre-scientific system of beliefs (which he calls the evangelical wing of the church) and the radical response of the "God is dead" theologians, which encompasses a range of agnostic positions,[14] and is implicitly atheistic. While affirming many of their criticisms of the traditional theology, Hick refuses to relinquish the transcendent (as many have) and clings to the New Testament picture of Christ as the origin of his faith in the living God of love.

The tools Hick brings to this constructive theological task are formidable. Thoroughly familiar with the linguistic contributions of Wittgenstein, the existential reflections of Tillich and others, the sociological theory of religion of Durkheim, and the psychological theory of religion of Freud and his legacy, he

---

[13]John Hick, *The Centre of Christianity* (London: SCM Press, 1977), declares that preserving a vital Christian faith will entail and revise perspective of the relation of the faiths, in which Christianity is dislodged from the center of the universe of faiths. A twentieth-century theology of religions must reflect the greatly expanded knowledge of the religious experience of all of humankind.

[14]Ibid., 11. When this slim, apologetically-oriented volume was written (first edition, 1968, entitled *Christianity at the Center*), the "God is dead" discussion was in full swing.

interfaces these and the insights of classical theology and philosophy with the fresh perspectives of phenomenologists of religion and his own penetrating analysis of the problems of religious language.

When dealing with the theology of religious pluralism, Hick does not attempt to establish the truth of the relevant Christian beliefs; he assumes them as a starting point of his inquiry.[15] Moreover, a very practical and pastoral interest can be found in Hick's writings and lectures. His "second-order" reflection on the nature and logic of faith is often superseded by his manifest care for the needs of others, whether it be a place of worship for the Sikh community in Birmingham, or educational or chaplaincy needs of the ethnic minorities in hospitals and schools, or in offering hope to people of a further experience of learning and encounter with God beyond death.

THE "COPERNICAN REVOLUTION" IN THEOLOGY

In the early 1970s Hick began to construct a Christian theology of religions. To that end, he found it necessary to make decisive shifts from what he has termed a Ptolemaic, one's-own-religion-centered, to a Copernican, God-centered, view of the religious life of humanity.[16] Several factors contributed to this shift.

---

[15]This is not to say that he does not in other circumstances argue for the reasonableness of holding Christian beliefs. See *God and the Universe of Faiths: Essays in the Philosophy of Religion* (London: Macmillan Press, 1973) 1-17, and *An Interpretation of Religion* (New Haven: Yale University Press, 1989) 210ff., in which he argues for the rationality of religious belief; however, Christianity instantiates no privileged status that can be claimed to be more believable.

[16]This perspective was first published in an essay in *God and the Universe of Faiths* entitled "The Copernican Revolution in Theology." He has further developed this construction in *Problems of Religious Pluralism* (New York: St. Martin's Press, 1985) 99ff.

Phenomenology of Worship

Initially, a phenomenology of worship was a persuasive component in Hick's reformulation. On phenomenological grounds, Hick asserts, one cannot distinguish a superior form of worship; the same kind of thing takes place in the synagogue, the mosque, the temple, as in the church. It is, in each case,

> human beings . . . coming together to open their minds to a higher reality, which is thought of as the personal creator and Lord of the universe, and as making vital moral demands upon the lives of men and women.[17]

The overlap and confluence of the faiths come in the dynamics of worship.

Ptolemaic Theology

Ptolemaic theology, in Hick's conceptual apparatus, is the doctrinal position summarized in the classic *extra ecclesiam salus*,[18] which was officially held in Roman Catholic theology until the Second Vatican Council 1963-65. Until the council's historic reformulation, "The Declaration on the Relation of the Church to Non-Christian Religions,"[19] various explanations were ventured to circumvent the stringency of Cyprian's dictum without repudiating it as dogma.[20]

---

[17]"Whatever Path Men Choose is Mine," 9. Cf. John Hick, "Towards a Philosophy of Religious Pluralism," *Neue Zeitschrift für Systematische Theologie and Religionsphilosophie* 22 (1980): 132, and his article "On Grading Religions," published in *Problems of Religious Pluralism*, 67ff. Cf. Raimundo Pannikar, *The Intra-Religious Dialogue* (New York: Paulist Press, 1978), who separates "faith" from "belief" as a means of enabling a non-pejorative religious encounter.

[18]*God and the Universe of Faiths*, 125.

[19]*The Declaration on the Relation of the Church to Non-Christian Religions* (Glen Rock NJ: Paulist Press, 1966). Cf. René Latourelle, ed., *Vatican II: Assessment and Perspectives*, vol. 1 (New York: Paulist Press, 1988), and Avery Dulles, *The Reshaping of Catholicism: Current Challenges in the Theology of the Church* (San Francisco: Harper and Row, 1988) for an updating on the effect of this and other Vatican II impulses.

[20]Two ideas utilized were: "implicit faith" and "baptism by desire." These were designed to incorporate those who by no fault of their own were outside the Roman Catholic Church.

Hick calls these attempts "epicycles"—reminiscent of the epicycles added to the old Ptolemaic picture of the universe to accommodate newly discovered knowledge about the movement and relationship of the planets.[21] This explanation of the universe grew increasingly cumbersome and finally people could discard it and assimilate the Copernican conception of the sun at the center of the universe.

God at the Center of the Universe of Faiths

Hick suggests that Christian theology must make the same conceptual shift; God is the center of the universe of faiths, not Christianity. Epicycles such as claiming members of other faiths as "anonymous Christians"[22] or suggesting that other religions provide "ordinary ways of salvation" over against the "extraordinary way" of the church[23] are useful in that they, in a provisional way, acknowledge salvation outside the church, but they do not go far enough.[24] They still "assume without question that salvation is only in Christ and through incorporation into his mystical body, the church."[25]

Hick contends that, from the Ptolemaic perspective, only a slender strand of the world's peoples have any hope of salvation, a position sensitive Christians can no longer tolerate. The Copernican Revolution would allow all the great world

---

[21]*God and the Universe of Faiths*, 124.

[22]Karl Rahner, *Theological Investigations*, vol. 5 (Baltimore: Helicon Press, 1966) 131.

[23]Hans Küng, "The World Religions in God's Plan of Salvation," *Christian Revelation and the World Religions*, Joseph Neuner, S.J., ed. (London: Burns and Oates, 1967) 51ff. See Paul Knitter's critique of Rahner and Küng in his article "Towards a Liberation Theology of Religions," in *The Myth of Christian Uniqueness*, John Hick and Paul F. Knitter, eds. (Maryknoll: Orbis Books, 1987) 182-83. Cf. Aloysius Pieris, "The Place of Non-Christian Religions and Cultures in the Evolution of Third World Theology," in *Irruption of the Third World: Challenge to Theology*, Virginia Fabella and Sergio Torres, eds. (Maryknoll: Orbis Books, 1983) 113-14.

[24]*God and the Universe of Faiths*, 124.

[25]Ibid., 126.

faiths to be different responses to the divine reality, all conditioned by the different streams of human culture within which they have developed.[26]

Conflicting Truth Claims About God?

In placing God at the center of the universe of faiths, the Copernican Revolution presents a problem; namely, the fact that the pictures of the divine reality held by the different religions are at great variance with one another. Can they all be true? Rather than regarding this disparity as the conflict of truth claims, Hick believes that because God is infinite, no one picture can comprehend the divine nature. The same divine reality has always been seeking to reveal God's own being to humankind, and the different perceptions of this revelation are due to differing mentalities and temperaments of the persons responding.[27] To seek to grade these perceptions may involve a "pretence to a divine perspective;"[28] therefore, the Christian must not absolutize a point of view, assuming that a contextualized perspective represents knowledge of the divine reality as it is in itself. Indeed, one community's affirmation does not contradict the affirmations of other communities, since each can be understood as expressing how God is related to them. Quite often this involves only one aspect of God's nature.

Moreover, Hick argues that even the claims that God is personal or impersonal are not, finally, mutually exclusive. He believes "that the sense of the divine as non-personal may indeed reflect an aspect of the same infinite reality that is encountered as personal in theistic religious experience."[29] Despite

---

[26]"Whatever Path Men Choose is Mine," 14.

[27]*God and the Universe of Faiths*, 138-39.

[28]John Hick, "On Grading Religions," *Religious Studies* 17 (1981): 451. See also his "Religious Pluralism and Absolute Claims," in *Problems of Religious Pluralism* (New York: St. Martin's Press, 1985): 46-65.

[29]*God and the Universe of Faiths*, 144.

Christianity's emphasis on God as personal Being, there is the recorded experience of God as other than personal, such as that expressed by the Christian mystics.[30]

CHRISTOLOGICAL PERSPECTIVE

The linchpin of Hick's relativistic assertions is his non-incarnational Christology. Understanding this facet of his thinking is of key importance to this study.

The Myth of Incarnation

Hick's schematization places Christianity as one way of salvation amidst others, and thus clearly clashes with the historic view of Christianity as the exclusive bearer of salvation. Christians have maintained this position because of their affirmation of Christ's divinity; however, Hick suggests that Christians have claimed more for Jesus than can be historically substantiated. His method for resolving this dilemma is his understanding of the nature or logic of the mythological language of divinity.[31]

Sounding very much like the doctrinal formulations of Maurice Wiles,[32] Professor Hick argues that the traditional Nicene and Chalcedonian incarnational Christology, the product of the Graeco-Roman world, is not the only way to

---

[30]Ibid., 144-45. Dorothee Soelle, *Strength of the Weak: Toward a Christian Feminist Identity* (Philadelphia: Westminster, 1984) 96-105, suggests a way of utilizing the resources of the mystics in appropriating a non-personal view of God as a means of overcoming exclusive gender-specific designations of God; however, these are not to be used exclusively, for God is also eternally Thou.

[31]See the essay, "Religions as Fact-Asserting," *God and the Universe of Faiths*, 18-36, for an explication of Hick's method. Gavin D'Costa, *John Hick's Theology of Religions* (Lanham/New York/London: University Press of America, 1987) 130ff., offers a helpful critique of Hick's use of incarnational language. Professor G.W.H. Lampe's book, *God as Spirit* (Oxford: Oxford University Press, 1977), also attempts to replace the model of incarnation as a way of understanding the presence of God in Jesus with that of inspiration.

[32]Maurice Wiles, "Does Christology Rest on a Mistake?" in *Christ, Faith and History*, S.W. Sykes and J.P. Clayton, eds. (Cambridge: Cambridge University Press, 1972).

conceptualize the lordship of Jesus.[33] Because "substance thinking" is too static and has no currency today, Hick believes it is more fruitful to use dynamic categories of action rather than of being because they more accurately reflect the biblical mode of thinking.[34] He suggests that in seeking to express what "incarnation" means today one should speak of the identity of divine and human activities of *agapé* love;[35] in Jesus' actions God's *Agapé* was enacting itself.

The doctrine of the divinity of Christ must be understood as a mythological expression of the Christian's total devotion to Jesus as Lord and Savior,[36] the one in whose presence he or she has found himself or herself to be at the same time in the presence of God. It was this experience of transforming salvation that prompted persons to use divinity language when speaking about Christ—something Jesus himself did not do, Hick claims.[37]

Hick does not believe that Jesus ever proclaimed himself to be God incarnate,[38] although he admits that he may have employed the title "Messiah"

---

[33]John Hick, "Jesus and the World Religions," *The Myth of God Incarnate*, John Hick, ed. (London: SCM Press, 1977) 168. Cf. the argument by Bernard Lonergan, *A Second Collection* (Philadelphia: Westminster Press, 1974) 22-27, which maintains that the Nicene Creed was metaphorical language for its most important doctrines, without mitigating its cognitive value.

[34]*God and the Universe of Faiths*, 149-51.

[35]Ibid., 165. An important article of Hick's is his contribution to the Farmer *Festschrift* in which he argued for the last time against a degree Christology. This marks an important transition in his thinking. See John Hick, "Christology at the Crossroads," *Prospect for Theology: Essays in Honour of H.H. Farmer*, F.G. Healey, ed. (London: Nisbet, 1966) 147-66.

[36]"Jesus and the World Religions," 178.

[37]"Whatever Path Men Choose is Mine," 15. C.F.D. Moule, "The Manhood of Jesus in the New Testament," in *Christ, Faith, and History: Cambridge Studies in Christology*, S.W. Sykes and J.P. Clayton, eds. (Cambridge: Cambridge University Press, 1972) 101, notes the difficulty the biblical writers have in reconciling the twin convictions of the humanity *and* divinity of Jesus.

[38]*God and the Universe of Faiths*, 163.

or the heavenly "Son of Man," which connoted a human being called to be God's special servant.[39] Hick argues for major christological development from the picture of Jesus recorded in Acts and the Synoptics, to the transcendent pre-existent Logos and the exalted Christological sayings placed on the lips of Jesus in the Fourth Gospel,[40] from whose texts the church has drawn its major support for its exclusivistic position and its exalted C'hristology.

The Gospel of John is a profound theological meditation, Hick argues, written late in the first century, expressing a Christian interpretation of Jesus. Moreover, Hick avers that John is a re-writing of Jesus' teaching.[41] In the Synoptics, the "Kingdom of God" is the focus, but in the Fourth Gospel, Jesus himself is the subject of his teaching and preaching; the church has followed John to the neglect of the more primitive strand in the first three gospels, in Hick's opinion.[42]

Certainly Jesus was more spiritually sensitive to God than his contemporaries and was aware of God's special claim upon his life in the same manner that Gautama or the Buddha was; subsequently, each human teacher was exalted into a divine figure of universal power, in the case of Christianity, to the Second Person of the Trinity.[43] Hick explains:

> Thus it was natural and intelligible both that Jesus, through whom men
> had found a decisive encounter with God and a new and better life,

---

[39]"Whatever Path Men Choose is Mine," 14. The "Son of Man" literature is quite extensive. Two studies are of particular import: M.D. Hooker, *The Son of Man in Mark* (London: S.P.C.K., 1967), and Barnabas Lindars, "Re-enter the Apocalyptic Son of Man," *New Testament Studies* 22 (no date) 52-72.

[40]Ibid. Cf. *God and the Universe of Faiths*, 114ff.

[41]"Jesus and the World Religions," 171-77.

[42]Ibid. It is, by no means, the consensus of contemporary gospel scholarship that John's Gospel is a later, non-historical account of Jesus' proclamation and ministry. John A.T. Robinson's, *The Priority of John* (London: SCM Press, 1985), argues cogently for the priority of the fourth gospel both historically and theologically.

[43]Ibid., 168, 171, 173.

should have come to be hailed as Son of God, and that later this poetry
should have hardened into prose and escalated from a metaphorical son
of God to a metaphysical God the Son, of the same substance as the
Father within the triune Godhead. This was an effective way, within that
cultural milieu, of expressing Jesus' significance as the one through
whom men had transformingly encountered God.[44]

Nevertheless, "incarnation has no *literal* meaning,"[45] Hick bluntly states;
it is a figure of speech or a piece of poetic imagery.[46] Indeed, whenever theologians have tried to articulate its meaning, its language has been pressed to the
point of heresy.[47] Thus it remains a "form of words without assignable
meaning."[48] The Chalcedonian formula stands, but uninterpreted. Hick concludes
that "the real point and value of the incarnational doctrine is not indicative but
expressive, not to assert a metaphysical fact, but to express a valuation and evoke
an attitude."[49]

---

[44]Ibid., 176.

[45]"Whatever Path Men Choose is Mine," 15. John Bowden, *Jesus: The Unanswered Questions* (Nashville: Abingdon Press, 1989) 82ff., argues that the problematic conception of incarnation was created through combining two very different spheres of thought: "the sphere of mythology and cosmic drama characteristic of the world of first-century Judaism, and the more sophisticated world of Greek metaphysical philosophy." See his analysis of the impact of the volume, *The Myth of God Incarnate*, edited by Hick (87ff.).

[46]Ibid.

[47]Ibid. Cf. "Jesus and the World Religions," 178-79, and his essay, "Is There a Doctrine of the Incarnation?" *Incarnation and Myth: The Debate Continued*, Michael Goulder, ed. (London: SCM Press, 1979) 48.

[48]"Jesus and the World Religions," 178.

[49]Ibid. Hans Küng struggles at length to give assignation to "incarnation" in his magisterial volume, *The Incarnation of God* (New York: Crossroad, 1977); interestingly, he returns to Hegel for assistance in speaking of the mystery of incarnation. Hegel argues, and Küng follows him, that the Spirit is immediately present in the historical existence of Jesus Christ in the shape of self-consciousness (209). God thus "passes through a 'life history'" (210) as the Absolute Being externalizes itself in the actual world.

Implications for Doctrine of Atonement

The doctrine of the atonement is suspect for Hick because

> in his own lifetime, and without any reference to his death, Jesus taught
> the love of God, and brought men and women into a new and reconciled
> relationship with him as their heavenly Father.[50]

There was no hint in Jesus' teaching, contends Hick, that during his ministry God was angry and unloving and that his death would be the means to rectify this alienation. Rather the ancient concept of benefit for Israel being provided through the sufferings of a righteous servant of God was re-stated through such texts as the "ransom" saying in Mark 10:45 and Matt 28:20. These came to be transposed, however, into a cosmic transaction which was the pivot for all relationships between God and humanity.[51]

Hick simply finds the evidence lacking for the idea that the death of Jesus transformed God's relationship to persons so that God was enabled to love them; besides, the idea that the Cross transforms God's nature is not theologically viable, because Jesus' revelation of the "loving Father" (to use Hick's language) contradicts it.[52] Further, most atonement theories (e.g., the classic or the satisfaction theories) are equally unsatisfactory for they are based on antiquated redemption myths, in Hick's estimation. They presuppose literal rather than metaphorical incarnation concepts which insert God temporarily into the human process, an idea which is indefensible logically.[53]

---

[50]John Hick, "Incarnation and Atonement: Evil and Incarnation," *Incarnation and Myth: The Debate Continued*, 77.

[51]Ibid., 78.

[52]Ibid., 82.

[53]Ibid., 81. Hick and the other contributors to *The Myth of God Incarnate* maintain that it is more accurate to assert God's continuing awareness and sympathy with the sufferings of God's children than to insist that only through the incarnation was there identification and co-suffering with them.

Hick distinguishes the revelatory understanding of the incarnation and cross from the transactional view. The latter, which insists that an unrepeatable debt for human sin was paid in the cross of Christ, if it be true, has only reached a limited minority of persons. Its culture-specific imagery of blood sacrifice has only infrequently hurdled the communication barriers between the different strands of humanity, in Hick's opinion.[54] Its historical particularity precludes a universal cognizance of its significance. A revelatory understanding of the cross is more tenable, for it allows God to reveal God's being through other key religious figures for the sake of other sections of humankind.[55]

Resurrection and Divinity

The divinity of Christ cannot be sustained by adducing the resurrection, Hick declares, because "we cannot ascertain today in what this resurrection-event consisted."[56] The raising of Jesus, because it was not a unique happening in first-century Palestine, gave him no distinctive status. Even if it could be adequately and accurately depicted, the resurrection still would not be proof of Jesus' divinity, for it was God who raised him, not his own divine nature.[57]

SOTERIOLOGICAL PERSPECTIVE

Salvation is the central business of religion,[58] Hick affirms, and thus must be characterized in such a way that men and women can readily identify it

---

[54]In contrast, René Girard, *The Scapegoat*, Yvonne Freccero, trans. (Baltimore: Johns Hopkins University Press, 1986), maintains that the innocent visitor whose blood is shed by violent, guilty persons is a major motif in all mythology. Collective violence demands a scapegoat.

[55]Ibid., 83.

[56]"Jesus and the World Religions," 170.

[57]Ibid., 171. Hick places the raising of Lazarus (John 11:1-44), a widow's son (Luke 7:11-17), and Jairus' daughter (Mark 5:35-43) on the same level as the resurrection-event of Jesus.

[58]*The Centre of Christianity*, 74.

in terms of the actual quality of human existence. As one might imagine, Hick deliberately sketches his concept of salvation with broad enough strokes to embrace all the religions.

"Salvation" presupposes a situation that needs redeeming, or perhaps, to be brought to completion. The reality of evil and suffering and death in the world raises significant questions about the meaningfulness of human existence and the actuality of a good God in the face of these tragedies. It is the witness of all the great world religions that human existence, as it is perceived by a wide variety of persons, is "fallen, wrapped in illusion, and full of suffering; and that nevertheless a far better state is possible, a state of perfection, fulfillment as a child of God."[59]

Historically, two explanations in the Christian tradition have dealt theologically with the mystery of evil and the necessity of salvation: the Augustinian and the Irenaean types of theodicy. Hick employs the latter in his typology of salvation, and this approach is given attention in the following section.

The Typology of Salvation: The Irenaean View

Hick distinguishes the Augustinian view from the Irenaean view. The Augustinian framework has the meaning of evil in the past; it bears the concept of a wholly good world in which Adam and Eve rebelled against the Creator, and thence disorder perverted the pristine state of righteousness. This theory does not allow any positive existence to evil (so as to avoid any hint of dualism), and it is simply regarded as a *privatio boni*—the absence of the proper goodness. Therefore, God is free from any responsibility for the existence of evil because all occurrences of natural evil and moral evil are linked to the fall of the primeval pair.[60] Hick assesses this approach as an inadequate and self-contradictory

---

[59]John Hick, "Present and Future Life," *Harvard Theological Review* 71 (1978): 10.

[60]*The Centre of Christianity*, 83.

mythological theodicy, and chooses, instead, to accentuate the model first proposed by Irenaeus and other Hellenistic fathers.[61]

Hick argues that the Irenaean view was forward-looking in its perspective, teleological and eschatological in nature. Depending on Gen 1:26, Irenaeus suggested that Adam and Eve were not perfect beings who fatefully fell, thereby foiling God's original intention for them; rather, they were created good (in God's *image*) as rational, personal, and moral beings, but they were immature and needed to grow towards God's *likeness*, ultimately to be revealed through Jesus Christ. In other words, this approach views the human being as still in the process of creation, with perfection to be attained in the future.[62] This view mirrors the Augustinian scheme in that each person is viewed as a "fallen" creature—centered upon himself or herself—and is thus "still involved in what theology calls original sinfulness, which is not the result of a primal calamity but represents a state in God's creative plan."[63] One grows towards the divine likeness through free moral responses to the giveness of the world's hardships and challenges.[64]

Furthermore, the world is so constructed as to be a place of "soul-making" or "person-making."[65] The universe is designed to train humankind ethically.[66]

---

[61]Hick cites Schleiermacher as a key proponent of the Irenaean form of theodicy; in his opinion, he was responsible for reviving it over against the dominant Augustinian position. See Hick's *Evil and the God of Love*, rev. ed. (New York: Harper and Row, 1978) 219-40, and Friedrich Schleiermacher, *The Christian Faith*, H.R. Mackintosh and J.S. Stewart, eds. (Philadelphia: Fortress Press, 1976) 233-304.

[62]*The Centre of Christianity*, 85. See also Hick's *Death and Eternal Life* (New York: Harper and Row, 1976) 252-53. This view is quite compatible with a theistic evolutionary framework, such as that of Teilhard de Chardin.

[63]*The Centre of Christianity*, 86. Cf. "Present and Future Life," 9.

[64]*Death and Eternal Life*, 48.

[65]*The Centre of Christianity*, 87.

[66]*Death and Eternal Life*, 244.

The evil in the world, for which God is ultimately responsible,[67] is not sent as punishment, but is the instrument of a loving Parent who is gradually creating "children of God" out of human animals.[68] Therefore, salvation can only be thought of as a process characterized by persons learning to respond maturely and morally to the hard demands of living responsibly in this sort of world. God's strategy is to overcome evil with good, and, Hick declares, "the meaning of our present earthly life lies precisely in this struggle."[69] God is ever-seeking to draw persons into the ultimate battle against evil.

The Structure of Salvation

By accentuating the Irenaean framework, Hick's soteriology has some nuances not found in the more dominant Augustinian perspective. Ostensibly the understanding of salvation seen through the lens of the Hellenistic fathers (Irenaeus, Clement, et al.) has more in common with the other great world religions than with its counterpart in the Christian tradition.

Salvation is the transformation of life. A comparative study of religions reveals a rather common soteriological structure: the offering of a transition from a "radically unsatisfactory state to a limitlessly better one."[70] Although each structure describes the human problem and the liberated state with its own graphic distinctiveness, the transition, in each case, is from self-centeredness to Reality centeredness.[71] Salvation is a transforming process whereby people

---

[67]Hick believes it to be much more consistent to say that God created a world in which evil can occur because of the profoundly good over-all strategy for human development. Augustinianism seeks to absolve God of any responsibility by making the human creature culpable, but it only succeeds in making God look vindictive because of its accompanying view of predestination: God created free beings whom God knew would choose wrongly; when they do, they are damned. Because God set the situation up in this fashion, God is responsible, in Hick's judgment.

[68]*The Centre of Christianity*, 74.

[69]Ibid., 87.

[70]"On Grading Religions," 452.

[71]Ibid., 453. By "Reality-centeredness" Hick means God, as defined by the different religions.

become—individually and corporately—the persons God wills to create.[72] Persons freely enter a more wholistic quality "through immeasurable choices of self-transcendence;"[73] a more liberated state is never imposed by God, but is gained through genuinely free human response.

Salvation is contextual. Hick firmly believes that one's birthplace is the major determinant as to how one understands and structures salvation.[74] It is evident to all that the different religions have their different means of expressing how God has acted savingly towards them.[75] When one is born to Buddhist parents in Sri Lanka, he or she becomes, predictably, a Buddhist. The birth of a child in an Islamic culture practically insures that this one will think of God as Allah the all-merciful and will see the way of salvation as submission to the divine will as revealed in the Qur'an.

In addition, there seems to be a cultural insulation that mitigates conversion from one of the great world religions to another, because missionary endeavor only appears to be fruitful among the peoples of the "primal" religions.[76] Clearly, most persons live out their lives of faith in the cultural stream of religion into which they were born. Hick thinks that this situation makes blasphemous the traditional idea in Christianity that only Christians have the possibility of salvation. More than seventy-five percent of the world's people would be excluded by geographical accident if that were true. Exclusivism with regard to salvation jeopardizes the Christian understanding of God,[77] Hick concludes.

---

[72]"Is There Only One Way to God?" 5. A recent work by Richard Viladesau, *Answering for Faith: Christ and the Human Search for Salvation* (New York and Mahwah: Paulist Press, 1987), grounds this search and actualization in a christologically defined anthropology.

[73]"Present and Future and Life," 11.

[74]*God and the Universe of Faiths*, 138.

[75]"Jesus and the World Religions," 181.

[76]"On Grading Religions," 456.

[77]"Is There Only One Way to God?" 6.

Salvation is the work of the Logos. It is possible, however, to express God's saving activity toward humankind as the work of the Logos as long as one does not contend that the Logos found expression only in Jesus of Nazareth.[78] The Christian can only say that in Christ he or she has experienced God's saving presence. The Christian errs when making the negative assertion that the Logos has worked through no other human vehicle than Christ and no other way of faith but the Christian way.

Salvation is a process that extends beyond death. If salvation is a process characterized as the transformation of life to a better quality of human existence, (e.g., to become children of God) based upon human choices, it appears that for the great majority of persons this salvation is never actualized, or at least the transformation is not completed at death.[79] For many whose whole lives have been marked by deprivation of food or peace, experiencing little of the material, cultural, and aesthetic offerings of this world, salvation is a truncated concept. In light of their frustrated desires and lack of realization of their human potential, Hick says it is proper and necessary to ask whether such actualization is to be accomplished instantaneously at each individual's death, as Roman Catholic theology has suggested, or whether it requires further living beyond death.[80] Hick prefers to accept "the unanimous witness of the great religious traditions to a further life or lives beyond death,"[81] believing such a view to make the most

---

[78]"Jesus and the World Religions," 181.

[79]*God and the Universe of Faiths*, 35.

[80]"Present and Future Life," 9.

[81]Ibid., 11. In this article, Hick interacts with scientists, philosophers, and theologians on the issues related to the mind/brain identity hypothesis. He criticizes both Wolfhart Pannenberg and Gordon Kaufman for accepting a naturalistic view of the human being, i.e., the concept of the end of the body being the end of the person. He believes that theologians posit a disembodied consciousness when imagining God, and thus should have some frame of reference for inferring a non-material human mind. The debate about the status of the mental life is far from over, Hick asserts, and feels it odd that so many theologians have prematurely adopted a monistic view.

sense of the toils and challenges of the environment in which persons live. Would there be any point to the struggle if there were no chance of completing this creative process? Hick says no.

Hick points to three great themes that run through all of the world's great religions which make further life for humans beyond death necessary: 1) the immense potentialities of the human spirit which are fulfilled in relationship with the divine reality; 2) the realization that this potential requires transcending the selfish claims of personal egos and moving into wholistic corporate forms of life; and 3) the transcendence of the isolated self-centered existence comes through the voluntary relinquishment of it.[82] He believes the Irenaean structure is the most constructive for achieving these goals; it is a framework over which all of the faiths can stretch the canvases bearing their visions of salvation.

Hick's rejection of juridical conceptions of salvation further augments the case for continued growth and development after the present life. By juridical, Hick means judging a person on the basis of his or her moral development or righteous acts without regard to individual circumstances and opportunities for growth. A notion such as purgatory limits the evaluation of one's personhood to the character of one's earthly life. It would be the grossest of injustices, Hick vehemently declares, to measure all by the same criteria given the vast differences of moral and spiritual advantage.[83]

The Universality of Salvation

Within the New Testament, one can find both universalist and non-universalist passages, Hick says. The standard argument for universalism is based

---

Hick also refutes the prevalent concept among theologians which asserts that a concern for personal immortality is an irreligious or selfish concern. He grants that it smacks of this if it is the perpetuation of our "grubby little egos" which is the chief concern; but, the concept itself is not immoral and irreligious.

[82]"Present and Future Life," 6-8. Hick contrasts the "eschatalogical myths" of the Indian and Semitic traditions in *An Interpretation of Religion*, 355ff.

[83]Ibid., 11. Hick is less interested in freeing God from responsibility for past and present evils than in showing how a certain hope for the future may keep faith from being falsified by those evils.

on the fact of a loving God who wills to save all persons. Because God is almighty and good, the divine goal will not be frustrated, and all will eventually be saved. The *contra* side of the argument adds the premise of the freedom of the human will, and, accordingly, concludes that some may not freely choose God's salvation. Hick's analysis seeks to push the debate past this impasse.[84]

Contradictory biblical evidence? Hick believes that universalism is not ruled out by the biblical evidence;[85] indeed, he believes that it best reflects the intention of the New Testament. Two sets of utterances speak to the problem, however, supporting the two sides of the antinomy. One group of statements is composed of the sayings of Jesus in which eternal damnation is a viable possibility for those who do not repent and turn to God, such as Luke 6:23-4, Matt 23:14, Matt 5:26, and Matt 18:34-5. Several of these are prophetic denunciations which serve as warnings and do not imply a final separation of the saved and the lost. Otherwise, it would seem that "the divinely ordained moral order of the world would be extremely crude if all the judgment sayings were rightly held to involve eternal heaven and hell."[86] It is more constructive, he believes, to see gradations of condemnation rather than a single dichotomy between infinite penalty and infinite reward.[87]

Whereas the judgment sayings are fairly common, Hick's analysis suggests that there is a paucity of passages which seem to point to eternal loss and punishment. He distinguishes only one passage in the synoptic tradition, Matt

---

[84]*Death and Eternal Life*, 242.

[85]Hick affirms the practical certainty, as opposed to the logical possibility, of universal salvation. This ". . . is an aspect of Christian hope" he argues in *Evil and the God of Love*, 381. Like John A.T. Robinson, Hick's views on universalism have been profoundly influenced by his teacher at Westminster College in Cambridge University, H.H. Farmer. See Farmer's *The World of God*, rev. ed. (London: Nisbet and Co., Ltd., 1955) 255-59. See Robinson's *In the End God* (New York: Harper and Row, 1968) 110-33.

[86]*Death and Eternal Life*, 244.

[87]Ibid.

25:41-46, in which an ultimate dual destiny seems to be clearly affirmed. Maintaining Marcan priority, he examines the context of the passage and thrust of Matthew's gospel and concludes the saying is not original in the *Sitz im Leben* of Jesus, but reflected the "life of the church during the post-apostolic age of persecution."[88]

More important for Hick is his argument for an all-loving God who would not allow everlasting suffering. Further, a doctrine of hell would imply the failure of God's purpose of redemption.

While the Fourth Gospel has more emphasis on eternal life and eternal death than the Synoptics, it also indicates that the division between the two has already, in some sense, been ratified.[89] The perspective of John, then, does not relate to the question of the freedom of human decision-making about one's relationship to God, Hick observes, and should not be adduced as evidence in the universalist/non-universalist contest. Concluding what he deemed a comprehensive examination of the non-universalist passages, Hick writes, "The confident assertion that Jesus threatened or predicted eternal torment is not so securely based as has often been assumed."[90] Even if Jesus did threaten eternal punishment, there is another strand of witness of the New Testament that implies the salvation of all persons and the restoration of the whole created order.[91]

In this regard, Paul's epistolary material is a primary source for Hick. The Pauline material contains a much earlier witness of the church, in his opinion,[92]

---

[88]Ibid., 246. D'Costa, *John Hick's Theology of Religions*, 57, observes the marginal role historical-critical studies of biblical material played in Hick's earliest christological writings. His article in *The Myth of God Incarnate* makes a shift from a more philosophical argument to one buttressed by biblical criticism.

[89]Ibid.

[90]Ibid.

[91]Ibid., 247.

[92]Ibid.

than that in the Gospels. Although Hick is reticent to trumpet Paul as an unequivocal universalist, he feels the inner logic of his writings unmistakably suggests universal salvation.[93]

Knowing that it would be methodologically unsound and too facile to pit the sayings of Jesus against those of Paul, Hick offers a different means of argument. It is necessary, he contends, to recognize that the two sets of statements "belong to quite different situational contexts and fulfil quite different functions."[94] Paul's statements are to be viewed as mature theological reflection for the church while the sayings of Jesus are undoubtedly more existential in tone, for he was wrestling with individuals who were heading towards destruction.[95] Moreover, they are not incompatible:

> The danger which Jesus declared so starkly is a most real danger. Unless you repent you will inevitably come to total and irretrievable misery and frustration. But it does not follow from the fact of this danger that you or I or anyone else is in fact never going to repent and be saved.[96]

Hick urges contemporary interpreters to employ Paul's perspective, which is to see the concrete life situations of individuals in relation to God's ultimate providence.

Having reviewed the relevant New Testament material, Hick turns to engage the problem of human freedom. From the outset, he dismisses any sort of "double decree" as antithetical to a proper doctrine of God.[97] Predestination

---

[93]Ibid., 248. Arland Hultgren, *Christ and His Benefits: Christology and Redemption in the New Testament* (Philadelphia: Fortress Press, 1987) 195ff. shares this view, granting the Pauline perspective a privileged status.

[94]Ibid.

[95]Ibid., 248-49.

[96]Ibid., 250.

[97]Ibid., 250-51.

couched in that perspective ineluctably belies freedom and responsibility, in his opinion.

Universalism and the doctrine of creation. One must look to the doctrine of creation, Hick advises, for the biblical solution to the problem of how one can posit universal salvation without having to forfeit human freedom through ascribing coercive activity to God.[98] Sounding much like Augustine, Hick describes creation as being bent towards God who has created human beings for Godself.[99] The *telos* of one's life, the inexorable pull in the direction of the actualization of one's proper good, is due to the divine structuring of human nature.[100] There is no need for coercion, for human nature was created to move towards God.[101] Only there will human hearts "find rest." God aids persons in fulfilling what their own inner natures desire to be, but that does not mean God has violated their freedom and responsibility.[102] Hick rightly accentuates the reality that human freedom is always contingent freedom because we are created beings, and he maintains that God can carry saving work to completion without negating genuine autonomous human response.

---

[98]Ibid., 251. Cf. "Present and Future Life," 10-11. See Hick's lengthy analysis of Augustine's treatment of this paradox in *Evil and the God of Love*, 59-69.

[99]Ibid. Cf. *Evil and the God of Love*, 48f.

[100]Ibid. See *God and the Universe of Faiths*, 96.

[101]Hick is well aware of the extended debate about the structure and content of the "image of God." He indicates that the Irenaean view moves beyond the Catholic/Reformed *cul-de-sac* which revolves around one's capacity to respond to God; the Irenaean view regards the image of God as a given (because the Fall is not given the same veracity as in the Augustinian view), and the likeness is the perfection of one's nature in relation to God, towards which each person instinctively moves.

[102]*Death and Eternal Life*, 253-56. Hick says that to be human presupposes forces beyond oneself and thus any usable view of human freedom must be compatible with that presupposition. Cf. Hendrikus Berkhof, *Christian Faith*, rev. ed. (Grand Rapids: Eerdmans, 1986), 187ff., for a helpful discussion of the human being as "respondable," which implies concomitant freedom.

ECCLESIOLOGICAL PERSPECTIVE

Hick has few constructive proposals for ecclesiology because a doctrine of the church occupies such a peripheral sphere in his theological program. He believes that the phase of "Ptolemaic Christianity" is summarized in *extra ecclesiam nulla salus*. Hence, most of his remarks about the church are denunciatory. The church is "the human corruption of the Kingdom of God which came on earth in the person of Jesus of Nazareth";[103] it is a "stumbling block to almost anyone who is drawn to Jesus;"[104] and it has tried to confine Jesus within its theoretical constructions.[105] All of these evils have contributed to an "ecclesiocentric" rather than a "theocentric" view of the universe of faiths, he asserts.[106]

The Church as a Human Community

Hick firmly believes that the church has been, throughout its history, something very different from what Jesus intended.[107] Like other human communities, it has developed along recognized sociological principles; and, thus, its structure is really no different from them.[108]

---

[103]*The Centre of Christianity*, 66-67.

[104]Ibid.

[105]"Jesus and the World Religions," 183.

[106]Hick criticizes Rahner for his imperialistic "ecclesiocentrism." See his *God Has Many Names*, 27, 68. Cf. D'Costa's analysis of Hick's understanding of *extra ecclesiam nulla salus* in *John Hick's Theology of Religions*, 73-85.

[107]*God and the Universe of Faiths*, 92.

[108]Cf. Peter Slater, *The Dynamics of Religion: Continuity and Change in Patterns of Faith* (London: SCM Ltd., 1978). Slater analyzes how persons keep alive the faith of ancestors and adapt it to present circumstances. He contends that the dynamics of religions can only be understood by reference to the present interplay of past and future considerations. Cf. W.C. Smith, *The Meaning and End of Religion: A Revolutionary Approach to the Great Religions of Tradition* (New York: Macmillan, 1962). Hick

The church was inevitable. The message of the Galilean was community-oriented; relationship with Jesus served as the presupposition for relationship with others. The church gives corporate expression to the power of transformation found in Jesus.

Hick can define "church" with little reference to the transcendent:

> So long as the person of Jesus of Nazareth is remembered, and gives rise
> to a continuing faith-response, the men and women in whom that faith-
> response occurs will be the church. . . .[109]

Originally a spirit-filled community built up around the apostolic core, by the time of Augustine the church had become "almost indistinguishably blended with the declining Roman Empire and the spirit that prevailed within it was that of imperial, and later, pontifical Rome."[110]

Summarizing the church's history as thoroughly corrupt, Hick gives little credence to the Spirit's continuing ministry through the church. He criticizes both Roman Catholic and Protestant provinces of Christianity for being "equally dominated by authoritarianism, attachment to property, and unimaginative lovelessness towards the outsider."[111]

The Mission of the Church

Hick regards the church's traditional view of its mission and missionary policies as defunct. The church must realize that its goal of "converting" the world has largely failed.[112] The miniscule percentage of converts to Christianity from

---

depends upon Smith's discussion of "cumulative traditions" for his own contribution to this area of study.

[109]*God and the Universe of Faiths*, 94.

[110]*The Centre of Christianity*, 67.

[111]Ibid., 68.

[112]"Jesus and the World Religions," 182.

the other world religions should have made clear long before now that "conversion" as the chief missionary endeavor is fallacious.

The shape of the church's mission must be restructured, Hick adamantly argues. The uniquely Christian gift to the world is Jesus, and the church should strive to bring people of the other faiths to know him and incorporate him into their religious life, "not to displace but to deepen and enlarge the relationship with God to which they have already come within their own tradition."[113] Christianity must welcome the different interpretations these religions will bring to the person of Jesus;[114] the fresh images cannot but be positive, in Hick's opinion. Any contemporary Christian mission strategy must be compatible with the recognition of other religions as valid ways of faith.

The Future of the Church

In the face of a rapidly growing secularization of society, many pre-secular forms of the church will die.[115] Hick believes that this is good and necessary if the church is going to have any authentically Christian witness in the years ahead. It is to be preferred to a myopic, entrenched, stagnant perseverance against culture rather than attempts to transform culture, to appropriate Richard Niebuhr's classic paradigms.

Hick submits two useful paths the church might take in its task of re-tooling for applicability to the needs of the present and future generations. First, it will be particularly significant for churches to strive towards ecumenicity. It is the most pragmatic way "to release the active core of the church . . . from the frustrating task of maintaining a self-defeating plethora of institutions."[116]

---

[113]Ibid., 181. J.A.T. Robinson, *Truth is Two-Eyed* (Philadelphia: Westminster Press, 1979) 120ff., sounds a similar note to Hick in this assertion, yet insists upon retaining the "decisiveness" of Christ.

[114]Ibid.

[115]*Christianity at the Centre*, 77.

[116]Ibid., 79.

Church reunion would permit the churches to reclaim their resources from self-serving purposes and put them more at the disposal of the needy of the world.

Second, Hick urges the church to move in the direction of an even larger global ecumenicity. The religions of the world must grow towards one another if they are to reflect their common origin in the different manifestations of the divine Logos.[117] As one might expect, Hick hopes that a common attitude and approach to the Divine may become ultimately possible.

EVALUATION

John Hick offers not an unattractive position in the quest for a tenable Christian theology of religious pluralism. In many respects, he has raised for the late twentieth century the same question of Lessing and Troeltsch as to whether any contingent historical fact can have more than relative significance. Indeed, he has presented a kind of meta-theology which strives to be universal, transcending what he sees as the scandalous particularity of the various religious systems. To be sure, his Copernican Revolution is a bold stroke, and it deserves a careful examination, for it advances an alternate route for those trudging the well-worn paths of Christian exclusivism.

The implications of Hick's argument urgently demand critical engagement because of their ravaging effects on traditional theological doctrines, especially Christology. Jesus would be stripped of time-honored dogmas about him as a consequence of Hick's new projection, which involves several assumptions about the nature of God and the impossibility of a christocentric theology of religions. Other issues such as Hick's biblical methodology, his understanding and use of mythological language, and the adequacy of his Christian perspective also require careful evaluation. In the material that follows, several general observations will precede a more detailed critique of his thought.

---

[117]Ibid., 80-81.

Hick's penetrating concern for a Christian evaluation of the adherents of non-Christian religions is laudable, and his writings have proved to be catalytic for many to re-think their pejorative stance over against these pious others. Reforms in the attitudes within the religious communities of Birmingham, to name one example, give practical evidence of his influence.[118]

"Ptolemaic Theology": A Caricature?

This writer believes that Hick is justifiably critical of those who have used *extra ecclesiam nulla salus* in its starkest form to deny that salvation is other than exclusively located within the visible structure of the Roman Catholic Church and of those who grant no valid perceptions of God outside Christianity. He ignores the fact, however, that the theological tradition of the church is much more diversified than his outlining of "Ptolemaic theology" portrays.[119] There have always been those within the Christian faith with a more inclusive attitude towards non-Christians who have, nevertheless, maintained Christ's uniqueness.[120]

Ostensibly he has erected a caricature ("Ptolemaic theology") that looks indefensible beside the ineluctable logic of the Copernican Revolution. To be sure, if Christianity were thoroughly exclusivisitic in the manner of his description, many Christians would like to find their place in his cartographical revision. If, as he has suggested, Christians have triumphalistically placed Christianity at the center, that does need correction. It would seem to be more accurate historically and theologically for Hick to admit that the majority of Christians have placed

---

[118]"Living in a Multi-cultural Society," 103-104; *God Has Many Names*, 38-40.

[119]Duncan B. Forrester, "Professor Hick and the Universe of Faiths," *Scottish Journal of Theology* 29 (1976): 67, believes Hick is unfair when he depicts Ptolemaic theology as the dominant expression of Christianity. Forrester says that "for a century and more among Protestants Hick's 'Ptolemaic theology' has been held by a small and uninfluential minority." The present writer thinks neither assessment is accurate.

[120]S. Mark Heim, *Is Christ the Only Way? Christian Faith in a Pluralistic World* (Valley Forge: Judson Press, 1985), delineates the varied options under this rubric in chapter seven, 111-27.

Christ at the center. In his Copernican Revolution, Hick subtly equates rejecting *extra ecclesiam nulla salus* to rejecting "salvation is through Christ alone." He does not sufficiently explain this identification. This step allows Hick to dispense with any attempt to construct a christocentric theology of religious pluralism.

Hick's criticism is more *a propos* when he castigates the practice of many "ptolemaic" Christian theologians who use inter-faith dialogue simply as a ploy for "conversions" of the non-Christians. Dialogue should be a means for a mutual and constructive search for truth.

Use of Mythological Language

Hick's definition of "myth" inadequately expresses the truth of the incarnation—that is, that God was in Christ—and probably should have been avoided. As he defines myth, it cannot be *literally* true; its truth lies in its power to evoke an appropriate attitude in its hearers.[121] The logical status of incarnational language is mythological rather than theoretical or literal. His sharp distinction between "literal" and "metaphorical" (which he uses interchangeably with mythological) usages of language lacks in precision.[122] He assumes that those who wish to speak of a "literal" incarnation only use it in a "wooden" fashion which no critically-minded person could countenance. The British philosopher of religion seems captive to a crude positivism when he asserts "the Christian image of a divine incarnation lacks a content or meaning in virtue of which the statement that Jesus is God made man could be literally true or false."[123]

---

[121]*God and the Universe of Faiths*, 176. Hick's definition of myth is closely akin to Paul Ricoeur's. See *The Symbolism of Evil*, Emerson Buchanan, trans. (Boston: Beacon, 1967). Through myth, Hick writes, we "relate ourselves to the (problematic) phenomenon or situation in question without being able to explain it." *God and the Universe of Faiths*, 166.

[122]Nicholas Lash, "Interpretation and Imagination," *Incarnation and Myth: The Debate Continued*, 21, has criticized Hick for assuming that "'literal' discourse is 'objective, fact-asserting,' whereas imaginative, metaphorical, symbolic or mythological discourse is 'subjective,' expressive of attitudes."

[123]*God and the Universe of Faiths*, 176. Perhaps if Hick had dealt more with the ontic nature of God he could better qualify that statement. The content of the myth is supplied by one's subject response, in Hick's opinion. Much more fruitful an approach is offered

Further, the issue of history is touched only tangentially in Hick's presentation. It seems to make no material difference whether there is any historical referent as the basis of the myth. Indeed, Hick implies that when there is myth (evidenced, for instance, by poetic form or messianic ideas) there is no history.

Hick correctly points to the problematic nature of religious language, but to use his definition of myth would mean that very little that is meaningful could ever be said about God. How can one be sure that the myths of Jesus are able to give any accurate information about the nature of God? Myth seems to tell more about the nature of the myth-maker than about ultimate reality![124] Any religious myth is true, Hick says, if one's capacity for faith and worship is activated. Are all responses to God equally valid? Arguably some are more in keeping with the character of God than others, but what can serve as criteria? Indeed, what is the importance of the cognitive aspect of faith and worship? These issues Hick needs to explore more fully.

Use of Scripture: Christological Implications

The logic and goal of Hick's presentation is to reduce or sufficiently weaken Christianity's traditional claims about incarnational Christology so as to be able to give all religious figures and their followers equal standing in his "universe of faiths." To see the validity of these conceptual shifts, it is necessary to offer a critique of his biblical methodology.

---

by J.A.T. Robinson, *The Roots of a Radical* (London: SCM Press, 1980) 61: a central conviction maintained ". . . by the assertion of the *incarnation*, not indeed of God *simpliciter*, as if Jesus were God dressed up and walking this earth, but of the Word, of God's creative, self-expressive activity from the beginning, fully and finally embodied in *this man. . . .*" For an insightful evangelical approach to the issue of myth, see Clark Pinnock, "Theology and Myth: An Evangelical Response to Demythologizing," *Bibliotheca Sacra* 128 (July-September, 1971): 221.

[124]For an opposite assessment, see Rudolf Otto, *The Idea of the Holy* (Oxford: Oxford University Press, 1923) 126.

Obviously, Hick does not regard the Bible as the sole Word of God. For Christianity, it is functionally what the *Bhagavad Gita* or the *Granth* is within their respective traditions—inspired writings that record God's revealing activity in their midsts.[125] To his credit, Hick does not have a static, rigid view of Scripture, but employs the tools of biblical criticism which give proper notice to the dynamic nature of the texts. The Scriptures provide a many-layered form of theological reflection, in Hick's opinion, and he evaluates their priority in a manner consonant with the methods of radical New Testament criticism.

In his denial that Jesus himself had a so-called "messianic-consciousness"[126] or awareness of his divine nature and his belief that its presence in the sources is due to an "acute Hellenization" of primitive Christianity, he reflects a generation firmly entrenched in Bultmann's thinking.[127] His handling of the New Testament materials is much too superficial to allow for such sweeping statements about Jesus' self-awareness.[128] He neglects the task of exegesis, for the most part.

Hick maintains that the Gospels are existentially oriented, more of an album of snapshots or a collection of stories fondly remembered and modified by the different Christian communities in retrospect than the Pauline epistles, which

---

[125]Günter Lanczkowski, *Sacred Writings: A Guide to the Literature of Religions*, Stanley Godman, trans. (New York: Harper Chapel Books, 1966).

[126]See Karl Rahner, "Dogmatic Reflections on the Knowledge and Self-Consciousness of Christ," *Theological Investigations*, vol. 5, Karl-H. Kruger, trans. (Baltimore: Helicon Press, 1966) 209-12. He argues for a structuring of the Hypostatic Union that allows for a growing consciousness of divine sonship in Jesus.

[127]See Martin Hengel, *The Son of God* (Philadelphia: Fortress, 1976) 17.

[128]See James D.G. Dunn, *Christology in the Making: A New Testament Inquiry into the Origins of the Doctrine of the Incarnation* (Philadelphia: Westminster Press, 1980) 253-54, for the fruit of his careful study on Jesus' self-awareness. He writes: "We cannot claim that Jesus believed himself to be the incarnate Son of God; but we can claim that the teaching to the effect as it came to expression in the later first-century Christian thought was, in the light of the whole Christ-event, an appropriate reflection of an elaboration of Jesus' own sense of sonship and eschatological mission."

are a significantly more mature form of theological reflection. Hick's chronology
and the accompanying assumptions about christological formulation within the
New Testament need rigorous questioning.[129]

In Paul's earliest letters, written approximately two decades after the
resurrection, a developed Christology is already in place.[130] Jesus' divine status
as part of the Trinity is accorded in 2 Cor 13:14, and in 1 Thess 1:10; he is
depicted as the agent of deliverance, to give only two examples. Perhaps the
divine status was not, therefore, a late construct formed by spurious
accretions,[131] as Hick assumes.

One can grant Hick's basic position on the Gospel of John, namely, that
it is considerably later than the Synoptics[132] and shows profound theological

---

[129]Charles Moule's influential book, *The Origin of Christology* (Cambridge: Cambridge University Press, 1977), offers a signal contribution to the incarnation debate generated by *The Myth of God Incarnate*. Moule contends throughout this slim monograph that christological development "only attempts to describe what was there from the beginning. They are not successive additions of something new, but only the drawing out and articulating of what is there. They represent various stages in the development of perception, but they do not represent the accretion of any alien factors that were not inherent from the beginning . . ." (2-3). In the present evaluation, the word "development" is being used in the same sense as Moule. Moule distinguishes this from what Hick and other *Myth of God Incarnate* essayists have suggested as an "evolutionary" christology. This is the tendency to explain the change from "invoking Jesus as revered Master to the acclamation of him as a divine Lord by the theory that, when the Christian movement spread beyond Palestinian soil, it began to come under the influence of non-Semitic Savior-cults and to assimilate some of their ideas . . ." (2). Martin Hengel's book, *The Son of God* (Philadelphia: Fortress Press, 1976), echoes Moule's contention. See also M. Hengel, "Christologie und neutestamentliche Chronologie," *Neues Testament und Geschichte*, H. Baltensweiler and B. Reicke, eds. (Zürich: Theologie Verlag, 1972) 43ff.

[130]Moule, *The Origin of Christology*, 6.

[131]See Michael Green's critique of Hick, "Jesus in the New Testament," *The Truth of God Incarnate*, Michael Green, ed. (London: Hodder and Stoughton, 1977) 20. See also R.F. Aldwinckle, "Reflections on Christology," *Perspectives in Religious Studies* 8 (1981): 88-91.

[132]A remarkable consensus of New Testament scholars supports this.

development,[133] without positing a yawning chasm between its Christology and that of the earlier gospels.[134] Hick has overstated the case to call John a "re-writing" of Jesus' teaching.[135] Moreover, it is difficult to read Matthew, Mark, and Luke without being made aware that a primitive, non-supernaturalist Christology is not to be found;[136] the impact of Jesus upon his contemporaries colors every account, and they struggle to find adequate language to express his significance.

Further, Hick treats the resurrection in a rather cavalier manner. He sees no substantial difference between the raising of Jesus and the raising of Lazarus or other first-century figures. Their "resurrections" are analogous to his.[137] He fails to mention that the Evangelists credit Jesus with raising Lazarus and others from the dead. The analogy hardly holds! Granted, Hick is probably correct that it was not simply because Jesus was raised from the dead that the early witnesses ascribed divinity to him; rather, it was the cumulative effect of his life and death and their experience of his continuing living presence with them that led them to confess his divine Lordship. Hick wants to sunder the impact of Jesus' ministry from his death by casting suspicion on the rationality of believing he was raised. All components must be included in the Christ-event. Hick has used a *divide et impera* technique, attacking the data one by one and ignoring the evidence of their cumulative force. In addition, he should have dealt with the prediction sayings of

---

[133]*God and the Universe of Faiths*, 116. Balance can be brought to Hick's presuppositions about dating by John A.T. Robinson's provocative book, *Redating the New Testament* (Philadelphia: Westminster Press, 1976) 262ff. Robinson believes the Fourth Gospel to be much more reliable a historical witness than it is usually counted.

[134]John A.T. Robinson, "The Use of the Fourth Gospel for Christology Today," *Christ and Spirit in the New Testament: Studies in Honour of C.F.D. Moule*, Barnabas Lindars and Stephen S. Smalley, eds. (Cambridge: At the University Press, 1973) 64, 67.

[135]*The Myth of God Incarnate*, 170-77.

[136]Moule, *The Origin of Christology*, 6.

[137]"Jesus and the World Religions," 170.

Jesus concerning his death (e.g., Matt 20:17-19, 26:12f.; Mark 10:33f.; Luke 18:31-34) as well as the evidence for the resurrection as a part of his critique.

Soteriology: Incarnation and Atonement

In his writings on the doctrine of the Incarnation, Hick has not fully explored the close link that exists between it and the doctrine of atonement. By reducing the incarnation to a mythological status, it can be argued that he has put in jeopardy Jesus' soteriological significance for humanity. If he is simply regarded as a man who serves as a paradigm for living a life of agapé love, is that a sufficient Christology to enable sinful, alienated men and women to transcend their guilt and embrace God?[138]

Hick mitigates traditional Christology and its claims concerning Jesus' atoning death by his suggestion that this position has been built on the assumption that God's relationship to humanity was transformed by Jesus' death. Hick misses a key contention of those who have maintained the relationship between incarnation and atonement: God is *never* the object of propitiation;[139] God is always the subject, and when there is an object, it is evil.[140] Consequently, no "moral exemplar" characterization of one dying sacrificially out of love for God can adequately inform persons of God's loving initiative towards estranged men and women. A functional Christology may derive a salvation scheme that says in

---

[138]In the article "The Non-Absoluteness of Christianity," Hick argues that Christian soteriology can no longer ". . . be established simply by defining salvation as inclusion within the scope of the divine pardon bought by Christ's atoning death" (23).

[139]Charles Moule, "Incarnation and Atonement: A Comment on Professor Hick's Critique of Atonement Doctrine," *Incarnation and Myth*, 85, strongly insists that the "translator is forced, by the way in which the 'propitiation' word-group is used, into rendering it not by 'propitiate' but by 'expiate': God is seen as himself taking the initiative in expiating sin and transforming *man's* relation to *him*."

[140]Ibid. Moule says there are remnants of the pagan notion of appeasing an angry God found in the Old Testament, but it is clearly wrong for Hick to assert that the traditionalists believe such is found in the New Testament or coheres with Jesus' revelation of God.

Christ God acted decisively and uniquely in history if it is maintained that the "humanity of God is that of a particular human being. . . ."[141]

As a proponent of the Irenaean scheme, Hick asserts that evil, suffering, and death are the natural concomitants of God's construction of a "person-making" world, and, hence, concludes that no perfect sacrifice which purports to overcome these negative experiences is necessary. It would countermand the whole order and means by which the Logos (as the divine attitude to humankind) aids humanity's movement towards being "at-one" with God. The evils which plague men and women will gradually disappear as the human race matures—without the instrumentality of atoning death. With this conclusion, it appears that Hick has side-stepped both the enduring reality of natural evil with its ambiguous relationship to the freedom of the human will as well as the possibility that God could actually experience death through the Son and not cease to be God.[142] Further, by allowing no unique ontological status to Jesus, he sketches a God (*deus ex machina*) who does not come to grips with moral evil as the passion narratives do. There the ultimate struggle to overcome evil with good

---

[141]Brian Hebblethwaite, "Incarnation and Atonement: The Moral and Religious Value of the Incarnation," *Incarnation and Myth*, 89.

[142]In "Evil and Incarnation," *Incarnation and Myth*, 80, Hick writes: "For whilst a human being can make the supreme sacrifice by giving his life for others, God cannot. God incarnate would know that his 'death' could only be temporary; for God cannot cease to be God, the eternal source of all life and being; and to speak literally of his death is to speak without meaning." Hick can make this blatant statement because he refuses to seek to understand Jesus' death in trinitarian terms. Of course, Hick is correct to reject a divine impassibility and a facile "death of Jesus" equals the "death of God" explanation. He also correctly affirms God's continuing suffering love in all of God's creation, but he does not deal sufficiently with the importance of the visibility the cross gives to this suffering love. Jürgen Moltmann's profound study, *The Crucified God*, R.A. Wilson and John Bowden, trans. (New York: Harper and Row, 1974) esp. 227-48, explicates how death has been taken up into the life of God, i.e., the trinitarian history of the God revealed in the Bible. Eberhard Jüngel, *God as the Mystery of the World*, D.L. Guder, trans. (Edinburgh: T. & T. Clark, 1983) insists that the self-sacrificial nature of the divine love is seen only in the love of God for the world—seen in both creation and cross. Cf. Paul Fiddes, *The Creative Suffering of God* (Oxford: Oxford University Press, 1988), who describes the God who suffers universally and yet is still present uniquely in the cross of Christ.

is portrayed. Can a purely human Christ render explicit illumination to humanity's depth of evil and bring about the salvation of men and women?

Affirmations about God

In his arguments concerning the salvific possibilities for persons who adhere to non-Christian religions, Hick presupposes the loving God and "Father" of Jesus and bases his conclusions on what is most consonant with that depiction of God. It would seem that Hick's posture in this is not without logical difficulty, for he has postulated over and over again the relativity of all of the religions' images of God. To attempt to argue conclusively about "how things really are" on the basis of one of these images seems to beg the question. How would Hick know God is loving and parental to all through the relativity of Jesus' revealing of God? One who holds a more traditional view of the incarnation is on stronger grounds logically. If Hick believes that all religions in their "experiential roots" are in contact with the same ultimate reality,[143] a relativistic assertion, how can he elevate the personal model of the Judeo-Christian tradition to the role of being the measure of the others?

Further, he maintains in other contexts that God is perceived both as personal and impersonal in the different religions (complementary truths, in his estimation) and consequently, that God is to be thought of as the "divine noumenon, experienced by mankind as a range of divine phenomena which take both theistic and non-theistic forms."[144] Is it not, by definition, impossible for God to take a non-theistic form? It would seem that whatever form God chooses to take is thereby transformed into a theistic form, whether personal or impersonal. Perhaps Hick's imprecision on this issue illustrates, to some extent, the difficulty of his theocentric map of the universe of faiths.

---

[143]*God and the Universe of Faiths*, 147.

[144]"Towards a Philosophy of Religious Pluralism," 146.

The present writer will not quibble with Hick's affirmation of God as loving and providential in relationship to the creation, but given Hick's confessed dependence on the biblical view of God, it is fair to question Hick's rather one-sided view of God. Hick believes that the Christian view of God rules out the concept of Christianity as *the* way of salvation. God's role in judgment is given little notice; the unrepentant cannot ultimately be disqualified from participating in the rule of God, in Hick's scheme. This neglect reveals the primary role reason plays in his theological formulations—even though he tacitly claims otherwise.[145] To acknowledge fully the judgment of God would make less tenable his conclusions about universal salvation. Obviously a rationalistic approach better suits Hick's purposes.

SUMMARY

Clearly, Hick's proposals would change drastically Christianity's self-consciousness and teachings; his position demands a thoroughgoing relativization of Christianity's claims about the uniqueness of Jesus Christ and his necessity for the salvation of humankind. While Hick prefers the term "pluralism," his position clearly entails the sacrifice of the bedrock affirmations of Christian faith. Pluralism means living with real distinctives, conflicting approaches and answers about the ultimate concerns of humanity. Hick is correct to maintain that the character of our world religiously is pluralist; however, one can acknowledge this reality without abandoning the heart of the Christian confession, Jesus is Lord. The present writer maintains that Hick has so relativized the role of Christ that a universal significance for him can no longer be held.

Is there enough continuity between its traditional shape and Hick's vision of it to merit calling it Christian? Brian Hebblethwaite, a continuing critic of Hick,

---

[145]J.J. Lipner, "Does Copernicus Help? Reflections for a Christian Theology of Religions," *Religious Studies* 13 (1977): 249. Lipner faults Hick for making rationality the chief criterion of the validity of a religion.

believes the incarnation and the Trinity are central to the Christian faith and that to deny these doctrines is to disqualify oneself from the label Christian.[146]

The effect of Hick's reductionist Christology is to leave no viable basis for a continuing devotion to the lordship of Jesus Christ which seems to jettison the core of Christian faith. Jesus becomes one figure in the pantheon of acceptable religious figures with no more compelling reason than any other to draw men and women to himself in faith.

To remain agnostic about the Trinity, Hick must, in essence forfeit any viable statements about the Spirit. It is easy to see why Hick ascribes no unique structure to the church. He does not grant that it is due to the continuing ministry of the Spirit of God that the church has persevered. True, it has often made a mockery of the merciful, inclusive, loving Jesus, but Hick disregards too much the abundant examples of self-less service the church has offered to the world.

Hick has correctly noted that the issue of Christ's finality is much more problematic than it used to be. He has challenged theologians to find more creative and relevant avenues to speak about God's movement toward humanity in the self-revelation of Jesus of Nazareth and the universal and cosmic import of this event.

---

[146]Brian Hebblethwaite, "The *Myth* and Christian Faiths," *Incarnation and Myth: The Debate Continued*, 16.

CHAPTER 6

TOWARDS A CHRISTOCENTRIC
THEOLOGY OF RELIGIOUS PLURALISM

Three distinctive options for dealing with the challenge of religious pluralism vis-à-vis Christianity's traditional claims have been sketched. Each offers a way for one to deal theologically with the phenomenon of the non-Christian religions, the historic formula *extra ecclesiam nulla salus*, and the question of the finality of God's revelation in Christ. As the evaluations of the exclusivist, inclusivist, and relativist perspectives have revealed, none is without its problems; yet, each delineates components that must construe a contemporary response to the question: "Is there salvation outside the church?" In this final chapter, I will venture my own response to the issues posed by this question. Obviously, it is far beyond the scope of a concluding chapter to construct a holistic theology of religious pluralism. Therefore, the proposal will necessarily take more the form of an outline than a comprehensive and systematic presentation.

Dialogue with the soteriological and ecclesiological paradigms of Brunner, Rahner, and Hick will inform and shape this constructive proposal, for their contributions certainly have positive implications for such a formulation. Insights drawn from their respective traditions and experiences will serve as the norms and criteria for this writer's presentation. Attention will also be given to the relevant biblical materials in order to formulate a more satisfactory answer, for surely theology of the Christian church demands extensive interaction with Scripture. Before attempting to construct guidelines for a christocentric theology of the world's religions as a means of engaging the problem of *salus extra ecclesiam*, a brief review of the strengths and weaknesses of the exclusivist, inclusivist, and relativist positions is in order.

THE CONTRIBUTION OF CHRISTIAN EXCLUSIVISM

As the critical evaluation of Christian Exclusivism revealed, Emil Brunner's position affords several important presuppositions for a christocentric theology of religious pluralism: a universal divine encounter of all persons with God; the affirmation that all stand in some relationship to God; the uniqueness and finality of Christ; the *ephapax* of Christ's atoning death, which Brunner defines in trinitarian terms;[1] the freedom and responsibility of each person in choosing salvation; the biblical doctrine of God's judgment upon those who refuse divine salvation;[2] and the significance of the church's contribution to salvation. While I clearly affirm these components of Brunner's position, several limiting factors remain.

Christian Exclusivism does more justice to the church's historic affirmation of the means of salvation than it does to the contemporary religious situation. Brunner pays scant attention to the vast number of persons who indeed may respond positively to the universal encounter with the Logos through general revelation. His position does not fully value the signs of God's saving presence and of positive human response which seem to pass the test of conformity to Jesus

---

[1]A very helpful approach is offered by Martin Hengel, *The Atonement: The Origins of the Doctrine in the New Testament,* John Bowden, trans. (Philadelphia: Fortress Press, 1981) 74. Cf. Donald G. Dawe, *Jesus: The Death and Resurrection of God* (Atlanta: John Knox Press, 1985) 65ff., for a discussion of the death of Jesus as the disclosure of God, an inductive trinitarian construction. In similar fashion, Elisabeth Moltmann-Wendel and Jürgen Moltmann, *Humanity in God* (New York: Pilgrim Press, 1983) 70ff., describe the "trinitarian story of Jesus" as the only way to fully understand the divine and human dimensions of Jesus' death as atonement.

[2]Emil Brunner, *The Christian Doctrine of Creation and Redemption. Dogmatics*, vol. 2, Olive Wyon, trans. (Philadelphia: Westminster Press, 1952) 118f.

Christ, even though they occur outside historic Christianity, as seen in the church. This affirmation creates a tension between creation and redemption as Brunner maintains that only the Word of God enables the response of repentance and faith. His view of the corruption of the formal image by sin disallows saving knowledge of God apart from the redeeming grace of the gospel of Jesus.[3] Yet the question remains: Could not the universal encounter with the Logos prompt men and women towards repentance and faith even if they had never heard of the only Savior? And does not repentance and faith, then, as Norman Anderson put it,

> open the gate, as it were, to the grace, mercy and forgiveness which he always longed to extend to them and which was to be made for ever available at the cross on which Christ "gave himself a ransom for all, to be testified in due time" (1 Tim 2:6 AV)?[4]

Sensing one's need of God (through whatever religious vehicle or through general revelation) and humbly casting oneself upon God's mercy are the mark of the Spirit's work and are ingredients of being saved. It should not be ruled out of hand, as Brunner does, that God is able to speak directly to the human heart, particularly when no other medium for the message is available. It would seem contrary to both Scripture and experience to suggest that adherents of other religions have no knowledge whatever of sin or of God. Indeed, the Apostle Paul seemed to assert in Rom 1:32 that all know something of the judgment of God on sin.[5]

---

[3]Brunner threatens to do what H. Richard Niebuhr, *The Purpose of the Church and Its Ministry* (New York: Harper and Row, 1956) 44, warns against: "The substitution of Christology for theology."

[4]Sir Norman Anderson, *Christianity and Comparative Religion* (Leicester: InterVarsity Press, 1970) 101.

[5]Robert H. Gundry, "Salvation According to Scripture: No Middle Ground," *Christianity Today* 22 (1977): 342-44, opposes such a view, believing that Paul only sought to emphasize that the "heathen, along with the Jews, stand under God's wrath because of their sin" (342), not that any have availed themselves of general revelation to know even this rudimentary fact. For a more positive assessment, see Arland J. Hultgren,

Further, Brunner's treatment of the biblical materials is uneven,[6] preferring to rest his position on some of the traditionally exclusivistic passages rather than to focus on the more problematic universalistic texts such as 1 Cor 5:18-19; 1 Cor 15:22f.; Rom 5:18; and Col 1:20. Seeking to preserve divine and human freedom, Brunner allows the two strands to stand unresolved alongside one another.[7]

More than Rahner or Hick, Brunner rightly emphasizes the significance for Christianity of the historical event of the atonement in the crucified Christ. He locates Christianity's distinctiveness from the "religions" in its proclamation of exclusive saving truth through the power of the cross. Jesus Christ is the center and key to the meaning of human existence, and he becomes this for the individual only insofar as the individual comes to explicit awareness of and contact with this unique savior. Consequently, Brunner offers no basis on which the efficacy of the atonement can extend to those who are not aware of it.

Would it not be more in keeping with the New Testament understanding of faith, however, to argue that the one who casts himself or herself upon God in repentance (such as the Publican in the Temple), regardless of specific awareness of Christ, has access to the mercy and forgiveness of God already actualized and shed abroad through Christ's atoning death? Does not Christ's representative atonement hold open a place before God, that is, create access, for the ones both

---

Christ and His Benefits (Philadelphia: Fortress Press, 1987) 55f. He believes this passage must be weighed in light of Paul's insistence on the grace of God for all who stand under judgment. He believes that knowledge of the universal judgment of God leads all to grateful response for God's encompassing salvation.

[6]See the critique of Brunner in George Rupp's *Christologies and Cultures* (Paris: Mouton & Co., 1974) 60-62.

[7]See John A.T. Robinson's critique of Brunner's "subtly unbiblical" approach in his *In the End God. Religious Perspectives*, vol. 20, Ruth Nanda Anshen, ed. (New York: Harper and Row, 1968) 113. Robinson believes Brunner's position rests on an inferior doctrine of God, for "the truth or falsity of the universalistic assertion, that in the end he is Lord entirely of a world wanting his lordship, is consequently decisive for the whole Christian doctrine of God" (114).

near and afar off (Eph 2:17-18) who share human solidarity with him and are those with whom Christ identified in his death *huper ēmon*?[8]

Brunner's christological position suggests a strict ecclesiocentric universe.[9] The normal corollary to his christological position is a literalistic interpretation of the maxim "No salvation outside the church." Brunner basically upholds this doctrine. Because of the church's integral connection with the saving events of the life of Jesus, it is the exclusive institution of salvation.

The *ekklesia* is essential to the experience of faith, in Brunner's thinking—a point he more consistently holds than either Rahner or Hick. He maintains that one does not receive salvation unless by the church to Christ. His exclusivism posits the church as the sole connecting link between the revelation of Jesus Christ and all subsequent eras. Where the church's witness is not known, one cannot encounter God in faith. This affirmation has the effect of subsuming all of God's redemptive activity in the world into the church, including that of the Logos. Brunner's position eventuates in a crude scenario: if the missionaries fail to preach in some obscure or off-limits locale, then it is simply too bad for those

---

[8]The idea that Christ holds open a place for persons before God is derived from Dorothee Sölle's approach in *Christ the Representative: An Essay in Theology after the "Death of God,"* David Lewis, trans. (London: SCM Press, 1967). What is necessary in a contemporary Christian theology of the atonement, in her opinion, is a recognition that the "mythical, fateful forces" (that which hinders human freedom as children of God) have been defeated or disarmed through Christ's liberated life, thus allowing one to respond freely to God's loving initiative (104-105). Sölle critiques any form of substitutionary atonement (especially that of Karl Barth) for its depersonalizing effect on humanity. She sums up Barth's view in the formula "without us—for us" (92). This view must be discarded, she insists, for it promulgates a human dependence without corresponding responsibility; it also lessens the unique irreplaceability of the individual. Cf. G.W.H. Lampe, *God as Spirit.* The Bampton Lectures, 1976 (Oxford: Clarendon, 1977) 5.

[9]Cf. Hans Küng's essay, "The World Religions in God's Plan of Salvation," *Christian Revelation and World Religions,* Josef Neuner, ed. (London: Burns and Oates, 1967) 25-66. Küng discusses the history and meaning of the phrase "No salvation outside the church" and shows it to be an ecclesiocentric view of the universe. Küng's most recent contribution to this important discussion is *Theology for the Third Millennium: An Ecumenical View* (New York: Doubleday, 1988). He describes the present as an "epochal threshold," a time in which a paradigm shift in the relation of the world religions is occurring (213f.).

dwelling there, because eternal salvation is not among their options. He makes no provision for one coming to faith if physically removed from a visible church.

Brunner refuses to employ the Augustinian distinction between *ecclesia invisibilis* and *ecclesia visibilis* because he deems this dual conception of the church as wholly foreign to the New Testament. Further, he believes such a dichotomy does not correspond to the nature of the *ekklesia* as the real fellowship of the reconciled. Indeed, Brunner's emphasis on the *Gemeinde* (fellowship of faith) maintains the balanced symmetry of his prevailing model of personal correspondence, that is, with God and with one's brother and sister. He is correct to argue that one becomes a part of the Body of Christ when one encounters God in faith; however, the extent of the *Corpus Christi* is solely defined by the dual criteria of the indwelling Word and Spirit in the Christian community. Brunner has no room for anything like Rahner's "anonymous Christian" in a scheme that makes the church constitutive of salvation.

In Brunner's estimation, the twofold distinction of visible and invisible, evidenced in Roman Catholic ecclesiology and followed by both Zwingli and Calvin, reflects the corruption of the Pauline definition of the *ekklesia*. It was a method by which Augustine could distinguish between what the church had become, namely, the hierarchically-structured, juristic institution, tainted by sin (*ecclesia visibilis*), and what the church should be as defined by the New Testament (*ecclesia invisibilis*).[10]

It appears that there is a need for some interpretive matrix that can deal with the persons of faith who are beyond the membership of the church which Christian Exclusivism simply cannot afford. The visible/invisible distinction is essentially encumbered with too much historical baggage and skirts the issue. Although the New Testament does not extensively treat this problem, it certainly does refer to godly persons (beyond the membership of the church) in the genre

---

[10]Cf. Jürgen Moltmann's reflection on the church "in the world" and "before God." He, like Brunner, will allow no dichotomized existence. See *The Church in the Power of the Spirit*, Margaret Kohl, trans. (New York: Harper & Row, 1977) 107.

of the "holy pagans" of the Old Testament.[11] Perhaps it is to these that Jesus refers in John 10:16: "But there are other sheep of mine, not belonging to this fold, whom I must bring in . . ." (NEB). Or perhaps in Mark 9:40 Jesus is alluding to persons with little comprehension who yet have drawn near to God: "For he who is not against us is on our side" (NEB). When the apostolic witness came to such as these, they received affirmation of the appropriate nature of their faith,[12] or were instructed further toward faith's completion.[13] Rahner's contribution deals expressly with such persons, collectively identifying them as "anonymous Christians" who, indeed, have both a relationship to Christ and to his church. To be sure, Brunner is correct to ascribe a normative role in salvation to the church, but the universal operation of the Holy Spirit should be affirmed as well. The structure of Brunner's *Dogmatics* implies that the Holy Spirit's action is totally mediated through the church.[14]

THE CONTRIBUTION OF CHRISTIAN INCLUSIVISM

Always concerned to give due credence to the church's historic pronouncements, Rahner has been equally concerned to engage current critical theological issues, for example, the soteriological significance of the incarnation for unbelievers and non-Christians. Whereas Brunner's position maintained both an exclusive Christocentric soteriology and a basically ecclesiocentric theology of religious pluralism, Rahner's Christian Inclusivism affirms an inclusive Christology and a "twofold distinction of the church as a visible society and as

---

[11]The term is Jean Daniélou's, *Holy Pagans of the Old Testament*, Felix Faber, trans. (London: Longmans, Green and Company, 1957).

[12]Acts 10:34.

[13]Acts 8:30-35; 17:25-27.

[14]See Emil Brunner, *The Christian Doctrine of the Chruch, Faith and the Consummation. Dogmatics*, vol. 3, David Cairns, trans. (Philadelphia: Westminster Press, 1962) 5.

humanity consecrated by Christ."[15] Holding these ecclesiological affirmations in tension, he can profess the necessity of the visible church (broadly interpreting *extra ecclesiam nulla salus* so as to further ecumenical concerns) and can argue for the possibility of salvation for persons outside the church. By viewing the church in a cosmic perspective, that is, as coterminous with all of humanity, he jettisons any vestige of ecclesiastical exclusivism.

The church is not, then, primarily a mediator of grace but the *result of grace*, in Rahner's thinking. It is the tangible sign in history of God's salvific work for all persons. *Extra ecclesiam nulla salus* comes to mean "Without the Church no salvation" in this scheme.[16] Christ is constitutive of salvation, and the church points to that reality. As Rahner puts it, "It is only in Jesus Christ that this salvation is conferred, and through Christianity and the one Church that it must be mediated to all men."[17] Rahner carefully measures his ecclesiological statements over against what he considers to be the absolute reference points: God's universal salvific will and Jesus Christ as the indispensable mediator of salvation.

Rahner's anthropology profoundly differs in emphasis from Brunner's. Following the Protestant tradition Brunner lays greater stress on the contradiction and guilt of human beings, while Rahner, true to a more optimistic Roman Catholic vision, extols the "supernatural existential" (God's self-communication) which grace infuses into all persons. Using this concept, he contends that every person is subject to the active and saving will of God. Unlike Brunner, Rahner insists that a person can respond in faith without the inbreaking of the Word

---

[15]Leo J. O'Donovan, S.J., ed., "A Changing Ecclesiology in a Changing Church: A Symposium on Development in the Ecclesiology of Karl Rahner," *Theological Studies* 38 (1977): 743.

[16]J. Peter Schineller, S.J., "Christ and Church: A Spectrum of Views," *Theological Studies* 37 (1976) 554.

[17]Karl Rahner, "The Church, Churches, and Religions," *Theological Investigations*, vol. 10, Graham Harrison, trans. (New York: Seabury Press, 1973) 31.

through hearing the gospel which, according to Brunner's perception, creates a capacity for faith in the individual. Rather, Rahner maintains that God's grace has already been poured out on the world through Christ's life and death. It is this distinctive understanding of nature and grace that permits Rahner to argue that all persons are already "dynamically finalized in the direction of ... God himself."[18] Therefore, one's being is never purely "natural" (in the sense of being unaffected by God's saving will for all). By overcoming the view that grace is extrinsic through positing its effective presence in every life, Rahner has strengthened the possibility that all can indeed positively respond to God's gracious summons which is experienced in the common life of human beings. Moreover, the summons ineluctably gives shape to each person's innermost being.

Both Brunner and Rahner characterize sin more as a state than as a collection of evil acts; however, Brunner draws a significant line of demarcation between the unregenerate and the regenerate person. Rahner, on the other hand, sees redemption as a gradual movement from non-reflective faith to reflective faith. His view does not necessitate the radical *metanoia* that Brunner made foundational to this theology by virtue of following the Reformation view of sin as disobedience, unbelief, and *hybris* that spawns arrogant rebellion against God. Rahner depicts sin as the refusal, through indifference or lack of courage, to respond to the call of absolute transcendence in history. If one continues to ignore one's graced openness to the horizon of transcendence (God), there remains a possibility of sin as a permanent existential, Rahner warns—but this is a minor theme in Rahner's soteriology. Rahner does not accentuate the guilt of humanity before God to the degree that Brunner does (which tends to make his position

---

[18]Karl-Heinz Weger, *Karl Rahner: An Introduction to His Theology* (New York: Seabury Press, 1980) 107. Cf. James A. Carpenter, *Nature and Grace* (New York: Crossroad, 1988) 68ff., who criticizes Rahner for subordinating creation in this formulation, and Eberhard Jüngel's essay, "Extra Christum Nulla Salus—A Principle of Natural Theology?" in *Eberhard Jüngel: Theological Essays*, J.B. Webster, ed. (Edinburgh: T. & T. Clark, 1989) 173-88, for his assessment that Rahner's form of natural theology basically collapses any distinction between "anonymous Christians" and confessing Christians.

overly optimistic). He is more concerned to elucidate the mystery and structure of the human being's positive relation to God.

Rahner insists that his theological anthropology is based on the human being *per se*, but others criticize him for extrapolating from the Christian vision and experience of humanity when he characterizes the courage and drive for authenticity with which all persons approach reality.[19] Brunner's anthropology, in my judgment, is more biblically and theologically sound.

A significant contribution of Rahner's inclusivist position is his attempt to establish a relationship between the atoning death and resurrection of Christ and the pre-Christians and extra-Christians. The historical Jesus of Nazareth can bring about salvation in these non-Christian contexts, Rahner argues, because Jesus Christ has redefined the horizon of their hope. All persons look for some form of completion or actualization of their hope, Rahner insists; in Christ the climax of history is revealed, and the shape and destiny of the world have been dynamically reoriented by grace.[20] The faith (either thematic or unthematic) with which people anticipate this completion has been determined by its *telos*, Christ himself.

Rahner's Christology demands that he seek to link all persons to the redemption provided in Christ; otherwise, a Christian provincialism cannot be avoided, and Christ holds only a relative importance if his redemption pertains exclusively to those who explicitly know of it. Thus, Rahner seems to be correct in giving Christ's action the unsurpassed significance of irrevocably reshaping the destiny of humankind. We can benefit from his insight that only a comprehensive

---

[19]Robert Kress, *A Rahner Handbook* (Atlanta: John Knox Press, 1982) 83-84.

[20]Rahner employs an eschatological theology of history which has marked similarities to the presuppositions of Wolfhart Pannenberg, i.e., that "history is the most comprehensive horizon of Christian theology." See Pannenberg's essay, "Redemptive Event and History," *Basic Questions in Theology: Collected Essays*, vol. I, George H. Kehm, trans. (Philadelphia: Fortress Press, 1970) 15. Stanley J. Grenz's new analysis of Pannenberg's theological contribution is extremely helpful for understanding Pannenberg's stress on "universal history." See his *Reason for Hope: The Systematic Theology of Wolfhart Pannenberg* (New York: Oxford University Press, 1989).

ontological movement in God, revealed in the incarnation, could bring about this salvific nuance. Rahner's position seems to suggest such an interpretation, and therefore he has effectively bridged the chasm between sacred history and secular history—a rift which has too long plagued Christian theology. He has planted Jesus Christ firmly in the stream of human history. Further, he has sought to maintain the supremacy of Christ by his argument that Christ is constitutive (but not normative) for all salvation.

But has Rahner really succeeded in preserving the necessity of Christ for salvation?[21] His theory of the omnipresence of grace seems to detract from his assertions of Christ's soteriological uniqueness. Although Rahner staunchly maintains that a person is graced with the "supernatural existential" because of what has been brought to fulfillment in Christ, his assertion that pre-Christians also have the "supernatural existential" seems to root grace more in the goodness of God's creative process than in the particular historical action of Jesus Christ as God Incarnate. In which is the universal possibility of salvation ontologically grounded?[22] Obviously, Rahner did not intend to pose such a dilemma; but, even though he attempted to interpret traditional Christian affirmations in evolutionary categories, it appears that he has not woven God's intention in creation and redemption together tightly enough. Moreover, the necessity of the particularity of the historical phenomenon of Jesus Christ is lessened if he does not insist that

---

[21]Russell R. Aldwinckle, *Jesus—A Savior or the Savior? Religious Pluralism in Christian Perspective* (Macon GA: Mercer University Press, 1982) 180-81. Aldwinckle believes that Rahner's eschatology suggests that "anonymous Christians" may utterly and efficaciously entrust themselves to God for eternal salvation at the point of death, without conscious committal to Christ. Only if Rahner would amend his view to stress the necessity for all men and women to have a saving relationship to Jesus Christ, either before or after death, could he safeguard Christ's soteriological necessity, in Aldwinckle's opinion.

[22]Rupp, *Christologies and Cultures* (Paris: Mouton, 1974) 213, notes Rahner's concern "to avoid grounding the universal possibility of salvation exclusively in the divine intention." Hence, Rahner's writings reveal an ambiguity between God and Christ as the bearer of the whole of salvation history as well as a lack of attentiveness to the voluntary nature of faith, a cornerstone of the Baptist tradition.

the universal possibility of salvation is clearly grounded in God, but not separate from Christ.

Rahner's inclusive understanding of the church as the "Body of Christ" and the "people of God" properly engages both the reality of consciously committed church members as well as those who are involved in a "Christology of quest" without being attached to a visible church. Rahner appropriately argues that individuals within this latter group are, nonetheless, standing in relationship to the church. But is it possible to reconcile Rahner's twofold distinction of the church as "visible society" with the responsibility of proclaiming salvation and the church as "humanity consecrated by Christ"? Does not the latter definition essentially compromise the distinctive New Testament understanding of *ekklesia*?

The church is portrayed in a variety of ways in the Pauline corpus alone, however. Hence, Rahner is not without scriptural warrant for his distinction, for the New Testament ostensibly refers to the church in both senses. 1 Thess 2:12; 2 Thess 1:5; Rom 14:17; and 1 Cor 4:20 point to the *ekklesia* as the present manifestation of the expected rule of the crucified Christ.[23] Two references in particular imply a more inclusive view of the church. Eph 2:11-15 explicates the unity of all humankind in Christ. Speaking to the gentiles, Paul informs them of the single new humanity Christ's death has formed:

> Remember then your former condition: you, Gentiles as you are outwardly, you, "the uncircumcised" so called by those who are called "the circumcised" (but only with reference to an outward rite)—you were at that time separate from Christ, strangers to the community of Israel, outside God's covenants and the promise that goes with them. Your world was a world without hope and without God. But now in union with Christ Jesus you who once were far off have been brought near through the shedding of Christ's blood. For he is himself our peace. Gentiles and Jews, he has made the two one, and in his own body of flesh and blood

---

[23]Moltmann, *The Church in the Power of the Spirit*, 76ff., depicts the church's inclusion in the messianic mission as a present reality, "corresponding to the rule of God" (84).

> has broken down the enmity which stood like a dividing wall between
> them; for he annulled the law with its rules and regulations, so as to
> create out of the two a single new humanity in himself. . . (NEB).

The gentiles are thus paradigmatic of the universal unity of humanity made possible by Christ.

Perhaps Rahner's view of the church as "humanity consecrated by Christ" mirrors the depiction of Col 1:20 of the reconciliation of the whole universe (*apokatallaxai ta panta*) through the shedding of Christ's blood on the cross.

Yet the question arises whether or not Rahner would have found it necessary to use the concept "church" (with the risk of stretching it beyond recognition) if he were not, to a major degree, still in the tradition of *extra ecclesiam nulla salus*. It would seem sufficient to underscore God's universal salvific will (which he repeatedly does) and the relationship that "anonymous Christians" have to the church as sacramental sign and grace without making "church" a non-discrete entity. His ecclesiological construal fails to maintain the New Testament tension (found especially in Paul) between the church's vocation to live *for* the world and to wage battle *against* the godlessness of the world.[24]

In sum, Rahner's chief contributions to a christocentric theology of religious pluralism are: his insistence that God's universal salvific will demands that geographical and historical accident should not preclude sharing in the redemption effected by Christ; his firm belief that Christ is constitutive of salvation; his view of the unity of human history; his affirmation that since all persons are oriented toward God, all are ineluctably seeking God, either consciously or unconsciously; his expansion of the strictures of traditional Roman Catholic ecclesiology to include all persons of faith; his view of the church as both the result of grace and the normative (not constitutive) expression of the reception of that grace; his affirmation of the grace-filled elements in all religions

---

[24]See J.C. Beker's helpful treatment of this dualism in *The Triumph of God: The Essence of Paul's Thought* (Minneapolis: Fortress Press, 1990) 29.

which mandates a non-judgmental attitude on the part of Christian theologians; and his concept of mission as chiefly proclamation of the Gospel rather than non-evangelistic humanitarian ventures. Rahner's inclusive position is not without problematic components, but surely it is a positive move beyond the Christian Exclusivism of Brunner and a more sensitive response to the complex problems posed by religious pluralism.

THE CONTRIBUTION OF CHRISTIAN RELATIVISM

John Hick's Christian Relativism offers a third option for dealing with the challenge of religious pluralism to the traditional affirmations of Christian theology. Most radical of the three paradigms, Hick's view urges contemporary Christian theologians to abandon what he deems outmoded and provincial ecclesiocentric and christocentric typologies in order to embrace a theocentric orientation as a more comprehensive and reasonable interpretive framework. Deeply immersed in the labyrinthine issues of a multi-faith world, Hick's argument has many compelling features; however, the toll his position exacts from fundamental Christian beliefs may be too great.[25]

Hick's "Copernican Revolution" advocates a theocentric position which regards Jesus Christ as the normative expression of God's salvific grace for Christians only. It is simply not possible, in Hick's opinion, to argue for a universal significance for Christ from the limited historical perspective of a Christian theologian. Although a reductionist Christology, this position offers, in the opinion of one writer, the advantage of recognizing "the incomprehensibility of God and the mystery of human subjectivity."[26] Hick, like Rahner, is insistent

---

[25]See the analysis and critique of Hick's pluralism in the review article by Francis X. Clooney, *Religious Studies Review* 15:3 (July 1989): 198-203.

[26]Schineller, "Christ and Church," 560. Hick's approach is much more sensitive to the socio-cultural factors in religious affirmations than are those of Brunner and Rahner; further, Hick reminds Christians of the provisional nature of their "doctrines of God."

that Christians lay aside the chauvinism that has, for the most part, colored their perceptions of other ways of faith. His methodology provides a corrective for the insensitive way many Christian theologians have lumped together non-Christian religions as miserable gropings toward God, as if they were practically devoid of knowledge of God.

Furthermore, this methodology also seeks to redress the cavalier manner with which many Christians have ignored the mystery and infinite transcendence of God through their substitution of a myopic Jesus-ology. This perspective allows Jesus to reveal God exhaustively—the historical Jesus of Nazareth subsumes all of the being of God. Hick argues that one religion's key revelatory paradigm can never fully apprehend the sovereign Creator and Redeemer of the universe.[27] Analogy is always necessary, and doxology is always appropriate when speaking of the primordial and even the consequent natures of God.[28] A theocentric orientation as outlined by Hick guards against the arrogance that presumes to speak of God in a univocal manner. Christology has functioned this way in much of the church's theology, in Hick's opinion.

Another strength of Hick's position is the emphasis he places on worship. Neglected by Rahner and Brunner in their evaluations of the non-Christian religions, the commonality that believers of disparate religious traditions seem to evidence in worship profoundly shapes Hick's relativist methodology.[29] Ostensibly different religions, many of which have experienced a striking renaissance in recent generations, are worshipping the same God through discrete,

---

[27]John Hick, *Problems of Religious Pluralism* (New York: St. Martin's Press, 1985) 94-95.

[28]The terminology is Alfred North Whitehead's, *Process and Reality* (London: Macmillan Company, 1929) 524f.

[29]Hick has been strongly influenced by W.C. Smith's stress on the priority of "personal faith" (the individual's own inner awareness of his or her relation to the divine) over against "cumulative tradition." See Smith's *The Meaning and End of Religion: A Revolutionary Approach to the Great Religious Traditions* (New York: Macmillan, 1962).

but overlapping conceptualities, Hick contends. This assessment elevates the truth that God indeed retains a witness in the kaleidoscope of human contexts and accentuates the possibility that God may be experienced as personal, as cosmic ground of being, or as the unitive, mystical reality.[30] Christian theology has rarely granted to all three modes the stamp of orthodoxy.

In the same vein, Hick has also put Christians on guard against any superficial understanding of the nature of religious language. Because of his analytic contribution, one can no longer blithely make religious pronouncements which disregard the accompanying responsibility of discerning which statements are fact-asserting and which utilize the non-factual language of myth, symbol, and poetry. But Hick does not take seriously enough that differences in myth and doctrine really *do* matter; because myths are not really truth-claims, in his opinion, they are "not of great *religious*, i.e., soteriological importance. . . ."[31] In effect, this position fails to acknowledge the key differences in world-views held by the major world religions. Hick's contention that truth is ultimately plural makes discriminating assessment problematic.

As constructive as some of these features are in fostering a more appreciative understanding of other religions, must one renounce the fundamental conviction that Christ and his church are the *sacramentum mundi*, that is, the necessary channel of grace for all of humankind, in order to benefit from these correctives of Hick's? Further, is it possible to move beyond the Ptolemaic exclusivism, which he so relentlessly criticizes, without capitulating to an unmoored relativism?[32] It is only possible if one retains the theological

---

[30]John Hick, "Towards a Philosophy of Religious Pluralism," *Neue Zeitschrift für Systematische Theologie und Religionsphilosophie* 22 (1980): 134.

[31]John Hick, *Problems of Religious Pluralism*, 94.

[32]My concern is not so much with Hick's definition of myth as it is with the appropriateness of describing the incarnation as "myth." One is on much safer ground, it seems, to describe the Genesis accounts of creation as myth, i.e., the story of God stooping in the mud to form human beings (archetypal history), than to assert that one is

irreducibility of Jesus Christ as constitutive for the salvation of all people, in my judgment. It is against this affirmation that Hick wages his strongest campaign.[33]

Although Hick's Copernican Revolution has several helpful implications for the formulation of a theology of religious pluralism, his opposition *in toto* entails a devastating blow to a christocentric approach: a non-incarnational Christology. Thus, all that Hick can say about Jesus Christ is that he is among the most outstanding religious figures known to humankind. The impact of his life has been sufficient to sustain a community gathered around his memory and instructed by his teachings. Teaching and modeling self-less love was his means of salvation. He revealed God as "the loving Father of all of humanity" (Hick's words), and Christians have genuinely encountered God through him.[34]

By placing God at the center of the "universe of faiths" and questioning Jesus' role as the sole mediator of God's salvation, Hick eliminates both the unique significance and universal efficacy of Christ's atoning death.[35] He can

---

making a mythical statement when, upon one's encounter with Jesus Christ, one describes him as Immanuel, God with us. In Hick's thinking, the truth of the myth does not matter, only the response it evokes is of consequence. It is a confession one makes in faith and does not connote, as Hick baldly puts it, that one is making the simple equation, Jesus is God. To reduce God's presence in Jesus of Nazareth to "a story told . . . which is not literally true" (*God and the Universe of Faiths*, 166) makes Christianity's foundation less tenable than orthodox Christology will allow. Hick delimits the concept "literal" to mean "substance"; however, one can maintain an incarnational Christology without making this assertion. Geoffrey Lampe's article in *The Myth of God Incarnate*, John Hick, ed., offers the language of "inspiration" by the Spirit as an alternative. While this is not classic Christology's understanding of incarnation, it is a way of dynamically interpreting Jesus' unique consciousness of God and the vital presence of God's Spirit in his life.

[33]See J.J. Lipner, "Does Copernicus Help? Reflections for a Christian Theology of Religions," *Religious Studies* 13 (1977): 255f.

[34]John Hick, "Incarnation and Mythology," in *God and the Universe of Faiths* (London: Macmillan Press, 1973) 172ff.

[35]See Geoffrey Wainwright, *Doxology: The Praise of God in Worship, Doctrine and Life* (London: Epworth Press, 1980) 68-69. Wainwright notes that "Hick's view of human history as the opportunity to discover God by faith and to grow in love towards him does, however, leave room for an abelardian view of the atonement" (68). (Continued)

sever the essential relationship between incarnation and atonement because his view of humanity and sin (which he calls Irenaean) does not posit a radical estrangement from God through rebellion that must be overcome by an objective work of redemption.[36] The structure of the "person-making" world needs no more than a purely human Jesus through whom God can function in a self-revealing manner to men and women. It is apparent that the consequences of Hick's relativized Christology are grave, and, to this writer unacceptable, for they demand a scuttling of many salient Christian beliefs. Salvation is always God's merciful gift; it does not hinge on a purely natural morality, as Hick's position would suggest. Even Rahner's "transcendental horizon" does not lapse into this anthropocentrism, reminiscent of Schleiermacher and Lessing. Hick is not satisfied if Christian theologians only make the conceptual shift that acknowledges that while there is salvation within other religions, it is all to be seen as the work of Christ—the point that Rahner makes. Sufficient evidence to sustain that lofty christological claim is not available and, thus, must be discarded, Hick concludes.

The contours of Hick's ecclesiology closely correlate to his Christology. Against any form of ecclesiocentrism, he argues that there is no unique community of salvation that must serve as the necessary means of salvation or as the sign of grace for the redemption of the world. Indeed, Hick excoriates the contemporary church of Jesus for being "a stumbling block to almost anyone who is drawn to him."[37] Obviously, the church has an attenuated significance in Hick's salvation-scheme, as does Jesus Christ. Therefore, Hick can advocate both a Christian ecumenicity among the plethora of churches and a global ecumenicity of the religions of the world, encouraging them all to affirm their genesis in the

---

(Continued) The present writer has noted already the inadequacies of Hick's non-incarnational soteriology and the limitations of the moral-exemplar theory of atonement in the evaluation section of chapter five of this study.

[36]Hick's essay on "Irenaean Theodicy" was published in *Encountering Evil*, Stephen Davis, ed. (Edinburgh: T. & T. Clark, 1981).

[37]John Hick, *The Centre of Christianity* (London: SCM Press Ltd., 1977) 67.

same God. Not only are Christian denominational differences of moot concern for Hick, but the larger divide between religious traditions seems to be of historical significance, but with little soteriological consequence. The result of Hick's projection is a relativism without a criteriological measure.[38]

PRESUPPOSITIONS FOR A CHRISTOCENTRIC THEOLOGY OF RELIGIOUS PLURALISM

At this juncture, it should be apparent that some form of Christian Inclusivism is the most appropriate option for a theological assessment of the issues pertaining to religious pluralism. Throughout its long history of development, the inclusivist approach has retained the central core of the Christian faith by professing Jesus Christ to be the unique mediator of God's salvific grace to all, and thus constitutive for salvation, without limiting the benefit of his sacrificial life and death to those who explicitly know and believe in it. This perspective has the advantage of retaining "respect for the stubborn complexities of religion's context and reason's demands."[39]

In addition, Christian Inclusivism has ascribed a normative role to the church as the expression of salvation through Christ without limiting it to the church's empirical membership. Drawing primarily from this tradition, in this last section I will present necessary presuppositions for the formation of a christocentric theology of religious pluralism.

---

[38]John Hick, "On Grading Religions," *Religious Studies* 17 (1981): 466-67.

[39]Francis X. Clooney, *Religious Studies Review* 15 (1989): 200. Hans Küng, *Theology for the Third Millennium*, echoes Clooney's contention:

> "After the discovery of the giant continents outside of Europe the world's religions were first and foremost external, *quantitative* challenge for Christendom. But they have now become an internal, *qualitative* challenge not just for some   enlightened spirits but for the Christian churches themselves" (233).

Hence Küng argues for "a generous, tolerant inclusivism . . ." (235).

A "Christocentric" Starting Point

Where one begins in constructing a theology of religious pluralism is not of mere methodological interest. Does one begin with Jesus Christ or with the transcendental reality (as Hick prefers)?[40] More specifically, can one argue cogently for God's universal salvific will without the undergirding of Christology? Although the Old Testament certainly contains some passages which indicate the universality of the deity's redemptive purposes (for example, Gen 12:3; Ps 47:9-10; Isa 19:16-25; 42:1-4; 45:20-25; and Jer 16:19-21), only the witness borne to the inclusive mercy of God through Jesus Christ to clarifies the reality of God's saving intent for all of humanity.

It is proper to attempt a christocentric theology of the non-Christian religions if one follows John A. T. Robinson's distinction in regarding Jesus Christ as "*totus Christus* and *totus Deus*, the one who is utterly expressive of Godhead, through and through, so that in him there is no unChristlikeness at all" rather than the restrictive "*totum Christi, totum Dei*, the exhaustive revelation and all sufficient act, so that apart from him there is nothing of God and no Christlikeness at all."[41] Jesus Christ does not subsume the deity (*totum Dei*), but thoroughly reveals God's purpose for humanity through one who was "born in the likeness of human beings" (Phil 2:7).

---

[40]That there are fundamental difficulties with Hick's doctrine of God has already been noted above. He consistently roots God's nature as loving and "fatherly" to all in the revelation of Jesus Christ. However, if there is no uniqueness or finality to Jesus which would render his perception of God as authoritative, Hick has chosen an amorphous starting point. If he claims his Judeo-Christian understanding of God to be the most accurate, he slips back into the exclusivism which he has criticized so vehemently. Clearly, the key problem for Christian theology is to articulate the universal significance of a particular individual, Jesus Christ, without lapsing into triumphal exclusivism.

[41]John A.T. Robinson, *Truth is Two-Eyed* (Philadelphia: Westminster Press, 1979) 104. Cf. Norman Pittenger, *The Word Incarnate* (London: Nisbet and Co., 1959) 249. Robinson can be called an "inclusivist" according to the typology utilized in the present study.

A christocentric theology should affirm the universal work of the Logos through human reason and all movements of the human spirit toward God. Certainly the Christ-event is not the only point in the fabric of human history where God has actively worked for the reconciliation of humanity; indeed, as Charles Moule eloquently reflects:

> it is impossible not to believe that God's creative work of reconciliation permeates the whole of his creation and all history, so that every act of self-sacrificing service and generous forgiveness by any one at any time is a part of it. But such a belief is not in the least incompatible with the belief that this continuous process comes to a complete and perfect expression at a particular point.[42]

A christocentric starting point allows a perspective from which to interpret the whole of God's redemptive action.

God's universal salvific will revealed through Christ. Jesus Christ is God's Word of clear explication about God's own universal salvific will. The theological concept refined during the exilic and post-exilic years that the nations (*ta ethne*) had a place in the salvation of Yahweh was inaugurated in the ministry of Jesus Christ, but not from the outset. Jesus focused his mission initially on the covenant people, Israel, proclaiming to them that God was acting to bring her to her true destiny.[43] Desiring to prepare the covenant people of God for their task of proclaiming to the nations God's salvation (which came about after his

---

[42]Charles Moule, "Incarnation and Atonement: A Comment on Professor Hick's Critique of Atonement Doctrine," in *Incarnation and Myth: The Debate Continued*, Michael Goulder, ed. (London: SCM Press Ltd., 1979) 86.

[43]George Eldon Ladd, *A Theology of the New Testament* (Grand Rapids: Eerdmans, 1974) 108. Although the Gospels record the blessing of the Syrophoenician woman (Mark 7:26) and the cure of the deaf-mute person (Mark 7:31-37), Ralph Martin, *New Testament Foundations*, vol. I (Grand Rapids: Eerdmans, 1975) 188, suggests that these are exceptions in the "essentially Jewish setting of the rest of the miracles in the historical career of Jesus." John Bowden, *Jesus: The Unanswered Questions* (Nashville: Abingdon, 1989) 165, observes the essentially antisemitic character of Christianity's interpretation of the ministry of Jesus—a distortion, in his opinion.

glorification), Jesus clearly insisted that his preaching of the rule of God was directed to the "lost sheep of the house of Israel" (Matt 15:24). Further, as Jeremias notes, during Jesus' lifetime he sent disciples to Israel alone.[44]

But the rejection of their messiah by the Jews is a recurring motif in the Gospels,[45] and a decisive shift in Jesus' ministry is recorded[46] when Israel's rejection of the rule of God became irreversible. Although Jesus continued to warn Israel of its need for repentance,[47] at the same time he began to announce that the gentiles would share in the eschatological rule of God.[48] Whereas the sending of the Twelve had signified the continuity between Israel and Jesus' disciples, Luke adduces the commissioning of the seventy[49] (*hebdomekonta*) as indicative of the universalizing sphere of Jesus' ministry.[50] Probably conscious

---

[44]Joachim Jeremias, *Jesus' Promise to the Nations* (Philadelphia: Fortress Press, 1958) 24. See Matt 10:5f.; 10:23. In addition, Jeremias maintains "that we have no support for the view that the early church embarked upon the Gentile mission immediately after the resurrection . . ." (25). Philip A. Cunningham, *Jesus and the Evangelists* (New York: Paulist Press, 1988), argues, *contra Jeremias*, that the resurrection inaugurated the inclusion of Gentiles as a sign of the messianic age (200-202).

[45]Matt 23:37ff.; Luke 4:16-30; Mark 6:1-6.

[46]Matt 21:43; Mark 12:1-9. Cf. G.D. Kilpatrick, "The Gentile Mission in Mark and Mark 13:9-11," *Studies in the Gospels: Essays in Memory of R. H. Lightfoot* (Oxford: Oxford University Press, 1955) 145-58. Looking at the ministry of Jesus as a whole, Daniel J. Harrington, S.J., *God's People in Christ: New Testament Perspectives on the Church and Judaism* (Philadelphia: Fortress Press, 1980) 28, concludes: "His preaching and his healing activity were available to all kinds of people (even tax collectors and sinners) and seem to point logically beyond the confines of Israel."

[47]Johannes Munck, *Paul and the Salvation of Mankind* (Richmond: John Knox Press, 1959) 257.

[48]Jeremias, *Jesus' Promise*, 48.

[49]Luke 10:1ff.

[50]Karl H. Rengstorf, "*hepta*," *Theological Dictionary of the New Testament*, vol. II, Gerhard Kittel, ed., Geoffrey W. Bromiley, trans. and ed. (Grand Rapids: Eerdmans, 1964) 634, writes: "When, therefore, Jesus sent out seventy messengers with His Word and in His power, against the background of the ideas of the time this raises the symbolical claim to hearing and obedience not merely on the part of Israel but of all humanity. . . ."

of his role as the Servant of the Lord[51] who would bring "justice to the nations," he sounds the clear note of God's universal saving will as ingredient to his message.[52] Even the predictions of his death carried the universal overtone as he envisioned his personal sacrifice for "the many,"[53] or as Matthew has it, "for many for the forgiveness of sins."[54]

The Pauline and Johannine literature also insist on a universal significance for Jesus' death. In John's theological reflection, Jesus says: "And I shall draw all to myself when I am lifted up from the earth."[55] Expressing a similar concept, Paul writes: "The death he died he died to sin, once for all, but the life he lives he lives to God"[56] (NEB). There is a marked continuity from what was, in many

---

[51]Jeremias, *Jesus' Promise*, 53. Ben Witherington, III, *The Christology of Jesus* (Minneapolis: Fortress Press, 1990) 267ff., discerns in the Gospel material a refined messianic-consciousness in Jesus' self-perception.

[52]Ibid., 70. Jeremias declares that Jesus believed that the Gentiles would only come to share in the *basileia* through God's "eschatological act of power, as the great final manifestation of God's free grace." His view has not received widespread support.

[53]Mark 10:45. The present writer is aware that many New Testament scholars brand these predictions sayings as *vaticinia ex eventu*, but maintains that subsequent attempts to construct a theology of Jesus' atoning death are rooted in his own perception of his death. See how Joachim Jeremias argues in his *New Testament Theology: The Proclamation of Jesus* (New York: Charles Scribner's Sons, 1971) 292ff., for the authenticity of the saying in the life of Jesus. Jeremias understands it to refer to Jesus' intention to offer his life in a representative way for the countless multitudes. In another book, *The Eucharistic Words of Jesus*, 3rd ed. (Philadelphia: Fortress Press, 1966) 181, Jeremias insists that the "for many" (*anti pollon*) of Mark 10:45 is a Semitic idiom which uses "many" for "all." See Charles Moule's interaction with Jeremias' contention in *The Origin of Christology* (Cambridge: Cambridge University Press, 1977) 119.

[54]Matt 26:28. Cf. Mark 14:24 and Matt 1:21.

[55]John 12:32. Arland Hultgren, *Christ and His Benefits* (Philadelphia: Fortress Press, 1987) 145ff., notes that even though the fourth gospel's proclamation of the meaning of Christ's death was crafted in a polemical setting, nevertheless the goal of his death is "clearly the salvation of all humanity" (154).

[56]Rom 6:10. Kenneth Grayston, *Dying We Live: A New Enquiry into the Death of Christ in the New Testament* (New York: Oxford University Press, 1990) 102, sees the key to this verse as its profound emphasis on the singularity of Christ: "it would not do to take some other hero or tragic person and use his example as a universal pattern."

respects, implicit in the Synoptic tradition to what is more "self-consciously articulated in the Fourth Gospel, the epistles, and the book of Revelation"[57] about the universality of Christ's atoning death.

Christ's death provides cosmic reconciliation. That the debates about the precise meaning of Jesus' death have been numerous indicates that this event was of such profound significance that none of the interpretations can adequately do it justice. Christians have, in the main, contended that the death of Jesus provides the all-sufficient condition for the forgiveness and reconciliation that humanity needs.

Earlier in this investigation, the link between incarnation and atonement was explored, and I am persuaded that for the death of Jesus to be viewed as unique and as an event in which God had definitively initiated reconciliation for all sinners,[58] that an incarnational Christology must be maintained. Because God wills salvation, Jesus died and rose again and it is incorrect to reverse the order and say, "because the crucifixion occurred, God wills the salvation of all." As Aldwinckle expresses it, "the uniqueness of the death of Jesus will depend upon the reality of God's action and presence in Jesus."[59] In this event God shares fully in the brokenness of the world, taking unto God's own self its sin. Without this affirmation, it makes little sense to argue for the universal efficacy of Jesus' death. The *locus classicus* for the assertion that the presence of God in Christ (and his purpose in dying) has effected a cosmic reconciliation is 2 Cor 5:19:

---

[57]Rupp, *Christologies*, 174. See Wolfhart Pannenberg, *The Apostles Creed*, Margaret Kohl, trans. (London: SCM Press, 1972) 88-89. Cf. Charles Davis, *Christ and the World Religions* (London: Hodder and Stoughton, 1970) 39.

[58]See Vincent Taylor, *Jesus and His Sacrifice* (London: Macmillan Press, 1937) 265. Paul S. Fiddes, *Past Event and Present Salvation: The Christian Idea of Atonement* (Louisville: Westminster/John Knox Press, 1989), also argues for the universal significance of Christ's death based upon the character of God and the demands of justice.

[59]Aldwinckle, *Jesus*, 68. Kenneth Surin, "Atonement and Christology," *Neue Zeitschrift für Systematische Theologie und Religionsphilosophie* 24 (1982): 131-49, argues that the doctrine of the atonement necessarily implies an ontological, incarnational Christology.

God was in Christ reconciling the world, no longer holding humanity's misdeeds against them. . . .

That Christ's death was of saving significance is put forward by all the major sections of the New Testament. Expressed by various images drawn from the theology of the Day of Atonement (Heb 2:17), Jewish sacrificial practices in general, biblical motifs that emphasize the Suffering Servant of Isa 53 (Luke 22:32ff.), and the paradigmatic contrast between Adam and Christ (1 Cor 15:20-24), each distinctive representation presupposes a "cosmic disorder."[60]

The cosmic disorder, most clearly articulated by Paul, encompasses more than the human predicament of guilt because of sin. To be sure, one stands unreconciled before God because of personal *adikia* and *asebeia*,[61] but Paul also contemplates[62] some "extra-terrestrial power . . . at work enslaving the world and corrupting its fair beauty by subjecting it to 'decay' as well as imposing a curse upon humanity. . . ."[63] The cosmic agencies—"thrones, dominions, principalities, authorities"[64]—though created by Christ, were, like sinful people, the object of his reconciling death on the cross.[65] Paul graphically portrays their

---

[60]See Ralph P. Martin, *Reconciliation: A Study of Paul's Theology*, New Foundations Theological Library, Peter Toon, ed. (Atlanta: John Knox Press, 1981) 49ff.

[61]Rom 1:18.

[62]Rom 8:19-23.

[63]Martin, *Reconciliation*, 53. Emil Brunner's biblical and theological treatment of the powers of evil is most helpful. See *The Christian Doctrine of Creation and Redemption*, Dogmatics: vol. II (Philadelphia: Westminster Press, 1952) 136-47. Cf. Walter Wink, *Unmasking the Powers* (Philadelphia: Westminster Press, 1986).

[64]Col 1:16.

[65]Col 1:20. Martin, *Reconciliation*, 54, explains the reason for the reconciliation of these powers. They were "created to be subservient to the cosmic Christ . . . but they have broken away from their primal station and 'deserted their appointed rank.' Their 'status' between creation and the time of Christ's triumph over them is one of rebellion, and the effect of his work is to neutralize or at least pacify that enmity against the day of their elimination."

defeat: "God disarmed the principalities and powers and made a public example of them, triumphing over them in him."[66] The apocalyptic motif of a ransom or redemption from the bondage of alien powers through the defeat of Satan or the principalities and powers of the present age is a key interpretation of the inclusive nature of the death of Jesus.[67]

Not only were these cosmic powers dealt a mortal blow, but human enslavement to death, sin, and the Law—the unrelenting triumvirate—were also overcome in Christ's redemptive death.[68] However, they were vanquished only in principle in the cross and resurrection of Jesus; their utter subjection "under Christ's feet" will not be until his final triumph.[69]

Christ's death creates a new context for faith. Maintaining the extensive efficacy for Jesus' death that the New Testament seems to warrant may demand a re-fashioned objective model of atonement. Obviously, using the term "objective" need not imply crude suggestions of an action that would transform God in the sense of propitiation, although an objective theory can glean helpful insights from the classic notion of Aulén, the satisfaction motif of Anselm, and the substitution ideas of Luther and Calvin, without making any of these theories (which are, for the most part, rejected by contemporary theologians) carry the full weight of explaining the soteriological significance of Christ's death. Nor should such a theory imply an abject passivity for humans as if the "great transaction" could be accomplished without personal response. Moreover, no dualism in the divine nature can be allowed in an attempt to state for moderns "the uniqueness

---

[66]Col 2:15. Kenneth Grayston, *Dying, We Live*, comments on this triumphal scene: ". . . if one is enslaved by a dark power, more than knowledge is needed . . ." (133).

[67]Gal 1:4; 1 Cor 15:24f.; John 12:31-32; 1 John 3:8; Heb 2:14-15. See Gustaf Aulén's classic, *Christus Victor*, A.G. Hebert, trans. (London: S.P.C.K., 1970) 66f. Joseph A. Grassi, *Rediscovering the Impact of Jesus' Death* (Kansas City: Sheed and Word, 1987) 94f., who interprets Luke's drama of the cross as a cosmic struggle with Satan.

[68]Col 1:21; Rom 6:9.

[69]1 Cor 15:54ff.

of the death of Jesus as an objective divine act through which the demands of God's holiness and the expression of God's self-giving love have both been adequately actualized. . . ."[70] Thus, "objective" implies the irrevocable reshaping of the human and divine situations.

I am employing the word "objective" in the sense of an ontological movement in the "trinitarian history of God," to use Moltmann's phrase,[71] in the triune God's utter identification with the suffering of alienated humanity.[72] Hence, in God's own life, something "objective" transpired in the new experience of human suffering in Christ and the consequent subjugation of the demonic powers of evil. Suffering love absorbed the hostility of the forces of enmity, and thereby stripped them of their ultimate potency. Their death-grip on vulnerable human beings was broken in the victory of Christ's resurrection. Therefore, the death of Jesus speaks not only of sin and forgiveness in the triumph over the evil with which humans have so readily co-operated, it also speaks about the problem of human suffering[73]—an issue that is inescapable for Christian theology of

---

[70]Aldwinckle, *Jesus*, 67. Paul Fiddes's discussion of objective and subjective dimensions in atonement in his *Past Event and Present Salvation* can help push us beyond any polarizing conundrum (26-28).

[71]Moltmann, *The Church in the Power of the Spirit*, 52f.

[72]The structure of this argument has been greatly influenced by Kenneth Surin's contention in his provocative article, "Atonement and Christology," 139, that the "divine identification with men's evil and suffering, in and through Jesus Christ, must be construed in ontological terms if it is to have salvific significance."

[73]Maurice Wiles, *The Remaking of Christian Doctrine* (London: SCM Press, 1974) 69. See also Dorothee Sölle, *Suffering*, Everett R. Kalin, trans. (London: Darton, Longman and Todd, 1975) 145-50. A contemporary Christian theodicy must be rooted in the suffering of the cross. In an often quoted passage, Elie Wiesel paints the reality of the suffering love of God in a story he relates in his wrenching book, *Night* (New York: Hill and Wang, 1960) 70f.

> The SS hung two Jewish men and a boy before the assembled inhabitants of the camp. The men died quickly but the death of the boy lasted half an hour. "Where is God? Where is he?" a man behind me asked. As the boy, after a long time, was still in agony on the rope, I heard the man cry again, "Where is God now?" And I heard a voice within me answer, "Here he is—he is hanging on this gallows. . . ."

religious pluralism. Thus, the "on behalf of" (*hyper*) language of the New Testament speaks of the definitive solidarity between God and humanity in the quintessential expression of suffering love, at the cross.[74] Further, this formula suggests an achieved fact that is universally accessible.

This event in God's life, manifested in Jesus Christ, is essentially bound up with the history of all of humanity. Rahner's concept of God's grace having been poured out on the world through Christ's life and death and "dynamically finalizing" persons in the direction of God is extremely helpful, for it seeks to describe the creation of a new context for human faith. In that the shape and destiny of the world has been dynamically reoriented by grace through the cosmic ramifications of Christ's atoning death, a new access (*ten prosagogen*) has been opened for relating to the One who has fully shared in the human condition. Jesus has served the priestly function of opening an approach to God for the people.[75]

Human response determines efficacy of atoning work. Christ's work, and its "outworking and appropriation,[76] as Elizabeth Moberly puts it, must not be considered in isolation. Redemption demands a response on the part of the one receiving its benefit. Repentance is the appropriate response toward God, and is, in Abelard's thinking, that to which the love of God is inexorably urging all persons.[77] The love of God, fully revealed in Jesus Christ, urges all to repent of sin through the inner yearning and movement of the graced human spirit. It is not enough to argue for the inclusive nature of Christ's atoning death without accentuating, as well, the personal freedom and responsibility of the individual to

---

[74]Moule, *The Origin of Christology*, 116-17.

[75]Heb 2:5. Cf. Rom 5:2; Heb 4:16; 1 Pet 3:18.

[76]Elizabeth R. Moberly, *Suffering, Innocent and Guilty* (London: S.P.C.K., 1978) 23.

[77]Peter Abelard, *Ethics*, Morris Ashcraft, ed., vol. 3, Christian Classics (Nashville: Broadman Press, 1981) 182. Abelard hints that the transforming power of the love of God will not simply repristinate the pre-fall dignity of the human being, but will make possible a new level of glorified existence.

"take hold of that for which Christ took hold" of him or her.[78] Salvation is necessarily participatory because of the free subjectivity of one's personhood.[79] The Bible pictures God as one who calls out to men and women (and even searches for them) while awaiting their response. And persons are not spared the consequences of their negative responses.

Of course, the age-old question is "How can one respond to a Savior of whom one has never heard?" Again, Rahner makes a valuable contribution to a christocentric theology of religious pluralism as he articulates the "searching christology" evident in all persons. He has stressed appropriately that historical or geographical contexts should not bar persons from the opportunity to respond to Christ, yet he has not fully sketched how it can be a possibility for all, particularly if one's response is in the inchoate form of unthematized faith.[80] A careful interpretation of Scripture reveals that it is surely within the biblical co-ordinates of truth to argue that ignorance does not disqualify one for grace; the intentionality of one's heart would be the more important criterion.[81] And we must remember Paul's instruction: "no one comprehends what is truly God's except the Spirit of God" (1 Cor 1:11, NRSV).

Furthermore, the New Testament narratives regarding the consummation of history as a temporal process unequivocally place Jesus as the central focus of all persons' confession of faith.[82] Therefore, it would seem fair to suggest that

---

[78]Phil 3:12.

[79]While God in Christ provides salvation which we cannot achieve for ourselves, there must be a participatory element to atonement as we are "crucified with Christ." See esp. Paul Fiddes's treatment of this concept in *Past Event and Present Salvation*, 77-79, and Dorothee Sölle, *Christ the Representative*, who goes further in her analysis, arguing for Christ's dependence on Christians' assent to his cruciform way of life in the world (123).

[80]Aldwinckle, *Jesus*, 180-81.

[81]The *Leitmotiv* of Abelard's entire *Ethics* is the centrality of *intention* rather than acts. Surely this salient feature of his views must be ingredient in a christocentric theology of religious pluralism.

[82]Phil 2:9-10; Rom 14:9; Eph 1:20-21.

those who do not know him have the inevitable eschatological opportunity for clarification of or confrontation with him who has been the unknown object of their faith.[83]

Several scholars suggest that the descent passage in 1 Pet 3:19, and the further note in 4:6 about the gospel being preached to the dead, are clues to the opportunity that remains after death for the unevangelized to encounter Christ.[84] Pannenberg, attempting to capture the contemporary relevance of the phrase in the Apostles' Creed about Christ's descent into hell (as well as attempting to address the question of those "who have never heard"), interprets the phrase to mean:

> what took place for mankind in Jesus also applies to the people who either never came into contact with Jesus and the message about him, or have never really caught sight of the truth of his person and his story.[85]

Dale Moody takes the latter passage as a clue to the possibility that "the dead who had no chance to hear the Gospel before they departed life" receive a "first chance" to encounter its truth.[86] The strength of Moody's suggestion is that it retains the biblical accent on *fides ex auditu.*

Scripture does not cancel out *a priori* the hopes of unevangelized persons for salvation because they do not know of Jesus Christ. Indeed, in addition to these clues of salvation from future judgment being made available in the realm of the dead for those who had not yet encountered Christ or his message, there are

---

[83]One who stands firmly within the evangelical wing of Christian theology, Clark Pinnock, "Why is Jesus the Only Way?" *Eternity* 27 (1976): 34, concurs: "Thus the desire to believe which is accepted in lieu of explicit faith in Christ, is finally completed at death when we all encounter the true God."

[84]These texts are notoriously difficult in translation, exegesis, and theological interpretation. Kenneth Grayston, *Dying, We Live*, 250-51, and his note on pages 446-47 can help us through the thicket of interpretation.

[85]Wolfhart Pannenberg, *The Apostles' Creed*, 94-95.

[86]Dale Moody, *The Word of Truth: A Summary of Christian Doctrine Based on Biblical Revelation* (Grand Rapids: Eerdmans, 1981) 496. Cf. W.J. Dalton, "Christ's Proclamation to the Spirits: A Study of 1 Peter 3:18-4:6," *Analecta Biblica* 23 (Rome, 1965).

examples of inclusion in the *basileia* on the basis of mercy[87] or by following the "light of nature" apart from the Law.[88]

It is more scriptural, in my judgment, to focus on the desire for salvation which exists in many human hearts than to stress that all the world religions are vehicles of salvation, as Rahner and Hick do.[89] It is fair to argue that one can encounter Christ at work in these non-Christian religions, but the goal of his work is the transformation rather than the ordaining of these ways of faith. Further, one must remain cognizant of the dialectic between salvation as an individual and as a universal affair when examining the salvific role of the non-Christian religions.[90]

In sum, not only must the presuppositions for a christocentric theology of religious pluralism stress that all participate in the cosmic disorder that needs God's redemption in Christ, but must also include the affirmation that all will

---

[87]Matt 25:34-40.

[88]Rom 2:14-16. Further, Acts 17:25-27 suggests that God has functioned providentially in behalf of the nations of the earth through making the divine being known. Some have questioned whether v. 27, "that they should seek God, in the hope that they might feel after God and find God, means God can be found by humans. The least that can be said is that the seeking after God can, at some point, converge with what has been provided in Christ. Cf. Bertil Gärtner, *The Areopagus Speech and Natural Revelation* (Lund: Gleerup, 1955) 228-41. Cf. Ulrich Wilckens, *Die Missionsreden der Apostelgeschichte: Form-und Traditions-geschichtliche Untersuchungen* (Neukirchen: Neukirchen Verlag, 1961) 99. Cf. Jean Daniélou, *Holy Pagans of the Old Testament*, Felix Faber, trans. (London: Longmans, Green, and Co., 1957) 4f.

[89]See R. Pannikar, *The Unknown Christ of Hinduism* (London: Darton, Longman, and Todd, 1974) 54, who believes one is saved through the cultural instruments of religion available. Cf. H.R. Schlette's contrasting conclusion in *Towards a Theology of Religions* (London: Burns and Oates, 1963) 25: "the fundamental attitude of the Old Testament and New Testament in regard to religions . . . is to be described as extremely negative." For example, he notes 1 Kings 11:1-13; Jer 2:26-29; 10:1-16; Isa 40:18-20; Ps 105; 113:10-16, etc. Yet these texts cannot be lifted from their *Sitz im Leben* as an ahistorical pronouncement, as Schlette's treatment suggests.

[90]See Samuel Amirtham, "The Challenge of New Religions to Christian Theological Thought," *International Review of Missions* 67 (1978): 399-406. S.J. Samartha, *One Christ—Many Religions* (Maryknoll NY: Orbis Books, 1991) says this dialectic will only be made possible if Christians will assent to a "revised christology" which takes full account of the reality of religious pluralism.

have an opportunity to respond to Christ. The discussion above has stressed the universality of Christ's work, creating a new context for faith in all persons through the outpouring of grace in the self-emptying death of Jesus Christ. The implication of maintaining an incarnational Christology and an eschatological dimension to a saving relationship with him is the firm belief that all salvation is through Jesus Christ; he is constitutive for reconciliation between God and humanity. This affirmation cannot help but shape Christian attitudes toward other ways of faith.[91] Most importantly, however, it is possible to insist on this cosmic role for Christ without denying the grace-filled elements in the non-Christian experience.

Attitudes Toward Other Ways of Faith

That the present global religious scene necessitates a major rethinking of Christian theology's assessment of other ways of faith has been consistently maintained in this study. A balanced christocentric theology of religious pluralism can neither view the non-Christian religions as a morass of evil idolatry (exclusivism) nor as simply a functionally-equivalent means for faith (relativism). In light of an increasingly sensitive retrospective look, much is being written of the "casualties" of the historic Christian missionary endeavor.[92] Perhaps these accusations are overdrawn by those desiring to exorcise their triumphal arrogance; nevertheless, the modern Christian, attempting to be faithful to Christianity's

---

[91]Langdon Gilkey warns that convictions such as the "sole efficacy or even superiority" of our Christian tradition renders any true religious dialogue impossible. See his essay, "Plurality and Its Theological Implications," 37, in *The Myth of Christian Uniqueness*, John Hick and Paul F. Knitter, eds. (Maryknoll NY: Orbis Books, 1987). Cf. Paul J. Griffiths' critique of Gilkey's position in his recent contribution, "The Uniqueness of Christian Doctrine Defended," in *Christian Uniqueness Reconsidered*, Gavin D'Costa, ed. (Maryknoll NY: Orbis Books, 1991) 157-73. In my perspective, genuine dialogue can only occur when those involved retain the integrity of their discrete perspectives which, for the Christian, entails an incarnational Christology with universal implications.

[92]Paul Tillich, *Christianity and the Encounter of the World Religions* (New York: Columbia University Press, 1963) and John V. Taylor, "Theological Basis of Interfaith Dialogue," *Christianity and Other Religions*, John Hick and Brian Hebblethwaite, eds. (Glasgow: Collins, 1980) 212-33.

traditional commitment to missions, is faced with repudiation and rejection on many fronts because of its former "theology of glory" approach, with its paternalistic, culture-exporting agenda.[93] In this vein, the Christian missionaries have seen themselves as the ones with the financial resources, the formal theological education, and the total message, which, in turn, meant they had *the* answers for *them* and the scheme to implement it. Even though at times the "two-realm" perspective (that salvation only involves something that occurs in the spiritual sphere) was overcome through the ministries of hospitals, agricultural programs, and educational institutions, there was often still lacking the self-emptying character that manifested Christ. The texture of the relationships lacked mutuality, for the Christians lacked the security and grace that could have allowed them to receive both spiritually and culturally. Protection of self from the vulnerability of being a fellow pilgrim in faith set limits to the quality and depth of sharing. Kenneth Kaunda criticizes the paternalism of past missionary pursuits:

> They gave many things but they did not give themselves. The relations tended to be one way, with the European dictating the degree of intimacy, deciding what he would give to, and what he would withold from the relationship.[94]

Stories like this are legion and should stand as stark reminders that the Christian attitude toward non-Christian religions and their followers needs to be etched with the humility of a thoroughgoing *theologia crucis*. Confession of past wrongs is appropriate, but Christians must not indenture themselves to a burden of debilitating guilt that eschews any missionary activity at all. Rather, a widened theological aperture is needed, for

---

[93]Luther W. Meinzen, "Reflections on Doing Theology in Mission," *Currents in Theology and Mission* 5 (1978): 173-79. Cf. Schlette, *Towards a Theology of Religions*, 27.

[94]Kenneth Kaunda, *A Humanist in Africa: Letters to Colin Morris* (London: SCM Press, 1966) 73. Cf. Wilfred Cantwell Smith, *The Faith of Other Men* (New York: The New American Library of World Literature, 1963) 105-28.

Western theology has not been able to develop a theology of history which would provide room for the nations and peoples of the extra-biblical traditions. The framework of Western theological systems simply excludes them from the *oikonomia* of God.[95]

Adherents of other ways of faith are persons for whom Christ died. Just as the Anabaptists had the impetus to preach the gospel to all because all had the opportunity to respond (due to their stress on the extensive implications of the atonement, the solidarity of all humankind, and universal election), so do contemporary Christians have a similar mandate. Using these three affirmations as pillars to uphold an inclusive missionary theology, the extremes of Calvinist particularism and non-missionary relativism can be corrected. The Christian must be frequently reminded that the gospel is directed toward a universal horizon.[96] Indeed, Moltmann views the critical co-ordinates of the relationship of the Christian faith to the world religions as: "attitudes and judgments which are based on Christianity's special promise and are directed toward the universal future of mankind in the kingdom of God."[97] Even though many contemporary persons are tacitly denying any religious faith, Christians must learn to identify and engage the unrequited yearnings of their innermost beings as an ingredient of the missionary task.[98] The "searching christology" in these persons, as well as in

---

[95]Choan-Seng Song, "New China and Salvation History—A Methodological Inquiry," *Living Faiths and Ultimate Goals*, S.J. Samartha, ed. (Maryknoll NY: Orbis, 1974) 73.

[96]Arguing for the *universalistic* sphere of the Gospel is quite different from affirming that all persons will be saved, i.e., *universalism*. See Hans Urs von Balthasar's excellent treatment of the question of *apokatastasis* in his brief monograph *Dare We Hope "That All Men Be Saved"?* (San Francisco: Ignatius Press, 1988).

[97]Moltmann, *The Church*, 150. See also Burlan A. Sizemore, Jr., "Christian Faith in a Pluralistic World," *Journal of Ecumenical Studies* 13 (1976): 405-19.

[98]Aldwinckle, *Jesus*, 78, argues that this is an appropriate overture and urges Christians to remember that "the Christian diagnosis is not peculiar in being time-conditioned and influenced by its cultural context." I would contend that the anthropology of Christian theology is the most coherent; however, this study cannot engage the thorny problems of belief and unbelief.

members of non-Christian religions, is a further indication of the universal
ramifications of Christ's death (although we cannot make ultimate soteriological
conclusions about their destiny).

Christ is already at work in the non-Christian religions. A christocentric
theology of religious pluralism must affirm with Irenaeus that "the Word of God
has never ceased to be present in the race of man."[99] Perhaps the Christian
theologian can more readily offer assent to this statement with regard to Judaism,
for there the continuity between it and the Christian faith is unmistakable. But the
statement of Irenaeus holds true for all the world's major religions. Past attempts
to relate the *individual* non-Christian to Christianity, especially prior to Vatican
II, were based on the unhistorical presupposition that "the individual was saved
in spite of pagan social environment rather than in any way because of it."[100]
God's seeking grace is expressed universally and thus one does not approach a
Muslim or Hindu as one already condemned before God (for not believing in the
only Son, John 3:17-18), but as one in whose context of faith the creative-
redemptive eternal Logos of God is drawing persons toward explicit faith in Jesus
Christ as Lord.

The task of the Christian, then, is to engender thematized faith in Christ
through a coherent theological anthropology based on his revealing of God's love
for sinful persons. Many will never respond to God in the basic intentionality of
their hearts apart from the midwifery of the Christian missionary, and we must
continue faithfully in our calling to bear witness. To say that Christ is already at
work in the non-Christian religions does not lessen the missionary task; rather, it
augments its viability, because the preaching of the Gospel enhances the
opportunity for salvation and increases the responsibility of the one hearing.

---

[99]*Adv. haer.* III, 16.1.

[100]Charles Davis, *Christ and the World Religions* (London: Hodder and Stoughton,
1970) 42.

Accordingly, the possessive exclusivism with which some Christians have regarded Christ as the property of the Christian faith[101] is a clinging sin that must go the way of the cross if Christians are to mature in their calling and function. Christ has bound himself to all of humankind, not just to Christians, in the solidarity of the incarnation; Christians, therefore, should acknowledge their basic commonality with all broken, suffering humanity. The threats to peace, threats to self-actualization, and threats to the continuation of a fit environment are a shared reality that need the varied insights of all religious traditions through which the one Christ is shaping persons of mercy, faith, and reverence. In this global context, Christianity, in particular, must consciously and responsibly strive for "an alteration of the whole atmosphere of life. . . ."[102] Indeed, qualitative mission will most likely take place in sharing the urgent task of rectifying humanity's most pressing problems.[103]

View of the Church

The central question pursued in this study has been: what is the proper response to the traditional formula "No salvation outside the Church," given the vast religious pluralism of today's global context? As the historical overview of the formula's theological development revealed, very few proclaim it today with Cyprian's stringency.[104] New theological currents and the broadened awareness of the world's religions have radically changed the meaning ascribed to the axiom.

---

[101]Amirtham, "The Challenge of New Religions to Christian Theological Thought," 403. Marjorie Hewitt Suchocki, "In Search of Justice," in *The Myth of Christian Uniqueness*, 149-61, argues for a strong connection between religious imperialism and sexism. Cf. Maura O'Neill, *Women Speaking Women Listening: Women in Interreligious Dialogue* (Maryknoll NY: Orbis Books, 1990).

[102]Moltmann, *The Church*, 152.

[103]Ibid. See John Macquarrie, *Principles of Christian Theology* rev. ed. (London: SCM Ltd., 1977) 446. I believe it is important to distinguish between the goals of dialogue and of missions. Dialogue presses toward understanding and mutual evaluation; Christian missions involves (without being limited to) proclamation of the gospel of Christ for the purpose of conversion to faith in him.

[104]See Karl Rahner and Herbert Vorgrimler, eds., "Church," in *Dictionary of Theology* (2nd ed.; New York: Crossroad, 1981) 71-78.

What theological content should it contain in a christocentric theology of religious pluralism? Methodologically, the christological perspective has been outlined first as it should primarily shape the ecclesiological structure. In the above discussion, it has been argued that there is only one economy of salvation in that Jesus Christ is the normative revelation of God and is constitutive of the work of God for human redemption. The world's salvation is tied to the particular, historical, enfleshed Logos, Jesus of Nazareth. And the church points to the salvation being effected by Christ.

Representative community in continuity with Christ.[105] Faith in Christ creates the church out of justified sinners and is the corporate expression of commitment to his path of suffering love. Salvation becomes available to the world predominantly through the church, for, in the main, it is the chief proclaimer of the gospel. But the mediation of salvation through the church's nurture and proclamation of the history and promise of Christ does not exhaust God's redemptive activity in the world through Christ. The Holy Spirit locates the church, which is the community and fellowship of Christ,[106] but is not sequestered to minister only through its temporal instrumentality. Thus, the church is representative rather than constitutive of salvation because not all who ultimately participate in God's salvific purpose are visibly attached to this community of faith which remains in direct continuity with the earthly ministry of Jesus Christ.[107] While maintaining that Jesus Christ is constitutive of the world's salvation, the church must be considered the normative expression of response to that fact and the chief vehicle for evangelization.[108]

---

[105]Schineller, "Christ and Church," 555.

[106]Moltmann, *The Church*, 33.

[107]*Dictionary of Theology*, 73.

[108]See Moltmann's definition of evangelization, *The Church*, 10.

Comprehensive in its definition. To grasp the overall historical character of the church, one must view it in a trifocal manner:

> in the inwardness of faith and grace, in the visibility of representational office and sacramental action, and in a growing participation (realized here and now in committed love) in the future aeon where sign and signified are no longer distinguished.[109]

In other words, the definition of the church should refer to its local manifestation and to its catholic nature, as well as to its eschatological dimension of consummation which will include those who come to faith in its founder in a post-mortem confrontation with Christ.[110]

Becoming incorporated in Christ's church should not be regarded as an optional aspect of participating in God's salvation, for, though faith requires a free and individual response, the redemption through Christ is essentially a corporate reality.[111] A key New Testament interpretation of the aim of Christ's sacrificial death was its creation and sanctification of his church unto eternal life;[112] consequently, the church has more than a peripheral role in the economy of redemption. It is both the goal of his redeeming work and the continuation of the Risen Christ's ministry. Therefore, salvation does not occur unrelated to Christ's church, although all do not have equal opportunity to become a part of its visible expression in this life.

Rahner's two-fold definition of the church as a "visible society" and as "humanity consecrated by Christ" threatens to obscure truly free personal response. Both Rahner and Hick fail to entertain seriously the notion that men and

---

[109]*Dictionary of Theology*, 74.

[110]This seems a more plausible solution than Rahner's argument for "anonymous Christians" which entails degrees of membership in the Church.

[111]1 Cor 6:15ff.; Eph 1:22f.; 2:17-19; 1 Pet 2:10.

[112]Eph 5:25ff.

women might refuse to repent and turn to God in love. Although the world-views (and concomitant theological anthropologies) Rahner and Hick employ have a deep attraction for contemporary persons in that they want to avoid impugning the justice of God or sacrificing the divine love, they obscure the biblical differences between earthly life and eternal life[113] by presupposing the natural immortality of the soul. Being "dynamically finalized" toward God through the efficacy of Christ's death does not, however, insure that one will utterly entrust all of one's being to this merciful God. One must leave open the "dark destiny" of eternal separation from God, as the New Testament frequently warns.[114]

CONCLUSION

Arguing from a christocentric vantage point, this study concludes that the question of *salus extra ecclesiam* must be answered negatively. Foundational to this investigation has been the elucidation of the reasons why *extra ecclesiam nulla salus* cannot be held in an exclusivistic manner in a religiously plural society, yet it has affirmed that there is no salvation that is unrelated to Christ's church. Obviously, since Vatican II, even for Roman Catholics the formula cannot connote "no salvation outside the church" if it means only the Roman Church. Nor can the formula be valid if it refers only to the present empirical membership of one of the various local manifestations of the Body of Christ.[115]

The maxim has always presupposed that there is no salvation apart from Christ, and that the church's mission was to live proleptically as a sign of redemption for the world and to proclaim to all that God's salvation is at hand.

---

[113]Moody, *The Word of Truth*, 500.

[114]Among the relevant passages are Matt 10:28; 25:41; Luke 8:31; Rom 2:6-8; 10:7; James 3:6; Rev 9:1; 17:8; 20:3.

[115]Contemporary western Christian theologians would benefit from a reacquaintance with the Orthodox concept of *oikonomia* when attempting to formulate a more comprehensive understanding of the church.

These fundamental tenets must be reaffirmed. Further, evidences of God's universal redemptive work in the world's great religions must be acknowledged with thanksgiving. If faithful to her raison d'être, the church must continually proclaim to all the fullness of God's revelation in Christ, with the goal that all might become incorporate in him. The Christian faith will survive in an increasingly secular society only if Christians remember that "Christ is greater than any institution claiming monopoly of his secrets . . ."[116] and that he alone heals human hurt and unlocks the mystery of understanding the inchoate yearnings of all persons.

Finally, Christians are not the gatekeepers of eternal life; God alone makes the ultimate judgment about the ones who are allowed to "enter into the joy of the Lord." This study has called for Christians to espouse a more inclusive theological approach to persons of other ways of faith as the appropriate stance of humility and love.

---

[116]Donald MacKinnon, "The Future of Man," *Explorations in Theology 5* (London: SCM Ltd., 1979) 10.

BIBLIOGRAPHY

A. BOOKS

Abbot, W. M., ed. *The Documents of Vatican II*. New York: Herder and Herder, 1966.

Abelard, Peter. *A Dialogue of a Philosopher with a Jew and a Christian*. Pierre J. Payer, trans. Toronto: Pontifical Institute of Medieval Studies, 1979.

_____. *Ethics*. Morris Ashcraft, ed. Christian Classics, Vol. III. Nashville: Broadman Press, 1981.

Aldwinckle, R[ussell] F. *More Than Man: A Study in Christology*. Grand Rapids: Eerdmans, 1976.

_____. *Jesus—A Savior or the Savior?* Macon GA: Mercer University Press, 1982.

Allen, E. L. *Christianity Among the Religions*. London: Allen and Unwin, 1960.

d'Alverny, M. T. "Deux traductions latines du Coran au Moyen Age." Vol. XVI, *Archives d'histoire et litteraire du Moyen Age*. Paris: 1948.

Altaner, Berthold. *Patrology*. Hilda C. Graef, trans. New York: Herder and Herder, 1960.

Althaus, Paul. *The Theology of Martin Luther*. Robert C. Schultz, trans. Philadelphia: Fortress Press, 1966.

Anderson, Gerald, ed. *The Theology of the Christian Mission*. Nashville: Abingdon Press, 1961.

_____ and Thomas F. Stransky, C.S.P., eds. *Christ's Lordship and Religious Pluralism*. Maryknoll: Orbis Books, 1981.

Anderson, Sir Norman. *Christianity and Comparative Religion.* Leicester: InterVarsity Press, 1970.

Aquinas, Thomas. *Summa Contra Gentiles.* Vernon J. Bombe, trans. New York: Image Books, 1956.

Arndt, W. F. and F. W. Gingrich, trans. and eds. *A Greek-English Lexicon of the New Testament and Other Early Christian Literature.* Chicago: University of Chicago Press, 1957.

Atkinson, James, trans. and ed. *Luther: Early Theological Works.* The Library of Christian Classics: Ichthus Edition. Philadelphia: Westminster Press, 1962.

Aulén, Gustaf. *Christus Victor: An Historical Study of the Three Main Types of the Ideas of the Atonement.* London: S.P.C.K., 1970.

Avis, Paul D. L. *The Church in the Theology of the Reformers.* Atlanta: John Knox Press, 1981.

Badham, Paul, ed. *A John Hick Reader.* Philadelphia: Trinity Press International, 1990.

Bainton, Roland. *Erasmus of Christendom.* New York: Charles Scribner's Sons, 1969.

Barth, Karl. *Church Dogmatics.* 4 Vols. G. W. Bromiley, trans. Edinburgh: T. & T. Clark, 1975.

Bauer, Walter. *A Greek-English Lexicon of the New Testament and Other Early Christian Literature.* Trans. and adapted by William F. Arndt. 2nd ed. rev. and aug. by F. Wilbur Gingrich and Frederick W. Danker. Chicago: University of Chicago Press, 1979.

Bede, The Venerable. *Historia Ecclesiastica.* B. Colgrave and R. A. B. Mynors, eds. Oxford: Oxford University Press, 1969.

_____. *Historiam Ecclesiasticum Gentis Anglorum.* Christopher Plummer, ed. London: Oxford University Press, 1896.

Beker, J. C. *The Triumph of God: The Essence of Paul's Thought.* Minneapolis MN: Fortress Press, 1990.

Berkouwer, G. C. *The Second Vatican Council and the New Catholicism*. Lewis B. Smedes, trans. Grand Rapids: Eerdmans, 1965.

_____. *The Work of Christ*. Cornelius Lambregtse, trans. Grand Rapids: Eerdmans, 1965.

Blair, Peter Hunter. *The World of Bede*. New York: St. Martin's Press, 1970.

Blass, F. and A. Debrunner. *A Greek Grammar of the New Testament and Other Early Christian Literature*. Trans. and rev. by Robert Funk. Chicago: University of Chicago Press, 1961.

Bleisten, Roman. *Bibliographie 1969-1974*. Freiburg: Herder, 1974.

_____ and Elmer Klinger. *Bibliographie Karl Rahner 1924-1969*. Freiburg: Herder, 1969.

Boullaye, H. Pinard de la, S.J. *L'Étude Comparee des Religions: Essai Critique*. 2 Vols. Paris: 1929-1931.

Bowden, John. *Jesus: The Unanswered Questions*. Nashville: Abingdon, 1989.

Braaten, Carl. *The Flaming Center: A Theology of the Christian Mission*. Philadelphia: Fortress Press, 1977.

Braden, Charles S. *These Also Believe: A Study of Modern American Cults and Minority Religious Movements*. New York: Macmillan, 1951.

Branick, Vincent P. *An Ontology of Understanding: Karl Rahner's Metaphysics of Knowledge in the Context of Modern German Hermeneutics*. St. Louis MO: Marianist Communications Center, 1974.

Bromiley, G. W., ed. *Zwingli and Bullinger*. The Library of Christian Classics: Ichthus Edition. Philadelphia: Westminster Press, 1953.

Brown, Peter. *Augustine of Hippo*. Los Angeles: University of California Press, 1967.

Brunner, Emil. *Das Symbolische in der Religiösen Erkenntis*. Tübingen: J. C. B. Mohr, 1914.

_____. *Die Christusbotschaft im Kampf mit den Religionen*. Stuttgart U. Basel: Evang. Missionsverlag, 1931.

_____. *Die Mystik und Das Wort*. Tübingen: J. C. B. Mohr, 1928.

_____. *Die Unentbehrlichkeit des Alten Testamentes für die missionierende kirche.* Basel: Evang. Missionsverlag, 1934.

_____. *Eternal Hope.* Harold Knight, trans. Philadelphia: Westminster Press, 1954.

_____. *God and Man: Four Essays on the Nature of Personality.* David Cairns, trans. London: SCM Press, 1936.

_____. "Intellectual Autobiography." Keith Chamberlain, trans. In *The Theology of Emil Brunner,* Charles W. Kegley, ed. *The Library of Living Theology,* Vol. III. New York: Macmillan, 1962.

_____. *Man in Revolt: A Christian Anthropology.* Olive Wyon, trans. London: Lutterworth Press, 1939.

_____. *Revelation and Reason: The Christian Doctrine of Faith and Knowledge.* Philadelphia: Westminster Press, 1946.

_____. *The Christian Doctrine of God.* Olive Wyon, trans. *Dogmatics,* Vol. I. Philadelphia: Westminster Press, 1950.

_____. *The Christian Doctrine of Creation and Redemption.* Olive Wyon, trans. *Dogmatics,* Vol. II. Philadelphia: Westminster Press, 1952.

_____. *The Christian Doctrine of the Church, Faith and the Consummation.* David Cairns, trans. *Dogmatics,* Vol. III. Philadelphia: Westminster Press, 1962.

_____. *The Divine-Human Encounter.* Amandus W. Loos, trans. Philadelphia: Westminster Press, 1943.

_____. *The Divine Imperative.* Olive Wyon, trans. Philadelphia: Westminster Press, 1947.

_____. *The Great Invitation and Other Sermons.* Harold Knight, trans. Philadelphia: Westminster Press, 1955.

_____. *The Letter to the Romans.* H. A. Kennedy, trans. Philadelphia: Westminster Press, 1959.

_____. *The Mediator: A Study of the Central Doctrine of the Christian Faith.* Olive Wyon, trans. London: Lutterworth Press, 1934.

_____. *The Misunderstanding of the Church*. Harold Knight, trans. London: Lutterworth Press, 1952.

_____. *The Predicament of the Church Today*. London: Lutterworth Press, 1940.

_____. *The Scandal of Christianity*. London: SCM Press, 1951.

_____. *The Word and the World*. London: Christian Movement Press, 1931.

Bull, George. *Vatican Politics at the Second Vatican Council 1962-5*. London: Oxford University Press, 1966.

Cairns, David. *The Image of God in Man*. 2nd ed. London: Fontana Library of Theology and Philosophy, 1973.

Calvin, John. *Commentary on the Epistle of Paul the Apostle to the Romans*. John Owen, trans. and ed. Grand Rapids: Eerdmans, 1948.

_____. *The Institutes of the Christian Religion*. John T. McNeill, ed. *The Library of Christian Classics*. 2 Vols. Philadelphia: Westminster Press, 1960.

von Campenhausen, Hans. *Men Who Shaped the Western Church*. Manfred Hoffman, trans. New York: Harper and Row, 1960.

Capéran, Louis. *Le Problème du Salut des infideles: Essai historique*. 2 Vols. Toulouse: Grand Seminaire, 1934.

Carpenter, James A. *Nature and Grace: Toward an Integral Perspective*. New York: Crossroad, 1988.

Carr, Anne. *The Theological Method of Karl Rahner*. H. Ganse Little, Jr., ed. American Academy of Religion Dissertation Series, 19. Missoula MT: Scholars Press, 1977.

Carver, W. O. *God and Man in Missions*. Nashville: Broadman Press, 1944.

_____. *Missions in the Plan of the Ages*. New York: Revell Company, 1909.

_____. *Missions and Modern Thought*. New York: Macmillan, 1910.

Chadwick, Henry. *Lessing's Theological Writings*. London: Adam and Charles Black, 1956.

Clayton, J. P., ed. *Ernst Troeltsch and the Future of Theology*. Cambridge: Cambridge University Press, 1976.

Coakley, Sarah. *Christ Without Absolutes: A Study of the Christology of Ernst Troeltsch.* Oxford: Clarendon Press, 1988.

Cobb, John B., Jr. *Christ in a Pluralistic Age.* Philadelphia: Westminster Press, 1975.

_____. *The Structure of Christian Existence.* Philadelphia: Westminster Press, 1967.

Congar, Yves, O.P. *The Wide World My Parish.* London: Darton, Longman and Todd, 1961.

Constable, Giles, ed. *The Letters of Peter the Venerable.* 2 Vols. Cambridge: Harvard University Press, 1967.

Courvoisier, Jacques. *Zwingli: A Reformed Theologian.* Richmond: John Knox Press, 1963.

Cragg, Kenneth. *The Christ and the Faiths.* Philadelphia: Westminster Press, 1986.

_____. *Christianity in World Perspective.* London: Lutterworth Press, 1968.

_____. *The Christian and Other Religions.* London: Mowbray, 1977.

Cranfield, C. E. B. *A Critical and Exegetical Commentary on the Epistle to the Romans.* 2 Vols. Edinburgh: T. & T. Clark, 1975-79.

Cross, F. L. and E. A. Livingston. *The Oxford Dictionary of the Christian Church.* 2nd ed. Oxford: University Press, 1978.

Cunliffe-Jones, Hubert, ed. *A History of Christian Doctrine.* Philadelphia: Fortress Press, 1978.

Dahl, Nihls A. *Studies in Paul: Theology for the Early Christian Mission.* Minneapolis: Augsburg, 1977.

Daniel, Norman. *Islam and the West: The Making of an Image.* Edinburgh: University Press, 1960.

Daniélou, Jean. *Holy Pagans of the Old Testament.* Felix Faber, trans. London: Longmans, Green and Co., 1957.

Davis, Charles. *Christ and the World Religions.* London: Hodder and Stoughton, 1970.

Dawe, Donald G. and John B. Carman, eds. *Christian Faith in a Religiously Plural World*. Maryknoll: Orbis Books, 1981.

D'Costa, Gavin, ed. *Christian Uniqueness Reconsidered: The Myth of Pluralistic Theology of Religions*. Maryknoll: Orbis Books, 1990.

_____. *John Hick's Theology of Religions: A Critical Evaluation*. Lanham/New York/London: University Press of America, 1987.

_____. *Theology and Religious Pluralism: The Challenge of Other Religions*. Oxford: Basil Blackwell, 1986.

The Declaration on the Relation of the Church to Non-Christian Religions. Glen Rock: Paulist Press, 1966.

deLubac, Henri. *Histoire et Espirit. l'intelligence de l'Écriture d'après Origène*. Paris: 1950.

Denney, James. *The Christian Doctrine of Reconciliation*. New York: George Doran, 1918.

Denzinger, Henry. *The Sources of Catholic Dogma*. Roy J. Defarrari, trans. New York: Herder, 1957.

Dewick, E. C. *The Christian Attitude to Other Religions*. Cambridge: Cambridge University Press, 1953.

Dillistone, F. W. *Jesus and His Cross: Studies in the Saving Work of Christ*. Philadelphia: Westminster Press, 1953.

Dodd, C. H. *The Epistle of Paul to the Romans*. London: Hodder and Stoughton, 1932.

_____. *New Testament Studies*. Manchester: University Press, 1953.

Dogmatic Constitution on the Church. Boston: Daughters of St. Paul, 1964.

Donceel, Joseph F., S.J. *The Searching Mind: An Introduction to a Philosophy of God*. Notre Dame: University of Notre Dame Press, 1979.

Douglas, J. D. *Let the Earth Hear His Voice: International Congress on World Evangelization, Lausanne, Switzerland*. Minneapolis: World Wide Publications, 1975.

Dunn, James D. G. *Christology in the Making: A New Testament Inquiry into the Origins of the Doctrine of the Incarnation.* Philadelphia: Westminster Press, 1980.

_____. *Unity and Diversity in the New Testament.* Philadelphia: Westminster Press, 1978.

Erasmus, Desiderius. *The Colloquies of Erasmus.* Craig R. Thompson, trans. Chicago: University of Chicago Press, 1965.

Estep, W. R. *The Anabaptist Story.* Nashville: Broadman Press, 1963.

Evans, Robert F. *One and Holy: The Church in Latin Patristic Thought.* London: S.P.C.K., 1972.

Farmer, H. H. *The World and God.* Rev. ed. London: Nisbet and Company, Ltd., 1955.

Fenton, Joseph E. *The Catholic Church and Salvation.* Westminster: Newman Press, 1958.

Fiddes, Paul S. *Past Event and Present Salvation: The Christian Idea of Atonement.* Louisville: Westminster/John Knox Press, 1989.

Fiorenza, Francis B. "Karl Rahner and the Kantian Problematic." In *Spirit in the World,* by Karl Rahner; William Dych, S.J., trans. New York: Herder and Herder, 1968.

Forsyth, P. T. *The Cruciality of the Cross.* London: Hodder and Stoughton, 1910.

Fremantle, Anne, ed. *A Treasury of Early Christianity.* New York: Viking Press, 1953.

Fuller, R. H. *The Mission and Achievement of Jesus.* Studies in Biblical Theology, 12. Chicago: A. R. Allenson, 1954.

Gärtner, Bertil. *The Areopagus Speech and Natural Revelation.* Lund: Gleerup, 1955.

Gelpi, Donald L. *Life and Light A Guide to the Theology of Karl Rahner.* New York: Sheed and Ward, 1966.

Gilkey, Langdon. *Naming the Whirlwind: The Renewal of God Language.* Indianapolis: Bobbs-Merrill, 1969.

_____. *Society and the Sacred: Toward a Theology of Culture in Decline.* New York: Crossroad, 1981.

Gill, Joseph, S.J. *Personalities of the Council of Florence.* New York: Barnes and Noble, Inc., 1964.

Goulder, Michael, ed. *Incarnation and Myth: The Debate Continued.* London: SCM Press Ltd., 1979.

Graf, G. *Die Arabischen Schriften des Theodor Abu Qûrra.* Paderborn: 1910.

Grassi, Joseph A. *Rediscovering the Impact of Jesus' Death.* Kansas City MO: Sheed and Ward, 1987.

Grayston, Kenneth. *Dying, We Live: A New Enquiry into the Death of Christ in the New Testament.* New York: Oxford University Press, 1990.

Green, Michael. "Jesus in the New Testament." In *The Truth of God Incarnate.* Michael Green, ed. London: Hodder and Stoughton, 1977.

Green, E. M. B. *The Meaning of Salvation.* Philadelphia: Westminster Press, 1965.

Greenslade, S. L., ed. *Early Latin Theology.* The Library of Christian Classics: Ichthus Edition. Philadelphia: Westminster Press, 1956.

_____. *Schism in the Early Church.* New York: Harper and Row, 1950.

Guthrie, Donald. *New Testament Theology.* Downers Grove: InterVarsity Press, 1981.

Hanson, R. P. C. "St. Cyprian," in *A Dictionary of Christian Theology*, Alan Richardson, ed. (Philadelphia: Westminster Press, 1969).

Harrington, Daniel J., S.J. *God's People in Christ: New Testament Perspectives on the Church and Judaism.* Philadelphia: Fortress Press, 1980.

Hebblethwaite, Brian. "Incarnation and Atonement: The Moral and Religious Value of the Incarnation." *Incarnation and Myth: The Debate Continued.* Michael Goulder, ed. London: SCM Press, 1979.

_____. "The *Myth* and Christian Faith." In *Incarnation and Myth: The Debate Continued.* Michael Goulder, ed. London: SCM Ltd., 1979.

Heidegger, Martin. *Being and Time.* John Macquarrie and Edward Robinson, trans. London: SCM Press, 1962.

Heim, S. Mark. *Is Christ the Only Way? Christian Faith in a Pluralistic World.* Valley Forge: Judson Press, 1985.

Hengel, Martin. *Acts and the History of Earliest Christianity.* John Bowden, trans. London: SCM Press, 1979.

_____. *The Atonement: The Origins of the Doctrine in the New Testament.* John Bowden, trans. Philadelphia: Fortress Press, 1981.

_____. "Christologie und neutestamentliche Chronologie." In *Neues Testament und Geschichte.* H. Baltensweiler and B. Reicke, eds. Zürich: Theologie Verlag, 1972.

_____. *The Son of God.* Philadelphia: Fortress Press, 1976.

Hick, John. *Arguments for the Existence of God.* New York: Seabury Press, 1971.

_____. *Biology and the Soul.* Cambridge: Cambridge University Press, 1972.

_____. *The Centre of Christianity.* San Francisco: Harper and Row, 1968, 1977.

_____, ed. *Classical and Contemporary Readings in the Philosophy of Religion.* Englewood Cliffs: Prentice-Hall, Inc., 1964.

_____. *Death and Eternal Life.* New York: Harper and Row, 1976.

_____. "Evil and Incarnation." In *Incarnation and Myth: The Debate Continued.* Michael Goulder, ed. London: SCM Ltd., 1979.

_____. *Evil and the God of Love.* Norfolk: Fontana Library, 1968.

_____. *Evil and the God of Love.* Rev. ed. New York: Harper and Row, 1978.

_____. *Faith and Knowledge.* 2nd ed. Ithaca: Cornell University Press, 1966.

_____. *Faith and the Philosophies.* New York: St. Martin's Press, 1964.

_____. *God and the Universe of Faiths: Essays in the Philosophy of Religion.* London: Macmillan Press, 1973.

_____. *God Has Many Names: Britain's New Religious Pluralism.* London: Macmillan, 1980.

_____. "Incarnation and Atonement: Evil and Incarnation." In *Incarnation and Myth: The Debate Continued.* Michael Goulder, ed. London: SCM Press, 1979.

_____. *An Interpretation of Religion*. New Haven: Yale University Press, 1989.

_____. "Irenaean Theodicy." *Encountering Evil*. Stephen Davis, ed. Edinburgh: T. & T. Clark, 1981.

_____. "Is There a Doctrine of the Incarnation?" In *Incarnation and Myth: The Debate Continued*. Michael Goulder, ed. London: SCM Press, 1979.

_____, ed. *The Myth of God Incarnate*. London: SCM Press, 1977.

_____. *Philosophy of Religion*. Englewood Cliffs: Prentice-Hall, 1963.

_____. "Pluralism and the Reality of the Transcendent." In *Theologians in Transition: The Christian Century "How My Mind Has Changed" Series*. James M. Wall. New York: Crossroad, 1981.

_____. *Problems of Religious Pluralism*. New York: St. Martin's Press, 1985.

_____ and Brian Hebblethwaite, eds. *Christianity and Other Religions*. Glasgow: Collins, 1980.

_____ and Paul F. Knitter, eds. *The Myth of Christian Uniqueness*. Maryknoll: Orbis Books, 1987.

_____ and Arthur McGill, eds. *The Many-Faced Argument*. New York: Macmillan, 1967.

Hill, David. *Greek Words and Hebrew Meanings*. Society of New Testament Studies Monograph Series, 5. Cambridge: Cambridge University Press, 1967.

Hillerbrand, Hans J. *The Reformation: A Narrative History Related by Contemporary Observers and Participants*. Grand Rapids: Baker Book House, 1978.

Hocking, W. E. *Living Religions and a World Faith*. New York: Macmillan, 1940.

Hourani, Albert. *Europe and the Middle East*. London: Macmillan Press, 1980.

Huizinga, Johan. *Erasmus and the Age of Reformation*. New York: Harper Torchbooks, 1957.

Hultgren, Arland. *Christ and His Benefits: Christology and Redemption in the New Testament*. Philadelphia: Fortress, 1987.

Humphreys, J. Edward. *Emil Brunner.* Bob E. Patterson, ed. Makers of the Modern Theological Mind. Waco: Word Books, 1976.

Hyma, Albert. *The Youth of Erasmus.* History and Political Science, 10. Ann Arbor: University of Michigan Press, 1930.

Imhoff, Paul and Hubert Biallowons, eds. *Karl Rahner in Dialogue: Conversations and Interviews 1965-1982.* New York: Crossroad, 1986.

Jeremias, Joachim. *The Central Message of the New Testament.* New York: Charles Scribner's Sons, 1965.

_____. *The Eucharistic Words of Jesus.* 3rd ed. Philadelphia: Fortress Press, 1966.

_____. *Jesus' Promise to the Nations.* London: SCM Press, 1958.

_____. *New Testament Theology: The Proclamation of Jesus.* New York: Charles Scribner's Sons, 1971.

John, Helen James. *Thomist Spectrum.* New York: Fordham University Press, 1966.

Jüngel, Ernst. "Extra Christum nulla salus—als Grundsatz naturlicher Theologie." In *Christentum innerhalb und ausserhalb der kirche.* Elmer Klinger, ed. Freiburg: Herdcer, 1976.

Jüngel, Eberhard. "Extra Christum Nulla Salus—A Principle of Natural Theology?" *Eberhard Jungel: Theological Essays.* J.P. Webster, ed. Edinburgh: T. & T. Clark, 1989.

_____. *God as the Mystery of the World.* D. L. Guder, trans. Edinburgh: T. & T. Clark, 1983.

_____. *Paulus und Jesus: eine Untersuchung zur Präzisierung der Frage nach dem Ursprung der Christologie.* Tübingen: J. C. B. Mohr, 1962.

Käsemann, Ernst. *Commentary on Romans.* Geoffrey Bromiley, trans. Grand Rapids: Eerdmans, 1980.

Kaunda, Kenneth. *A Humanist in Africa: Letters to Colin Morris.* London: SCM Press, 1966.

Kegley, Charles W., ed. *The Theology of Emil Brunner*. The Library of Living Theology, Vol. III. New York: Macmillan, 1962.

Kent, John H. S. "Christian Theology in the Eighteenth to Twentieth Centuries." In *A History of Christian Doctrine*. Hubert Cunliffe-Jones, ed. Philadelphia: Fortress Press, 1978.

Kilpatrick, G. D. "The Gentile Mission in Mark and Mark 13:9-11." *Studies in the Gospels: Essays in Memory of R. H. Lightfoot*. Oxford: Oxford University Press, 1955.

King, John J. *The Necessity of the Church for Salvation in Selected Theological Writings of the Past Century*. Washington: Catholic University of America Press, 1960.

Kitagawa, Joseph M., ed. *The History of Religions: Essays on the Problem of Understanding*. Chicago: University of Chicago Press, 1967.

Klassen, Walter, ed. *Anabaptism in Outline: Selected Primary Sources*. Scottsdale: Herald Press, 1981.

Knitter, Paul F. *No Other Name? A Critical Survey of Christian Attitudes Toward the World Religions*. Maryknoll: Orbis Books, 1985.

Knox, John. *St. Paul and the Church of the Gentiles*. Cambridge: Cambridge University Press, 1961.

Kraemer, Hendrik. *The Christian Message in a Non-Christian World*. Grand Rapids: Kregel Publications, 1938.

_____. *Religion and the Christian Faith*. London: Lutterworth Press, 1956.

_____. *World Culture and World Religion: The Coming Dialogue*. Philadelphia: Westminster Press, 1960.

Kress, Robert. *A Rahner Handbook*. Atlanta: John Knox Press, 1982.

Kritzeck, James. *Peter the Venerable and Islam*. Princeton: Princeton University Press, 1964.

Küng, Hans. *The Church*. Garden City: Image Books, 1976.

_____. *Does God Exist?* Edward Quinn, trans. London: Collins, 1980.

_____. *On Being a Christian.* Edward Quinn, trans. New York: Doubleday and Company, 1976.

_____. *Theology for the Third Millennium: An Ecumenical View.* New York: Doubleday, 1988.

_____. "The World Religions in God's Plan of Salvation." In *Christian Revelation and World Religions.* Joseph Neuner. London: Burns and Oates, 1967.

Ladd, George Eldon. *A Theology of the New Testament.* Grand Rapids: Eerdmans, 1974.

Lampe, G. W. H. *God as Spirit.* The Bampton Lectures, 1976. Oxford: Clarendon Press, 1977.

_____, ed. *A Patristic Greek Lexicon.* Oxford: Clarendon Press, 1960-68.

Lash, Nicholas. "Interpretation and Imagination." In *Incarnation and Myth: The Debate Continued.* Michael Goulder, ed. London: SCM Press, 1979.

Lanczkowski, Günther. *Sacred Writings: A Guide to the Literature of Religions.* Stanley Godman, trans. New York: Harper Chapel Books, 1966.

Levi-Provencal, E. *Histoire de'Espagne musulmane.* 3 Vols. Paris: 1950-57.

Lewis, H. D. and R. L. Slater. *World Religions.* London: Watt, 1966. Lehman, Helmut and Jaraslov Pelikan, eds. *Luther's Works.* 55 Vols. Philadelphia: Muhlenberg Press, 1961.

Lindbeck, George A. *The Nature of Doctrine: Religion and Theology in a Postliberal Age.* Philadelphia: Westminster, 1984.

Lindsell, Harold. *An Evangelical Theology of Missions.* Grand Rapids: Zondervan Publishing House, 1970.

Littell, Franklin H. *The Anabaptist View of the Church.* Hartford: American Society of Church History, 1952.

Luscombe, D. E. *The School of Peter Abelard.* Cambridge: At the University Press, 1969.

_____, ed. *Peter Abelard's Ethics.* Oxford: At the Clarendon Press, 1971.

Luther, Martin. *On War Against the Turks*. C. M. Jacob, trans. *Works of Martin Luther*, Vol. V. Philadelphia: A. J. Holman Company, 1931.

Lyonnet, Stanslas and Leopold Sabourin. *Sin, Redemption, and Sacrifice: A Biblical and Patristic Study*. Rome: Pontifical Biblical Institute, 1970.

McCallum, J. Ramsey. *Abelard's Christian Theology*. Merrick: Richwood Publishing Company, 1976.

McCool, Gerald A., ed. *A Rahner Reader*. London: Darton, Longman and Todd, 1975.

McKim, Donald K. *A Guide to Contemporary Hermeneutics: Major Trends in Biblical Interpretation*. Grand Rapids: Eerdmans, 1986.

McShane, Philip. *The Shaping of the Foundations: Being at Home in the Transcendental Method*. Washington DC: University Press of America, 1976.

MacKinnon, Donald. "Subjective and Objective Conceptions of Atonement." In *Prospect for Theology: Essays in Honour of H. H. Farmer*. F.G. Healey, ed. London: Nisbet, 1966.

_____. "The Future of Man." In *Explorations in Theology 5*. London: SCM Ltd., 1979.

Macquarrie, John. *Principles of Christian Theology*. London: SCM Ltd., 1977 (rev. ed.).

Marenbon, John. *Early Medieval Philosophy (480-1150): An Introduction*. London: Routledge, 1988 (rev. ed.).

Martin, Ralph. *New Testament Foundations*. Vol. I. Grand Rapids: Eerdmans, 1975.

_____. *Reconciliation: A Study of Paul's Theology*. Peter Toon, ed. New Foundations Theological Library. Atlanta: John Knox Press, 1981.

Maurer, Christian. "Syneidēsis." *Theological Dictionary of the New Testament*. Vol. 7. Gerhard Friedrich, ed.; G.W. Bromiley, trans. Grand Rapids: Eerdmans, 1971. Pp. 899-919.

Mensching, Gustav. *Tolerance and Truth in Religion.* H.J. Klimheit, trans. Birmingham: University of Alabama Press, 1971.

Metz, Johannes B. "An Essay on Karl Rahner." In *Spirit in the World,* by Karl Rahner. William Dych, S.J., trans. New York: Herder and Herder, 1968.

Meyendorff, John. *Byzantine Theology: Historical Trends and Doctrinal Themes.* New York: Fordham University Press, 1974.

_____. *Christ in Eastern Christian Thought.* Washington: Corpus Books, 1969.

_____. *Introduction a l'étude de Gregoire Palamas.* Paris: 1959.

_____. *St. Gregory Palamas and Orthodox Spirituality.* Adele Fiske, trans. Crestwood: St. Vladimir's Seminary Press, 1974.

_____. *A Study of St. Gregory Palamas.* George Lawrence, trans. London: Faith Press, 1964.

Migne, J. P., ed. *Patrologiae Cursus Completus. Series Graecae.* 161 Vol. in 166. Paris: Petit-Montrouge, 1857.

_____, ed. *Patrologiae Cursus Completus. Series Latina.* 221 Vols. Paris: Petit-Montrouge, 1852-60.

Moberly, Elizabeth R. *Suffering, Innocent and Guilty.* London: S.P.C.K., 1978.

Moltmann, Jürgen. *The Church in the Power of the Spirit.* Margaret Kohl, trans. New York: Harper and Row, 1977.

_____. *The Crucified God.* R.A. Wilson and John Bowden, trans. New York: Harper and Row, 1974.

Moody, Dale. *The Word of Truth: A Summary of Christian Doctrine Based on Biblical Revelation.* Grand Rapids: Eerdmans, 1981.

Morgan, Robert and Michael Pye, eds. *Ernst Troeltsch: Writings on Theology and Religion.* Atlanta: John Knox Press, 1977.

Moule, Charles F. D. "Incarnation and Atonement: A Comment on Professor Hick's Critique of Atonement Doctrine." In *Incarnation and Myth: The Debate Continued.* Michael Goulder, ed. London: SCM Press, 1979.

_____. *The Origin of Christology.* Cambridge: Cambridge University Press, 1977.

Munck, Johannes. *Paul and the Salvation of Mankind.* Frank Clarke, trans. Atlanta: John Knox Press, 1959.

Neill, Stephen. *Christian Faith and Other Faiths: The Christian Dialogue with Other Religions.* London: Oxford University Press, 1961.

_____. *Jesus Through Many Eyes.* Philadelphia: Fortress Press, 1976.

_____. *Salvation Today.* Nashville: Abingdon, 1976.

Neuner, Joseph, ed. *Christian Revelation and World Religions.* London: Burns and Oates, 1967.

Newbigin, Lesslie. *The Finality of Christ.* London: SCM Press, 1969.

_____, *The Open Secret.* Grand Rapids, Eerdmans, 1978.

Niebuhr, H. Richard. *The Purpose of the Church and Its Ministry.* New York: Harper and Row, 1956.

Ott, Heinrich. "Existentiale Interpretation und Anonyme Christlichkeit." In *Zeit und Geschichte: Festschrift für R. Bultmann.* E. Dinkler, ed. Tübingen: 1964.

Otto, Rudolf. *The Idea of the Holy.* Oxford: Oxford University Press, 1962.

Ozment, Steven. *The Age of Reform 1250-1550.* New Haven: Yale University, 1980.

Pannenberg, Wolfhart. *The Apostles' Creed.* Margaret Kohl, trans. London: SCM Press, 1972.

_____. "Redemptive Event and History." In his *Basic Questions in Theology: Collected Essays*, Vol. I. Philadelphia: Fortress Press, 1970.

_____. "Toward a Theology of the History of Religions." In his *Basic Questions in Theology: Collected Essays*, Vol. II. Philadelphia: Fortress Press, 1971.

Pannikar, Raimundo. *The Intro-Religious Dialogue.* New York: Paulist Press, 1978.

_____. *The Unknown Christ of Hinduism.* London: Darton, Longman, and Todd, 1964.

Parrinder, Geoffrey. *A Dictonary of Non-Christian Religions.* Philadelphia: Westminster Press, 1971.

_____. *Comparative Religion*. London: Allen and Unwin, 1962.

Pauck, Wilhelm. "The Church-Historical Setting of Brunner's Theology." In *The Theology of Emil Brunner*. Charles W. Kegley, ed. The Library of Living Theology, Vol. III. New York: Macmillan, 1962.

Pederson, Phillip E., ed. *What Does This Mean? Luther's Catechisms Today*. Minneapolis: Augsburg Publishing House, 1979.

Peers, E. Allison. *Fool of Love: The Life of Ramon Lull*. London: SCM Ltd., 1946.

_____. *Ramon Lull: A Biography*. London: S.P.C.K., 1924.

Pegis, Anton C., ed. *Basic Writings of Saint Thomas Aquinas*. 2 Vols. New York: Random House, 1945.

Pelikan, Jaraslov. *Obedient Rebels: Catholic Substance and Protestant Principle in Luther's Reformation*. New York: Harper and Row, 1964.

_____. *The Emergence of the Catholic Tradition (100-600)*. Vol. I, *The Christian Tradition*. Chicago: University of Chicago Press, 1971.

_____. *The Spirit of Eastern Christendom (600-1700)*. Vol. II. *The Christian Tradition*. Chicago: University of Chicago Press, 1974.

_____. *The Growth of Medieval Theology (600-1300)*. Vol. III, *The Christian Tradition*. Chicago: University of Chicago Press, 1978.

Petit, Louis, et al. *Oeuvres completes de Georges (Gennade) Scholarios*. 8 Vols. Paris: 1928-1936.

von Rad, Gerhard. *Old Testament Theology*. 2 Vols. D.M.G. Stalker, trans. Edinburg: Oliver and Boyd, 1962-65.

Rahner, Karl. "Anonymous and Explicit Faith." In his *Theological Investigations*, Vol. 16. David Morland, trans. New York: Seabury, 1979.

_____. "Anonymous Christianity and the Missionary Task of the Church." In his *Theological Investigations*, Vol. 12. David Bourke, trans. London: Darton, Longman and Todd, 1974.

_____. "Anonymous Christians." In his *Theological Investigations*, Vol. 6. Karl-H. Kruger and Boniface Kruger, trans. Baltimore: Helicon Press, 1969.

_____. "Atheism and Implicit Christianity." In his *Theological Investigations*, Vol. 9. Graham Harrison, trans. London: Darton, Longman and Todd, 1972.

_____. *The Christian of the Future*. W.J. O'Hara, trans. New York: Herder and Herder, 1967.

_____. "Christianity." In *Encyclopedia of Theology: The Concise Sacramentum Mundi*. Karl Rahner, ed. New York: Crossroad, 1982.

_____. "Christianity and the Non-Christian Religions." In his *Theological Investigations*, Vol. 5. Karl-H. Kruger, trans. Baltimore: Helicon Press, 1966.

_____. *The Church After the Council*. Davis C. Herron and Rodelinde Albrecht, trans. New York: Herder and Herder, 1966.

_____. "The Church, Churches, and Religions." In his *Theological Investigations*, Vol. 10. Graham Harrison, trans. London: Darton, Longman and Todd, 1972-73.

_____. "The Church's Commission to Bring Salvation and the Humanization of the World." In his *Theological Investigations*, Vol. 14. David Bourke, trans. London: Darton, Longman and Todd, 1976.

_____. "Controversial Theology on Justification." In his *Theological Investigations*, Vol. 4. Baltimore: Helicon, 1966.

_____. "Dogmatic Reflections on the Knowledge and Self Consciousness of Christ." In his *Theological Investigations*, Vol. 5. Karl-H. Kruger, trans. Baltimore: Helicon Press, 1966.

_____. *Foundations of the Christian Faith*. William V. Dych, trans. New York: Seabury Press, 1978.

_____. *Hearers of the Word*. New York: Herder and Herder, 1969.

_____. *Ignatius of Loyola*. Rosaleen Ockenden, trans. London: Collins, 1979.

_____. "The Individual in the Church." In his *Nature and Grace*. New York: Sheed and Ward, 1963.

_____. "Jesus Christ in the Non-Christian Religions." In his *Theological Investigations*, Vol. 17. Margaret Kohl, trans. New York: Seabury Press, 1981.

_____. "The Meaning of Frequent Confessions of Devotion." In his *Theological Investigations*, Vol. 3. Baltimore: Helicon, 1967.

_____. *Mission and Grace*. Cecily Hastings, trans. London: Sheed and Ward, 1963.

_____. "Observations on the Problem of the 'Anonymous Christian.' " In his *Theological Investigations*, Vol. 14. David Bourke, trans. London: Darton, Longman and Todd, 1976.

_____. "On Conversions to the Church." In his *Theological Investigations*, Vol. 3. Baltimore: Helicon, 1967.

_____. *On the Theology of Death*. New York: Seabury Press, 1973.

_____. "On the Theology of the Incarnation." In his *Theological Investigations*, Vol. 4. Kevin Smyth, trans. London: Darton, Longman and Todd, 1966.

_____. "The One Christ and the Universality of Salvation." In his *Theological Investigations*, Vol. 16. David Morland, O.S.B., trans. London: Darton, Longman and Todd, 1979.

_____. "The Position of Christology in the Church Between Exegesis and Dogmatics." In his *Theological Investigations*, Vol. 11. David Bourke, trans. London: Darton, Longman and Todd, 1974.

_____. "Reflections on Methodology in Theology." In his *Theological Investigations*, Vol. 11. David Bourke, trans. London: Darton, Longman and Todd, 1974.

_____. *Re-Thinking the Church's Mission*. New York: Paulist Press, 1966.

_____. "Selbstporträt." In *Forsher und Gelehrte*. W. Ernst Böhm, ed. Stuttgart: Battenberg, 1966.

_____. *Spirit in the World.* William Dych, trans. New York: Herder and Herder, 1968.

_____. "Transcendental Theology." In *Encyclopedia of Theology: The Concise Sacramentum Mundi.* Karl Rahner, ed. New York: Crossroad, 1982.

_____. "Universal Salvific Will." In *Encyclopedia of Theology: The Concise Sacramentum Mundi.* Karl Rahner, ed. New York: Crossroad, 1982.

_____ and Wilhelm Thüsing. *A New Christology.* New York: Seabury Press, 1980.

_____ and Herbert Vorgrimler, eds. *Dictionary of Theology.* 2nd ed. New York: Crossroad, 1981.

Ray, Roger D. "Bede, the Exegetic, as Historian." In *Famulus Christi: Essays in Commemoration of the Thirteenth Centenary of the Birth of the Venerable Bede.* Gerald Bonner, ed. London: S.P.C.K., 1976.

Rengstorf, Karl H. "Hepta." *Theological Dictionary of the New Testament.* Vol. 2. Gerhard Kittell, ed.; Geoffrey W. Bromiley, ed. and trans. Grand Rapids: Eerdmans, 1964, 627-34.

Reumann, John. *Creation and New Creation.* Minneapolis: Augsburg Publishing House, 1973.

_____. "Reconciliation." *The Interpreter's Dictionary of the Bible.* Supplementary Volume. Keith Crim, et al., eds. Nashville: Abingdon Press, 1976.

Ricoeur, Paul. *The Symbolism of Evil.* Emerson Buchanan, trans. Boston: Beacon, 1967.

Ridderbos, Herman. *Paul: An Outline of His Theology.* John Richard DeWitt, trans. Grand Rapids: Eerdmans, 1975.

Riesenfeld, Harald. "Hyper." *Theological Dictionary of the New Testament.* Vol. 8. Gerhard Friedrich, ed. and Geoffrey Bromiley, trans. Grand Rapids: Eerdmans, 1962, 507-16.

Ritschl, Albrecht. *The Christian Doctrine of Justification and Reconciliation.* H.R. Mackintosh and A.B. Macauley, trans. Edinburgh: T. & T. Clark, 1902.

Roberts, Alexander and James Donaldson, eds. *The Ante-Nicene Fathers.* 10 Vols. New York: Charles Scribner's Sons, 1885-87.

Roberts, Louis. *The Achievements of Karl Rahner.* New York: Herder and Herder, 1967.

Robinson, H. Wheeler. *Suffering Human and Divine.* New York: Macmillan, 1939.

Robinson, John A.T. *In the End God.* Rutha Nanda Anshen, ed. Religious Perspectives, Vol. 20. New York: Harper and Row, 1968.

_____. *Redating the New Testament.* Philadelphia: Westminster Press, 1976.

_____. *Truth is Two-Eyed.* London: SCM Press, 1979.

_____. "The Use of the Fourth Gospel for Christology Today." In *Christ and Spirit in the New Testament: Studies in Honour of C. F. D. Moule.* Barnabas Lindars and Stephen S. Smalley, eds. Cambridge: At the University Press, 1973.

Röper, Anita. *The Anonymous Christian.* Joseph Donceel, trans. New York: Sheed and Ward, 1966.

Ruether, Rosemary Radford. *Faith and Fratricide.* New York: Seabury Press, 1974.

Rupp, E. Gordon, and Philip S. Watson, eds. *Luther and Erasmus: Free Will and Salvation.* The Library of Christian Classics: Ichthus Edition. Phildelphia: Westminster Press, 1969.

Rupp, George. *Christologies and Cultures: Toward a Typology of Religious World Views.* Paris: Mouton, 1974.

Rust, Eric C. *Salvation History: A Biblical Interpretation.* Richmond: John Knox Press, 1962.

_____. *Religion, Revelation, and Reason.* Macon GA: Mercer University Press, 1981.

Sahas, Daniel J. *John of Damascus on Islam.* Leiden: Brill, 1972.

Samartha, S. J., ed. *Dialogue Between Men of Living Faiths: Papers Presented at a Consultation Held at Ajaltoun, Lebanon, March 1970.* Geneva: World Council of Churches, 1971.

_____, ed. *Faith in the Midst of Faiths*. Geneva: World Council of Churches, 1977.

_____. *Living Faiths and Ultimate Goals: Salvation and World Religions*. Maryknoll: Orbis Books, 1974.

_____. *One Christ—Many Religions*. Maryknoll: Orbis Books, 1991.

Sanders, E. P. *Paul and Palestinian Judaism*. Philadelphia: Fortress Press, 1977.

Schaff, Philip. *A Select Library of the Nicene and Post-Nicene Fathers*. 2nd Series. 14 Vols. New York: The Christian Literature Company, 1892-96.

_____ and Henry Wace, eds. *A Select Library of the Nicene and Post-Nicene Fathers*. 14 Vols. New York: The Christian Literature Company, 1887-89.

Schleiermacher, Friedrich D. E. *The Christian Faith*. H.R. Mackintosh, ed. Philadelphia: Fortress Press, 1976.

Schlette, H. R. *Colloquium Salutis—Christen und Nichchristen Heute*. Cologne, 1965.

_____. "Einige Theisen zum Selbstverständnis der Theologie angesichts der Religionen." In *Gott in Welt II*. J.B. Metz, ed. Freiburg: Herder, 1964.

_____. *Towards a Theology of Religions*. W.J. O'Hara, trans. London: Burns and Oates, 1963.

Schoonenberg, Piet. *Man and Sin*. Notre Dame: University of Notre Dame Press, 1965.

Schrotenboer, P. G. *A New Apologetics: An Analysis and Appraisal of the Eristic Theology of Emil Brunner*. J.H. Kok N.V. Kampen: 1955.

_____. "Emil Brunner." In *Creative Minds in Contemporary Theology*. Phillip E. Hughes, ed. Grand Rapids: Eerdmans, 1966.

Seeberg, Reinhold. *The History of Doctrines*. 2 Vols. Charles E. Hay, trans. Grand Rapids: Baker Book House, 1977.

Slater, Peter. *The Dynamics of Religion: Continuity and Change in Patterns of Faith*. London: SCM Press, 1978.

Smart, Ninian. "The Relation Between Christianity and Other Religions." In *Soundings*. A.R. Vidler, ed. Cambridge: Cambridge University Press, 1962.

_____. *The Religious Experience of Mankind.* New York: Scribners, 1969.

_____. *In Search of Christianity.* San Francisco: Harper and Row, 1979.

_____. *World Religions: A Dialogue.* London: Pelican, 1960.

Smith, W. C. "The Christian in a Religiously Plural World." In *Christianity and Other Religions.* John Hick and Brian Hebblethwaite, eds. Glascow: Collins, 1980.

_____. *The Faith of Other Men.* New York: Harper and Row, 1962.

_____. *The Meaning and End of Religion: A Revolutionary Approach.* New York: Macmillan, 1962.

_____. *Questions of Religious Truth.* New York: Scribners, 1967.

_____. *Religious Diversity.* New York: Crossroad, 1976.

_____. *Towards a World Theology: Faith and the Comparative History of Religions.* Philadelphia: Westminster Press, 1981.

Snaith, Norman. *The Distinctive Ideas of the Old Testament.* London: Epworth Press, 1944.

Sölle, Dorothee. *Christ the Representative: An Essay in Theology after the "Death of God."* David Lewis, trans. London: SCM Press, 1967.

_____. *Suffering.* Everett R. Kalin, trans. London: Darton, Longman and Todd, 1975.

Song, Choan-Seng. "New China and Salvation History—A Methodological Inquiry." In *Living Faiths and Ultimate Goals.* S.J. Samartha, ed. Maryknoll: Orbis Books, 1974.

Southern R. W. *Western Society and the Church in the Middle Ages.* Vol. II. *The Pelican History of the Church.* Middlesex: Penguin Books, 1970.

_____. *Western Views of Islam in the Middle Ages.* Cambridge: Harvard University Press, 1962.

Spinka, Matthew, ed. *Advocates of Reform: From Wyclif to Erasmus.* The Library of Christian Classics: Ichthus Edition. Philadelphia: Westminster Press, 1953.

Stackhouse, Max L. *Apologia: Contextualization, Globalization, and Mission in Theological Education*. Grand Rapids: Eerdmans, 1988.

Stevens, G. B. *The Christian Doctrine of Salvation*. The International Theological Library. Edinburgh: T. & T. Clark, 1905, 1910, 1930.

Stevenson, J., ed. *Creeds, Councils, and Controversies: Documents Illustrative of the History of the Church A.D. 337-461*. New York: Seabury Press, 1966.

Stott, John R. W. and Robert Coote, eds. *Down to Earth. Studies in Christianity and Culture: The Papers of the Lausanne Consultation on the Gospel and Culture*. Grand Rapids: Eerdmans, 1980.

Straw, Carole. *Gregory the Great: Perfection in Imperfection*. Berkeley: University of California Press, 1988.

Swidler, Leonard, ed. *Toward a Universal Theology of Religion*. Maryknoll: Orbis Books, 1987.

Sykes, S. W., and J. P. Clayton. *Christ, Faith and History: Cambridge Studies in Christology*. Cambridge: Cambridge University Press, 1972.

Taylor, John V. *The Go-Between God: The Holy Spirit and the Christian Mission*. New York: Oxford University Press, 1972.

_____. "Theological Basis of Interfaith Dialogue." In *Christianity and Other Religions*. John Hick and Brian Hebblethwaite, eds. Glascow: Collins, 1980.

Taylor, Vincent. *The Atonement in the New Testament*. London: Epworth Press, 1941.

_____. *Forgiveness and Reconciliation*. London: Macmillan Press, 1941.

_____. *Jesus and His Sacrifice*. London: Macmillan Press, 1937.

TeSelle, Eugene. *Augustine the Theologian*. New York: Herder and Herder, 1970.

Theisen, Jerome P., O.S.B. *The Ultimate Church and the Promise of Salvation*. Collegeville MN: St. John's University Press, 1976.

Thielicke, Helmut. *The Evangelical Faith*. Vol. 3. Geoffrey W. Bromiley, trans. and ed. Grand Rapids: Eerdmans, 1982.

Thomas, M. M. *Man and the Universe of Faiths.* Madras: Christian Literature Society, 1975.

Thomas, Owen C. *Attitudes Toward Other Religions: Some Christian Interpretations.* New York: Harper and Row, 1969.

Thompson, Craig R. *Inquisitio De Fide: A Colloquy by Desiderius Erasmus Roteradamus 1524.* Yale Studies in Religion, 15. New Haven: Yale University Press, 1950.

Tillich, Paul. *Christianity and the Encounter of the World Religions.* Columbia: Columbia University Press, 1963.

_____. *The Future of Religions.* Jerald C. Brauer. New York: Harper and Row, 1966.

_____. "Some Questions on Brunner's Epistemology." In *The Theology of Emil Brunner.* C.W. Kegley, ed. *The Library of Living Theology,* Vol. III. New York: Macmillan, 1962.

_____. *Systematic Theology.* Vol. I. Chicago: University of Chicago Press, 1951.

Toynbee, Arnold. *Christianity Among the Religions of the World.* New York: Scribners, 1957.

Tracy, David. *Blessed Rage for Order: The New Pluralism in Theology.* New York: Seabury Press, 1975.

_____. "Defending the Public Character of Theology." In *Theologians in Transition.* James M. Wall, ed. New York: Crossroad, 1981.

Troeltsch, Ernst. *Christian Thought.* London: University of London Press, 1923.

_____. *The Absoluteness of Christianity and the History of Religions.* David Reid, trans. London: SCM Press, 1972.

de Vaux, Roland. *Studies in Old Testament Sacrifice.* Cardiff: University of Wales Press, 1964.

Vidler, Alec R. *The Modernist Movement in the Roman Church.* Cambridge: Cambridge University Press, 1934.

Viladesau, Richard. *Answering for Faith: Christ and the Human Search for Salvation.* New York: Paulist Press, 1987.

Visser't Hooft, W. A. *No Other Name: The Choice Between Syncretism and Christian Universalism.* Naperville: SCM Book Club, 1963.

von Balthasar, Hans Urs. *Dare We Hope "That All Men Be Saved"?* San Francisco: Ignatius Press, 1988.

Vorgrimler, Herbert. *Karl Rahner, His Life, Thought and Works.* Edward Quinn, trans. London: Burns and Oates, 1965.

_____. *Understanding Karl Rahner: An Introduction to His Life and Thought.* John Bowden, trans. New York: Crossroad, 1986.

Wainwright, Geoffrey. *Doxology: A Systematic Theology.* London: Epworth Press, 1980.

Watt, W. M. *Free Will and Predestination in Early Islam.* London: Luzac, 1948.

Weger, Karl-Heinz. *Karl Rahner: An Introduction to His Theology.* London: Burns and Oates, Ltd., 1980.

White, Hugh Vernon. "Brunner's Missionary Theology." In *The Theology of Emil Brunner.* C.W. Kegley, ed. *The Library of Living Theology*, Vol. III. New York: Macmillan, 1962.

Whitehead, Alfred North. *Process and Reality.* London: Macmillan, 1929.

Wiesel, Elie. *Night.* New York: Hill and Wang, 1960.

Wilckens, Ulrich. *Die Missionsreden der Apostelgeschichte: Form-und Traditions-geschichtliche Untersuchungen.* Neukirchen: Neukirchen Verlag, 1961.

Wiles, Maurice. "Does Christology Rest on a Mistake?" In *Christ, Faith and History.* S.W. Sykes and J.P. Clayton, eds. Cambridge: Cambridge University Press, 1972.

_____. *Explorations in Theology.* Vol. 4. London: SCM Press, 1979.

_____. *The Remaking of Christian Doctrine.* London: SCM Press, 1974.

Williams, A. L. *Adversus Judaeos: A Bird's-Eye View of Christian Apologiae Until the Renaissance.* Cambridge: At the University Press, 1935.

_____. *Justin Martyr: The Dialogue with Trypho.* London: S.P.C.K., 1930.

Williams, George Huntston. "Erasmus and the Reformers on Non-Christian Religions and *Salus Extra Ecclesiam.*" In *Action and Conviction in Early Modern Europe: Essays in Memory of E. H. Harbison.* Theodore K. Robb and Jerrold E. Siegel, eds. Princeton: Princeton University Press, 1969.

_____. *The Radical Reformation.* Philadelphia: Westminster Press, 1961.

_____ and Angel M. Mergal, eds. *Spiritual and Anabaptist Writers.* The Library of Christian Classics: Ichthus Edition. Philadelphia: Westminster Press, 1957.

Williams, S. K. *Jesus' Death as a Saving Event: The Background and Origin of a Concept.* Harvard Dissertations in Religion, 2. Missoula MT: Scholars Press, 1975.

Willis, John R., S.J., ed. *The Teachings of the Church Fathers.* New York: Herder and Herder, 1966.

Witherington, Ben III. *The Christology of Jesus.* Minneapolis: Fortress Press, 1990.

Young, Frances. *Sacrifice and the Death of Christ.* London: S.P.C.K., 1975.

Young, Robert C. *Encounter with World Religions.* Philadelphia: Westminster Press, 1970.

Zaehner, R. C. *At Sundry Times.* London: Faber and Faber, 1958.

Zwingli, Ulrich. *Commentary on True and False Religion.* S.M. Jackson, ed. Durham: Labyrinth Press, 1981.

B. PERIODICALS

Aldwinckle, Russell F. "Gods Many and Lords Many," *Theodolite* 5 (1980): 5-10.

_____. "Reflections on Christology," *Perspectives in Religious Studies* 8 (1981): 88-96.

Allen, Diogenes. "A Christian Theology of Other Faiths," *Theology Today* 38 (1981): 305-13.

Amirtham, Samuel. "The Challenge of New Religions to Christian Theological Thought," *International Review of Mission* 67 (1978): 399-406.

Bainton, R. H. "The Parable of the Tares as the Proof Text for Religious Liberty to the End of the Sixteenth Century," *Church History* 1 (1932): 67-89.

Blue, J. Ronald. "Untold Billions: Are They Really Lost?" *Bibliotheca Sacra* 138 (1981): 338-50.

Bluhm, Heinz. "Luther's View of Man in His First Published Work," *Harvard Theological Review* 41 (1948) 103-22.

Brachen, Joseph A., S.J. "Salvation: A Matter of Personal Choice," *Theological Studies* 37 (1976): 410-24.

Bradley, Denis J. M. "Rahner's Spirit in the World: Aquinas or Hegel?" *The Thomist* 41 (April 1977): 167-99.

Brunner, Emil. "Der Neue Barth: Bemerkungen zu Karl Barths Lehre vom Menschen," *Zeitschrift für Theologie und Kirche* 48 (1951): 97-100.

_____. "Ecclesia and Evangelism," *Japan Christian Quarterly* 21 (1953): 154-59.

_____. "One Holy Catholic Church," *Theology Today* 4 (1947): 318-31.

_____. "Secularism as a Problem for the Church," *International Review of Missions* 19 (1930): 495-511.

_____. "Toward a Missionary Theology," *Christian Century* 66 (1949): 816-18.

Burns, J. Patout, S.J. "The Economy of Salvation: Two Patristic Traditions," *Theological Studies* 37 (1976): 598-619.

Clooney, Francis X. "Christianity and World Religions: Religion, Reason, and Pluralism," *Religious Studies Review* 15 (1989): 198-203.

Davies, Brian A. "A Modern Irenaean Theodicy: Professor Hick on Evil," *New Blackfriars* 57 (1976): 512-19.

Dunning, T. P. "Langland and the Salvation of the Heathen," *Medium Aevum* 12 (1943): 45-54.

Egan, Harvey. "Book Review: *Foundations of Christian Faith*," *Theological Studies* 38 (1977): 555-59.

Eichhorst, Calvin J. "From Outside the Church to Inside, Toward a Triumph of Grace in Catholicism," *Dialog* 12 (1973): 190-96.

Forrell, George W. "Luther and the War Against the Turks," *Church History* 14 (1945): 256-71.

Forrester, Duncan B. "Professor Hick and the Universe of Faiths," *Scottish Journal of Theology* 29 (1976): 65-72.

Gerrish, B. A. "Jesus, Myth, and History: Troeltsch's Stand in the 'Christ-Myth' Debate," *The Journal of Religion* 55 (1975): 13-35.

Groh, Dennis E. "Tertullian's Polemic Against Social Co-optation," *Church History* 40 (1971): 7-14.

Gundry, Robert H. "Salvation According to Scripture: No Middle Ground," *Christianity Today* 22 (1977): 342-44.

Haight, Roger D., S.J. "Mission: The Symbol for Understanding the Church Today," *Theological Studies* 37 (1976): 620-51.

Heim, S. Mark. "Thinking about Theocentric Christology," *Journal of Ecumenical Studies* 24 (1987): 1-52.

Hendry, George S. "An Appraisal of Brunner's Theology," *Theology Today* 19 (1963): 523-31.

Hentz, Otto, S.J. "Feature Review: *Foundations of Christian Faith: An Introduction in the Idea of Christianity*," *Thought* 53 (December 1978): 433-41.

Hick, John. "Is There Only One Way to God?" *Theology* 85 (1982):4-7.

_____. "Learning from Other Faiths: IX The Christian View of Other Faiths," *Expository Times* 84:2 (November 1972): 36-39.

_____. "Living in a Multi-Cultural Society: II Practical Reflections of a Theologian," *Expository Times* 89 (January 1978): 100-104.

_____. "On Grading Religions," *Religious Studies* 17 (1981): 451-67.

_____. "Present and Future Life," *Harvard Theological Review* 71 (1978): 1-15.

_____. "Towards a Philosophy of Religious Pluralism," *Neue Zeitschrift für Systematische Theologie und Religionsphilosophie* 22 (1980): 131-49.

_____. "Whatever Path Men Choose is Mine," *The Modern Churchman* 18 (Winter 1974): 8-17.

Jüngel, Eberhard. "Das Verhältnis von 'ökonomischer' und 'immanenter' Trinität," *Zeitschrift für Theologie und Kirche* 72 (1975): 353-64.

Knowles, M.D. "The Censured Opinions of Uthred of Boldon," *Proceedings of the British Academy* 37 (1951): 305-42.

Kritzeck, James. "Moslem-Christian Understanding in Medieval Times," *Comparative Studies in Society and History* 4 (1962): 388-401.

Küng, Hans. "Towards a New Consensus in Catholic (and Ecumenical) Theology," *Journal of Ecumenical Studies* 17 (1980): 1-17.

Lindbeck, G. "The Thought of Karl Rahner," *Christianity and Crisis* 25 (October 18, 1965): 211-15.

Lipner, J. J. "Does Copernicus Help? Reflections for a Christian Theology of Religions," *Religious Studies* 13 (1977): 243-58.

Luecke, Richard H. "God and Evil," *The Christian Century* 84 (March 1967): 377-78.

Luz, Ulrich. " 'Theologia crucis' als Mitte der Theologie des Neuen Testaments," *Evangelische Theologie* 34 (1974): 116-40.

Meinzen, Luther W. "Reflections on Doing Theology in Mission," *Currents in Theology and Mission* 5 (1978): 173-70.

Meyendorff, John. "Byzantine Views of Islam," *Dunbarton Oaks Papers* 18 (1964): 155-32.

Munro, D. C. "The Western Attitude Toward Islam During the Period of the Crusades," *Speculum* 6 (1931) 329-45.

O'Donovan, Leo, S.J. "A Changing Ecclesiology in a Changing Church: A Symposium on Development in the Ecclesiology of Karl Rahner," *Theological Studies* 38 (1977): 736-62.

_____. "Living into Mystery: Karl Rahner's Reflections at 75," *America* 140 (March 1979): 177-80.

Pearson, Larz, O.P. "Karl Rahner: A Neo-Augustinian Thomist," *The Thomist* 43 (January 1979): 178-94.

Pelikan, Jaroslav. "Form and Tradition in Worship: A Theological Interpretation," *Essays Presented at the First Liturgical Institute, 1949*, 150:22-23 (Valparaiso).

Pinnock, Clark. "Why is Jesus the Only Way?" *Eternity* 27 (1976): 13-34.

Rahner, Karl. "A Basic Interpretation of Vatican II," *Theological Studies* 40 (1970): 716-727.

Richards, Glyn. "Towards a Theology of Religions," *Journal of Theological Studies* N.S. 31 (1980): 44-60.

Riesenhuber, Klaus, S.J. "Der anonyme Christ nach Karl Rahner," *Zeitschrift für katholische Theologie* 86 (1964): 286-303.

Rupp, E. G. "Luther and the Doctrine of the Church," *Scottish Journal of Theology* 9 (1956): 384-92.

Rupp, George. "Religious Pluralism in the Context of a Emerging World Culture," *Harvard Theological Review* 66 (1973): 207-18.

Schineller, J. Peter, S.J. "Christ and Church: A Spectrum of Views," *Theological Studies* 37 (1976): 545-66.

Sizemore, Burlan A., Jr. "Christian Faith in a Pluralistic World," *Journal of Ecumenical Studies* 13 (1976): 405-19.

Starkey, Peggy. "Biblical Faith and the Challenge of Religious Pluralism," *International Review of Missions* 71 (January 1982): 66-77.

Stuhlmacher, Peter. "The Gospel of Reconciliation in Christ: Basic Features and Issues of a Biblical Theology of the New Testament," *Horizons in Biblical Theology* 1 (1979): 161-90.

Surin, Kenneth. "Atonement and Christology," *Neue Zeitschrift für Systematische Theologie und Religionsphilosophie* 24 (1982): 131-49.

_____. "Creation, Revelation and Analogy," *The Journal of Theological Studies* 32 (1981): 401-42.

Tappeiner, Daniel A. "Sacramental Causality in Aquinas and Rahner: Some Critical Thoughts," *Scottish Journal of Theology* 28 (1975): 243-57.

Tooley, M. "John Hick and the Concept of Eschatological Verification," *Religious Studies* 12 (June 1976): 177-99.

Whiteley, D. E. H. "St. Paul's Thoughts on the Atonement," *Journal of Theological Studies* 8 (1957): 240-55.

Wiles, M. F. "The Theological Legacy of St. Cyprian," *Journal of Ecclesiastical History* 14 (1963): 139-49.

Wilken, Robert L. "The Making of a Phrase," *Dialogue* 12 (1973): 174-81.

Williams, G. H. "Sectarian Ecumenicity: Reflections on a Little Noticed Aspect of the Radical Reformation," *Review and Expositor* 64 (1967): 141-60.

Young, Frances M. "Redemption—The Starting Point of Christian Theology," *The Expository Times* 88 (October 1976-September 1977): 260-64.

C. UNPUBLISHED SOURCES

Rainwater, Robert E., Jr. "The Theology of John Hick: A Critical Analysis." Dissertation. The Southern Baptist Theological Seminary, 1980.